Storytelling

can change the world

'Changing the world is the only fit work for a grown man or woman.'

HOWARD LUCK GOSSAGE, QUIRKY, GAME-CHANGING ADMAN

Other books by this author

The Field by the River, Anova Books, London, hardback, 2008, softback, 2009, and Kindle, 2013.

The Zen of Fundraising, Jossey-Bass, San Francisco, softback, 2006.

Tiny Essentials of an Effective Volunteer Board, The White Lion Press, London, softback, 2004.

Relationship Fundraising, second edition, Jossey-Bass, San Francisco, hardback 2002. The White Lion Press, London, hardback, 1992.

Friends for Life, The White Lion Press, London, hardback, 1996.

How to Produce Inspiring Annual Reports, Directory of Social Change, London, softback, 2000, with Karin Weatherup.

Website and blog, www.kenburnett.com

Storytelling

can change the world

Ken Burnett

The White Lion Press Limited, London
www.whitelionpress.com

ISBN: 978-0-9553993-5-0

First printed 2014

British Library Cataloguing-in-Publication Data.
A catalogue record for this book is available from the British Library.

Cover illustration by Roy Williams

Design and print production by Bradbury and Williams

Printed and bound in the United Kingdom by
CPI Group (UK) Ltd, Croydon CRO 4YY

This book is dedicated to
Marie, Joe and Charlie.

Acknowledgements

With grateful thanks to Marie Burnett, Roy Williams, Jane Fricker, Karin Weatherup, Lisa Sargent, Mary Stringer, Fergal Byrne, Aline Reed, Indra Sinha and Alan Clayton for their helpful guidance and general brilliance during the process of creating this book.

Thanks too to all the other writers whose work informed and inspired me, particularly those individuals and organisations who generously gave me permission to quote their work so that I might seem more clever and well informed. For a list of permissions see page 268.

The 'turning point' stories that divide the chapters are all real examples of tales that provoked change and, one way or another, involved me through my work or personally. They are included merely as examples, to add colour and context.

What others have said about this book

'I really like this book for its important history and exquisite examples, stories to make us laugh and cry, tips to do the right things in the right way and how it's inspired us to change the world.'

SIMONE JOYAUX, AUTHOR, *FIRE YOUR LOUSY BOARD MEMBERS* AND OTHER BOOKS, USA.

'Change in the world begins with change in oneself. Thus the real object of all cause advertising is not to tell people about what is happening in the world, but to lead them to ask what, if anything, they are prepared to do about it. It is not ultimately about slave labour camps, butchered seal pups, or blinded gas victims, it is about what sort of person each of us wants to be. The question applies as much to the storyteller as to the hearer. To be a change-maker, first change yourself. For a start, read this book.'

INDRA SINHA, AUTHOR, *ANIMAL'S PEOPLE,* SHORTLISTED FOR THE MAN BOOKER PRIZE 2007, UK.

'A big thanks is in order. What you have here is a compendium of everything known about storytelling in the fundraising context. It's an amazingly helpful desk reference. I found new details about familiar subjects (emotions, for instance); unfamiliar insights; good swift kicks in the pants ... every page has something worth hearing for the first or the hundredth time.

'You've written a classic. A very full meal.'

TOM AHERN, AUTHOR, *MAKING MONEY WITH DONOR NEWSLETTERS* AND OTHER BOOKS, USA.

'Passion is a word not often associated with business schools and it should be! This latest book from Ken Burnett has it ripping from every page. At a time when cynicism and lack of trust rules, this book, through its style of telling you about compelling acts of innovation and courage, shows we can still make the world a better place.'

PROFESSOR PAUL PALMER, CASS BUSINESS SCHOOL, LONDON, UK.

'Stories are the secret reservoir of values. Change the stories individuals and nations live by and you change the individuals and nations.'

BEN OKRI, WRITER

Contents

Other books by this author 2
Acknowledgements 6
What others have said about this book 7
Preface: *The worst story in the world* 14
Amnesty's whole page press ad. 15

Part 1 Why we tell stories 23

TURNING POINT. Charlie and the human rights lawyers of Guatemala 24

1. How transformational storytelling could be just right for you 25

The best way to bring about change
Looking forward to the age of opportunity
Entertainment or action: why there are only two types of story
Your story is all about its audience
Stories have influence
This book is all about you
The truth, told well, really will change the world
The most sincere form of flattery
Beware, handle stories with care
Now, meet the author
Chapter's end: actions and key messages 39

TURNING POINT. Kristiansand creates 5,348 jobs in less than a month. But not for Norwegians 40

2. Can storytelling really change the world? 42

Quick wins at school
The campaign for less boring higher education lectures
Banishing dull
Stories inspire, encourage and unite
Good written communication is a commercial necessity
Business is being choked by boring reports and tedious writing
Dismal, dull presentations
More opportunities for storytellers
The information explosion
The change enabler
Chapter's end: actions and key messages 61

TURNING POINT. The king's portrait 62

3. The best sales opportunities you'll ever have 63
Employers and employees are changing
The changing customer
The changing world of work
Good can be good for business
Stories encourage safety and sales
Corporate social responsibility is dead
Kellogg's campaign to give a child a breakfast
All kinds of organisations use storytelling to change their world
The best sales opportunity of all
More than a thank you
Feedback is the magic ingredient…
…but speed is the essence
Understanding the need and reward cycle
Five secrets of sales success
A few more reasons why businesses should tell their stories quickly
Chapter's end: actions and key messages 85

TURNING POINT. End MS in our lifetimes 86

4 The story of the story 88
The natural way we learn and teach
Everyone is a storyteller; everywhere is their stage
How stories shape us
But…it's just a story!
The story paradox: happy endings and endless discord
Bad news, dramas and disagreements
Dreaming of a deeper meaning
Chapter's end: actions and key messages 101

Part 2 Making the difference 102

TURNING POINt. Fundraising is fudge 104

5 Understanding your audience 105
Too much information, not enough stories
Our audience is individual, all different yet all the same
Why does everyone everywhere support the Lifeboats?
Funnily enough, it isn't about money
Always treat your audience with respect
When brevity is best
Long stories vs short
How to find your angle, style, content…
… and to stay 15 minutes ahead
Chapter's end: actions and key messages 116

TURNING POINT. A letter in praise of telemarketing without a script 117

6 Adding purpose and fulfilment 118
What most people really want
The progress paradox
Look! Storytellers can offer meaning…
Types of tale
On doing without
Chapter's end: actions and key messages 129

TURNING POINT. Finding the image that's just right 130

7 A life-stage fairytale: how Beryl and Clive found the meaning of life 133
When planets align
Once upon a time
Fairytales have meaning too
Chapter's end: actions and key messages 141

Part 3 Brilliant emotional storytelling 143

TURNING POINT. The Lord's sister explains the joys of earmarking 144

8 The truth, told well 146
Inspiring people to change the world
'The truth, told well'
The emotion words
The moody leader
Emotion vs intellect: making the emotional case
Not sentimental, really quite practical
Understanding the emotional brain
What are emotions?
Going over the top
Chocolate moments
Six questions to ask before you start your story…
…and the world-changer's seven most powerful words
Effective storytelling is all in the mind
An emotional letter worth copying
Chapter's end: actions and key messages 171

TURNING POINT. A close encounter with a hairy youth 172

9 Where the story turns 173

Building Sleeping Beauty's palace
Measuring commitment
Communications equals lifetime value
Chunking up and down
More than just thank you and welcome
Make a specific offer, define it clearly and give it a price
How your stories spread
How are you going to use the Internet to change the world?
How are you going to use mobile communications devices to change the world?
Getting your stories published
Chapter's end: actions and key messages 189

TURNING POINT. The worst tourist in the world 190

10 Things we get wrong and how we can put them right 192

The power of reciprocity and making the right offer
The most important word in storytelling
Drowning in useless words
You can't fake sincerity
Plan your rituals and cover your walls with inspiration
Mastering the art of communication
Appoint a tone-checker, today
Our most irresistible urge
Plan for approvals
The most difficult, most important part of the process
The art of briefing
Getting the thanking wrong
Keep it to a simple thank you
Good enough is not good enough
A few other most importants
Chapter's end: actions and key messages 210

'You don't write because you want to say something. You write because you have something to say.'

F SCOTT FITZGERALD

TURNING POINT. How Bata shoes came to be known as the shoes of Africa 211

11 Cornerstones of successful storytelling 212

Elmore Leonard's ten rules of writing
There are no rules, but...
Trust to their imaginations
More advice from writers
A quick skirt through the bleedin' obvious
Make it readable
Keep it short
Get to the point
Jargon, gobbledegook and long words
Smile, or whatever
Beat this, if you can
Talk to your readers in their language, not yours
'Persuade by illuminating, inspire by surprising'
Make a specific request and spell out what you need
Build trust and confidence
Leave them feeling wonderful
Make your stories sparkle
Ten keys to a successful headline
'Dear friend' and other abominations
Pattern interruptions
Great openers
Don't let your audience off the hook
Join the fight to keep the word 'yes'
Thirty-two more secrets of successful storytelling
Bacon, eggs and burning your boats
Finally, read copiously
Chapter's end: actions and key messages 241

'An awful lot of storytelling isn't really about making people understand, it's about making people care.'

STEVEN MOFFAT, TELEVISION WRITER AND PRODUCER, AUTHOR OF SEVERAL EPISODES OF *DR WHO*

Part 4 Stories that will stick 243

TURNING POINT. When our audience enters the twilight zone 244

12 Keeping the change working 246

First, we have to stop people from wanting to cross the road
Try and try again: the power of persisting
Storytellers safeguard history
Targeting those most likely to change
In a changing world, how do we keep people changing the world?
The habit of helping
The man who made the world smile more brightly
Becoming the world's best
Smile – you've just done good
The power of belief
It's how you tell 'em
Why our stories will change the world
The storyteller's responsibilities and opportunities
The Swedish story: proof that stories do last
Chapter's end: actions and key messages 265

Introducing the Online Story Bank 266

Permissions. 268

Start your story here 270

'All the stories I would like to write persecute me. When I am in my chamber, it seems as if they are all around me, like little devils, and while one tugs at my ear, another tweaks my nose, and each says to me, "Sir, write me, I am beautiful".'

UMBERTO ECO, *THE ISLAND OF THE DAY BEFORE*

PREFACE
The worst story in the world

Just as this book was being prepared to pass for press I found myself involved in the task of telling a truly transformational story on behalf of a magnificently brave and effective organisation, Amnesty International. For a press advertisement, Amnesty's UK Section had commissioned me and my friend and colleague Indra Sinha to tell the story of what we've come to know as the darkest corner of our planet, the gulag of North Korea, the hellish forced labour camps of so-called Supreme Leader Kim Jong-un.

It would by any standards be an ambitious advertisement, for we wanted to do more than just campaign, build Amnesty's brand and fundraise, all in the same ad. More important even than achieving these three objectives, we wanted to tell the world a difficult, horrific story that urgently needed telling. And we had to tell it in a way that had never been told before.

We immersed ourselves in researching the stories that have emerged from inside those terrible places, then roped in creative director Neil Godfrey and special effects photographer Neil Barstow to produce the most powerful tale we could tell in a bold, long-copy departure from accepted press advertising practice. The first double-page ads appeared in leading UK quality newspapers just before Christmas 2013. The shorter version opposite was produced a few weeks later to coincide with the unveiling of the report from a special UN Commission of Inquiry. We couldn't have told this story without key Amnesty people, the final members of our team.

Prior to unveiling the first draft of our ad to a roomful of Amnesty communications people I explained that I've long believed fundraising organisations such as theirs have the best stories in the world to tell and the best of reasons for telling them. I then ventured my opinion

ADVERTISEMENT

North Korea's leaders would do almost anything to prevent people reading this, so when you've read it please pass it on.

As you read this, some 100,000 people are locked in North Korea's brutal slave labour camps, where most will die of cold, hunger, exhaustion, disease, torture, or execution.

Amnesty has worked for years to close the camps, but the regime flatly denies that they exist. Inside the country there were dreadful rumours – but if no one guessed the whole truth, maybe it was because the truth was too horrific to imagine.

관리소 YODOK

Kwanliso (Political Prison Camp) 15 at Yodok encloses 370 square kilometres of mountains and river valleys, its perimeter stitched together by razor wire, booby traps and high-voltage fences. What we know of it comes from the very few people who have been released *and* who later fled North Korea. All were held in a sector reserved for those whose crimes are *less* serious. Those accused of *serious* crimes, most inmates, are sent to Yodok's 'Total Control Zone' where conditions are harsher. We don't know what happens there because no one who goes in there ever comes out again.

연좌제 KANG

Kang Cheol-hwan was nine when he and his family were sent to Yodok. His grandpa vanished first. No one knew what his crime was, but you can be sent to the camps for joking about the leader, owning a Bible, or just 'gossiping'.

North Korea's doctrine of 'guilt by association' punishes three generations of an offender's family, so security police soon came knocking for Kang, his granny, father, sister and brothers.

Yodok specialises in hideous surprises. Guards might order a new arrival to bury a dead body and wear the corpse's clothes. There was no way to wash their clothes, so prisoners wore them filthy, teeming with lice and fleas, and waited for rainstorms to do their laundry and ease the itching.

위험한 WORK

In *kwanliso* 14 at Kaechon, Mrs L., a housewife from Pyongyang, had spent all day carrying loads of human dung to the camp's huge cesspool. She was very tired. The lid of the tank stuck. She climbed up to push the door open, slipped, plunged into the deep pool of liquid faeces and vanished under the surface. A guard yelled, 'Stop! Let her die there unless you want to die the same way!' She was left to drown in shit.

At Kaechon bodies were often buried in the prison orchard, whose apples, peaches, pears, and plums are famous for their size and extraordinary sweetness, and reserved for senior party and police officials.

치명적인 HUNGER

In Yodok starving inmates hunted any animal that 'flew, crawled, or grew in the field.' 'We had no food,' Kang says. 'We'd eat anything we could lay hands on, frogs, rats, snakes, insects.' A starving prisoner chewed a guard's leather whip. Badly beaten, he was made to eat intestinal worms picked from a latrine and died soon after.

Mothers tried to keep their children alive by catching pregnant rats. The placentas and tiny foetuses were believed to cure disease and made rich eating. Kang caught frogs and worms and centipedes and learned to relish salamanders, which were thought to provide the vitamins necessary for survival.

His first attempt to eat one was a failure. 'I pushed it into my mouth, but I could not swallow. The creature was struggling to get out of my mouth. I was frightened, I closed my eyes and bit it hard. My mouth was suddenly full of bitter and stinking juice and I had to spit it out.' A friend taught Kang that the only way to eat one was to hold the tail and gulp it down.

도주 SHIN

Shin Dong-hyuk knew no life other than that of *kwanliso* 14 at Kaechon. A slave while still in the womb, he was born in Kaechon's Total Control Zone and was destined to live out his whole life and die there.

Shin grew up eating bark off trees and searching cow dung for undigested seeds. Aged ten, he was set to work in a coal mine, had part of a finger axed off for breaking a sewing machine, saw a girl his age beaten to death for stealing five kernels of corn and was made to watch his mother and brother being executed by a firing squad.

In January 2005 Shin and his friend Park braved Kaechon's 3,000 volt fence. Park died quivering on the wire. Shin scrambled over his body, lived, and found his way to Seoul, where he found that many people didn't, or didn't *want*, to believe his horrific story.

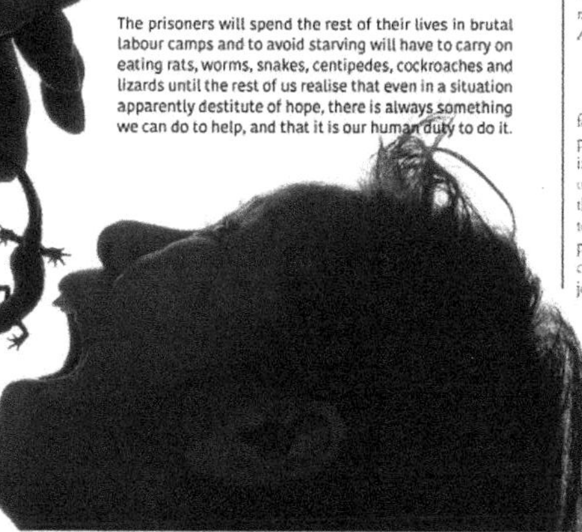

The prisoners will spend the rest of their lives in brutal labour camps and to avoid starving will have to carry on eating rats, worms, snakes, centipedes, cockroaches and lizards until the rest of us realise that even in a situation apparently destitute of hope, there is always something we can do to help, and that it is our human duty to do it.

The North Korean regime claims that the defectors are liars: 'There is no human rights issue in this country as everyone leads the most dignified and happy life.' In June last year the regime warned would-be defectors: 'Sordid human scum will never be able to look up to the sky and will never find an inch of land to be buried after their death.'

항성 STAR

Now please imagine Yodok under a thick blanket of snow. It's a night of brilliant stars but the prisoners, unheeding, shiver in their unheated huts. High above, unseen by them, a tiny point of light is moving across the sky. Amnesty shines a light into the darkness of the North Korean gulag by keeping watch on the camps from space, using satellites to overfly them. Photos taken by Amnesty's Science for Human Rights programme reveal that the regime is *expanding* some of the camps. By demonstrating the reality of North Korea's gulag, and making the survivors' terrifying witness impossible to ignore we chivvy and chip at Supreme Leader Kim Jong-un's pride. And the Supreme Leader wobbles. *Kang says the notorious Seungbori prison was closed after an Amnesty report exposed the goings-on there.*

너희 YOU

North Korean defector Joo Il Kim, a former army captain, likens the plight of the prisoners to that of 'a person who has fallen in a deep hole. It's not easy to hear the voices of those who have fallen in the hole, but when they are heard, it's up to the people outside to raise the alarm and get help. The more people who know, the better. So if you see a campaign for human rights in North Korea, join it, tell your friends, do whatever you can.'

One day, and it may be sooner than you think, the walls of silence and fear in North Korea will crumble and the prisoners will be free. On that day of celebration, imagine their joy when they realise that their long nightmare has ended at last. Together we *can* and *will* get these vile camps closed forever.

Please pick up your pen, fill in the coupon and become a part of this crucial work. *Please*, do it now.

'I want to support Amnesty and help close the labour camps in North Korea'

To donate £10 now text YODOK7 to 70505* or visit amnesty.org.uk/yodok

I would like to help by donating ☐£15 ☐£25 ☐£50 ☐£75 ☐£100 ☐£500 ☐Other £........

☐Here's my cheque to Amnesty International or ☐ Please charge my Visa☐ Mastercard☐ Other☐

Card No: ____|____|____|____ Expiry date __|__ Date of birth (if under 18) __|__|__

Title (Mr/Mrs/Miss/Ms) ______ Name: ....

Address: ....

....

Postcode: .... Telephone No: ....

Signature: .... Date__|__|__

Gift Aid it.

Please fill in the coupon and post (no stamp needed) to: Freepost RSHR-JYYA-UGXC, North Korean Appeal, Amnesty International UK, PO Box 36, Sheffield, S98 1DB

Amnesty International UK Charity No: 1051681

that this particular story – such is the horror of it – might well qualify as the worst story in the world.

To prove the point I then read to them the entire text of the ad aloud, all 2,300 words of it. When I'd finished there was a long silence. A few tears were quietly brushed away. Such emotion from this audience seemed to me to signal that, most probably, we had a success on our hands.

Before I attempt to summarise reactions to this advertisement and the hurdles we had to overcome to create it, please if you can bear it, read the single-page ad. It's not for the faint-hearted, yet it is the truth. And it's from the truth, told well, that great change comes.

The single-page ad text

North Korea's leaders would do almost anything to prevent people reading this, so when you've read it please pass it on.

As you read this, some 100,000 people are locked in North Korea's brutal slave labour camps, where most will die of cold, hunger, exhaustion, disease, torture, or execution. Amnesty has worked for years to close the camps, but the regime flatly denies that they exist. Inside the country there were dreadful rumours – but if no one guessed the whole truth, maybe it was because the truth was too horrific to imagine.

관리소 YODOK

Kwanliso (Political Prison Camp) 15 at Yodok encloses 370 square kilometres of mountains and river valleys, its perimeter stitched together by razor wire, booby traps and high-voltage fences. What we know of it comes from the very few people who have been released and who later fled North Korea. All were held in a sector reserved for those whose crimes are less serious. Those accused of serious crimes, most inmates, are sent to Yodok's 'Total Control Zone' where conditions are harsher. We don't know what happens there because no one who goes in there ever comes out again.

연좌제 KANG

Kang Cheol-hwan was nine when he and his family were sent to Yodok. His grandpa vanished first. No one knew what his crime was, but you can be sent to the camps for joking about the leader, owning a Bible, or just 'gossiping'. North Korea's doctrine of 'guilt by association' punishes three generations of an offender's family, so security police soon came knocking for Kang, his granny, father, sister and brothers.

Yodok specialises in hideous surprises. Guards might order a new arrival to bury a dead body and wear the corpse's clothes. There was no way to wash their clothes, so prisoners wore them filthy, teeming with lice and fleas, and waited for rainstorms to do their laundry and ease the itching.

위험한 WORK

In *kwanliso* 14 at Kaechon, Mrs L., a housewife from Pyongyang, had spent all day carrying loads of human faeces to the camp's huge cesspool. She was very tired. The lid of the tank stuck. She climbed up to push the door open, slipped, plunged into the deep pool of faeces and vanished under the surface. A guard yelled, 'Stop! Let her die there unless you want to die the same way!' She was left to drown in shit.

At Kaechon bodies were often buried in the prison orchard, whose apples, peaches, pears, and plums are famous for their size and extraordinary sweetness, and reserved for senior party and police officials.

치명적인 HUNGER

In Yodok starving inmates hunted any animal that 'flew, crawled, or grew in the field.' 'We had no food,' Kang says. 'We'd eat anything we could lay hands on, frogs, rats, snakes, insects.' A starving prisoner chewed a guard's leather whip. Badly beaten, he was made to eat intestinal worms picked from a latrine and died soon after.

Mothers tried to keep their children alive by catching pregnant rats. The placentas and tiny foetuses were believed to cure disease and made rich eating. Kang caught frogs and worms and centipedes and learned to relish salamanders, which were thought to provide the vitamins necessary for survival.

His first attempt to eat one was a failure. 'I pushed it into my mouth, but I could not swallow. The creature was struggling to get out of my mouth. I was frightened, I closed my eyes and bit it hard. My mouth was suddenly full of bitter and stinking juice and I had to spit it out.' A friend taught Kang that the only way to eat one was to hold the tail and gulp it down.

도주 SHIN

Shin Dong-hyuk knew no life other than that of *kwanliso* 14 at Kaechon. A slave while still in the womb, he was born in Kaechon's Total Control Zone and was destined to live out his whole life and die there.

Shin grew up eating bark off trees and searching cow dung for undigested seeds. Aged ten, he was set to work in a coal mine, had part of a finger axed off for breaking a sewing machine, saw a girl his age beaten to death for stealing five kernels of corn and was made to watch his mother and brother being executed by a firing squad.

In January 2005 Shin and his friend Park braved Kaechon's 3,000 volt fence. Park died quivering on the wire. Shin scrambled over his body, lived, and found his way to Seoul, where he found that many people didn't, or didn't want to, believe his horrific story.

The North Korean regime claims that the defectors are liars: 'There is no human rights issue in this country as everyone leads the most dignified and happy life.' In June last year the regime warned would-be escapers: 'Sordid human scum will never be able to look up to the sky and will never find an inch of land to be buried after their death.'

항성 STAR

Now please imagine Yodok, under a thick blanket of snow. It's a night of brilliant stars but the prisoners, unheeding, shiver in their unheated huts. High above, unseen by them, a point of light is moving across the sky. Amnesty is shining a light into the darkness of the North Korean gulag. We keep watch on the camps from space, using satellites to overfly them. Photos taken by our Science for Human Rights programme show that the regime is actually expanding some of the camps. By demonstrating the reality of North Korea's gulag, and making the survivors' terrifying witness impossible to ignore we chivvy and chip at Supreme Leader Kim Jong-un's pride. And the Supreme Leader wobbles. Kang says the notorious Seunghori prison was closed after an Amnesty report exposed the goings-on there.

너희 YOU

North Korean defector Joo Il Kim, a former army captain, likens the plight of the prisoners to that of 'a person who has fallen in a deep hole. It's not easy to hear the voices of those who have fallen in the hole, but when they are heard, it's up to the people outside to raise the alarm and get help. The more people who know, the better.

'So if you see a campaign for human rights in North Korea, join it, tell your friends, do whatever you can.'

One day, and it may be sooner than you think, the walls of silence and fear in North Korea will crumble and the prisoners will be free. On that day of celebration, imagine their joy when they realise that the long nightmare has ended at last. Together we can and will get these vile camps closed forever. Please pick up your pen, fill in the coupon and join us in this good work. Please, do it now.

Above the illustration sat a stark caption.

> **The prisoners will spend the rest of their lives in brutal labour camps and to avoid starving will have to carry on eating rats, worms, snakes, centipedes, cockroaches and lizards until the rest of us realise that, even in a situation apparently destitute of hope, there is always something we can do to help, and that it is our human duty to do it.**

A reply coupon followed, so that those who wanted to could make a donation, under the headline, 'I want to support Amnesty and help close the labour camps in North Korea.'

The British public, thus confronted over their breakfast tables, responded in droves. This first test showed that an earlier effective means of supporter recruitment – long-copy 'story' ads – could be capable of resurrection. With some lessons learned the second test, eight weeks later, did significantly better. So Amnesty found that it could recruit new supporters cost-effectively while campaigning powerfully, emotionally and in detail to their most important audiences. In addition to direct response the advertisement brought Amnesty benefits in media coverage, awareness, supporter inspiration and staff motivation. Future campaigns will refine and improve both the storytelling and the means whereby people respond, so Amnesty will continue to improve how it gets its stories through in what is, without doubt, an ever more noisy, cluttered and competitive world.

For sure it was a story well worth telling, despite the many difficulties. It took a combination of bravery, idealism, fine writing, persistence, rigorous attention to detail and sheer bloody-mindedness to get into print.

In an article in *Third Sector* magazine reviewing these ads Amnesty International UK's director, Kate Allen, said: 'Human interest stories and empathy have always been at the heart of how we campaign, and these are undiluted stories that can't fail to move the reader. Stories are our stock in trade. It's a simple formula and that's what Amnesty is, stripped back: a story and a refusal to accept the status quo.'

A comment in that *Third Sector* article from Peter Gilheany, director of Forster Communications, observed that while these advertisements break the conventional rules of direct response press advertising, they really work. 'It's not an approach you can employ too often, he said, '...but every now and then it is good to give your complacent assumptions about the right way of doing things a hefty kick up the backside, which is exactly what these adverts do.'

Peter may be right, and you can't use this style of story too often. Though, Indra Sinha's been doing it successfully these past 20 years and more.

Stories of this kind are invariably a challenge to tell. Issues of acceptability, sensitivity, permissions, verification, anonymity, creating powerful images by reconstruction, timing, copy approval, coupon construction and more all combine to make an already difficult story even more difficult to pull together. But tough though they are at the time, when a great story is told the trials and challenges all fall away into insignificance. And the results really make a difference.

This book is dedicated to telling similarly difficult yet life-changing stories, whether heart-warming or painful, upsetting or uplifting. It is for all stories that raise spirits, expose issues and shine light upon the limitless potential of life, as well as for all other equally important stories that have not yet been written, have not yet been told.

Ken Burnett, London, August 2014

PART ONE

Why we tell stories

TURNING POINT

Sometimes a true story can have life-changing consequences. I've chosen to tell this tale here because it's personal and it makes the point that underpins this book.

Charlie and the human rights lawyers of Guatemala

My youngest son, Charlie, was just 14 years old when I came home from visiting some development projects in Guatemala and Haiti. I'd been particularly impressed by a group of human rights lawyers I'd met in Guatemala and the stories they told me of the persecution they'd endured from the military dictatorship there. Impassively they told me of the cloud of disappearances, threats and killings under which they and their families had lived and worked for years as they struggled to document and oppose the regime's widespread human rights abuses – massacres, rapes, torture and acts of genocide against the indigenous tribal people. In return for their devoted fight for the rights of the weakest in their society these brave lawyers were hounded by their own government, abducted, imprisoned, tortured and forced into exile. Several of their friends and colleagues paid for their courage with their lives. The quiet dignity and dedication in the stories told me by these unassuming men and women made a massive impression on me and somehow, when I got back, I managed to convey that to my family, particularly to young Charlie.

That day Charlie decided he would become a human rights lawyer. Now a dozen years later with his masters in human rights law and two further law degrees under his belt he's just completed his training with a specialist human rights law firm in London, preparing for his life's work, setting wrongs to right. He's already handled several difficult, challenging cases, a few of them quite dramatic, even heartbreaking, and he's helped win some, too. He earns half what his friends in corporate law get paid and I feel bad about that. But I'm hugely proud of him and his decision, of his single-minded dedication and persistent application to tread a difficult path that grew from that simple story, which he's since seen through to such a great end. Those lawyers from Guatemala inspired Charlie, not only changing his life, but the lives of many others and will go on changing lives for the better for years to come.

All from a short, transformational story.

1. How transformational storytelling could be just right for you

'There is nothing to writing.
All you do is sit down at a typewriter
and bleed.'

ERNEST HEMINGWAY

Chances are that, as you're reading this book, you too are, or want to be, a transformational storyteller. So you probably already know that one of the best tools we have to help change this flawed world is a story, told well. It's widely accepted that people respond differently to stories from any other kind of information that comes their way. And for the five key stages of recruiting others to change the world – engagement, involvement, inspiration, influence and action – nothing works as well with almost any audience, anywhere, as simply telling a transformational story. Just how, where, when and why these stories have such impact is the subject of this book. Its purpose is to help you tell your stories better.

For clarity I should perhaps attempt a definition. Transformational storytelling involves using a story to make a difference, implicitly a positive difference, to change someone or something for the better. Stories told well in particular ways have potential to make things happen, to shake things up. The change may be large or small, temporary or permanent, actual or intangible, personal or public. Potentially powerful, transformational stories work best when told carefully, deliberately and responsibly.

Invariably I aim to satisfy the five key stages when structuring any story.

ENGAGEMENT. Engagement is attention plus emotion. How will I attract and interest my audience, to stir their emotions and secure their attention?

INVOLVEMENT. How do I keep that attention at least long enough to get my points across?

INSPIRATION. Can I raise their sights, lift their ambitions and fire their aspirations?

INFLUENCE. How will I inform and shape my audience's thinking, feelings and intentions? Can I convert involvement and inspiration into commitment?

ACTION. What actions will flow from the story, to bring about the desired change?

The most important decisions for the transformational storyteller are, what is my story about and what do I intend it to achieve?

The story that Cecil Jackson Cole told his three fellow volunteers on the Oxford Committee for Famine Relief in the last days of the Second World War was a transformational story. They'd set up the committee to provide relief supplies for the Greek people, who were being starved by Britain's blockade of their Nazi-occupied country. Now news had reached them that the war had ended, so the committee was all set to disband. Then CJC told them, 'There's a world of need out there, so we must go on.' That's how Oxfam was formed.

Founding moments often emanate from transformational stories. The story that lawyer Peter Benenson told in *The Observer* newspaper in 1961 about two Portuguese students imprisoned by their government for raising a glass to toast freedom is one for sure, for it led to the founding of Amnesty International.

Though penned by William Shakespeare 200 years after the battle, Henry V's St Crispin's Day speech to English troops before Agincourt is a transformational story because it remains the most rousing evocation to men at arms, inspiring them to risk their all for king and country. Exhorting the few likely survivors to show off their scars with pride, the king inspired his apprehensive troops to unexpected valour by telling them that 'Gentlemen in England now a-bed shall think themselves accurs'd they were not here, and hold their manhoods cheap, whiles any speaks that fought with us upon Saint Crispin's day.'

The equally thrilling story of Rosa Parks, arrested because she wouldn't give up her seat on the bus to a white person, that too changed the mood of a nation, so changing the world forever.

Since Twitter arrived in all our lives stories in 140 characters or less have often led the news, changing the world with the sheer weight of their instant global chatter. Witness the wave of change that swept the Middle East in the so-called Arab spring.

The Parable of the Talents, as told by Jesus of Nazareth, was surely transformational for its warning of the dire consequences if we fail to use properly the gifts and skills we've been given.

A single, appropriately captioned image can change a mood in a moment, such as when Amnesty matched that unforgettable image of the young man facing down a row of tanks in Beijing's Tiananmen Square with the headline, 'What are *you* doing this weekend?'

So, transformational stories are all around. They don't always have such impact and importance, though at times they might, and more even. Such stories are as old as life and as ubiquitous as conversation. They come in all shapes, styles and sizes. There's no right or wrong way to tell them, though learning to construct and spin transformational stories effectively will enable anyone to multiply the difference he or she can make. More examples, with varying degrees of impact and influence, will appear throughout this book.

Without thinking much about it I told my son Charlie the story you've just read, about the human rights lawyers in Guatemala. It transformed his life. That story has stuck with him, affecting who he is and what he stands for. Now, as a result of that story, he's changing the lives of others too and will do for years to come. Not to mention its effect on the rest of our family. Telling that story had influence and positive repercussions far beyond my expectations or intention. I now appreciate that a large part of that story's impact was the timing and the telling of it. And I've realised that I use storytelling often, both at work and socially, in a variety of different ways to produce any of a complex range of effects and outcomes.

The best way to bring about change

These realisations were the genesis of *Storytelling Can Change the World.* Though not all are as dramatic or as positive as Charlie's there are many stories in this book, each different, each a turning point in one way or another. All of them I hope add up to a convincing case for a particular kind of storytelling that will productively and profitably repay any efforts readers put in to master this book's simple, practical guidance.

Storytelling is the most important skill for any would-be influencer. It can quickly get you and your listener on the same side, to the same place. But there's more. To win the sale, secure a donation, spark some buzz, plant a seed, inspire extra effort, turn an argument... you need to change people, sometimes only slightly and for a short while, but often more deeply and durably. We do that best by telling them stories.

Effective, transformational storytelling is the topmost end of this enviable, practical ability. It's the most versatile, most valuable asset for anyone working as a teacher, influencer, or leader in any number of professional and technical business areas. It's particularly useful for those who aspire to effortlessly and painlessly persuade others to willingly do something that otherwise, most likely, they would not. The subtle skill that is transformational storytelling is indispensable for all who would entertain, inform or influence anyone else. As the phrase suggests, it's what we have to learn to do and use if we would bring about real change.

Why transformational storytelling works so well isn't in doubt. Receptiveness to stories is hard-wired into our DNA. Stories engage us easily, draw us in naturally, excite our curiosity, pique our interests and lead us to the satisfying conclusion that we can do something now, to make a difference.

In the modern world of massive information overload stories get through where wodges of bumph and formal reports, however filled with information, won't. Stories stick where whatever's picked up from sitting through lessons and lectures quickly fades. They're how people learn. Transformational stories have an extra dimension, the power to move people to make change.

So *Storytelling Can Change the World* could be the most timely 'how to' business book of the twenty-first century. It's for anyone who wants to get into real communications – to be not merely giving out, but actually getting through. It shows how, while entertaining and helping others, you can make a real difference in the world just by doing something you love and revel in.

The book is structured in several stages:

- *Once upon a time:* why telling stories is useful, profitable and fun. There's a lot on this in chapters 2, 3 and 4.

- *The pot of gold:* how your business, school, cause, or enterprise can harness transformational storytelling to build relationships, motivate staff, students, customers and prospects, while making a difference too. Read about this in chapters 2 and 3.

- *Adding purpose, fulfilment and the meaning of life:* how storytelling can add interest and engagement, so delighting and uniting people behind common aims and dreams. Chapters 2, 3, 6 and 7 show how this happens.

- *Unlocking the dream:* how to tell your stories well, when and to whom. See chapters 5, 7 and 9 for this.

- *All in the mind:* passion, emotion and the truth told well. How you can appeal not just to the hearts but also to the brains of your audience. Chapter 8 has lots on tickling the brain and tugging at heartstrings.

- *Magic moments:* key components upon which your stories turn. That's what chapter 9 is all about.

- *Stories that stick:* adding painful itch, soothing scratch and something unexpected. How to brief a writer, increase impact and lift response. What makes a story real. See chapter 10 for such things.

- *A practical treasure chest:* secrets of the storyteller's art and craft, top tips and helpful hints from other writers on how to write, plus suggested keys to effective transformational storytelling. Chapters 11 and 12 have lots on this.

From the start this book shows how storytelling makes a difference across a range of commercial activities. Struggling students learn more when their lessons are presented as stories, good causes recruit lifetime donors and advocates through storytelling, which can also help any business improve how it attracts, engages and retains customers.

Looking forward to the age of opportunity

And there's much more. Storytelling is key to a vast, largely unrecognised potential for social change. In our society wealth and opportunity appear to accumulate inexorably to the affluent elderly. Down the ages it's seemed that just as people reach financial security, soon afterwards their life will naturally decline and end. All that appears now to have changed. Now, 60 is the new 40 and there are some even who claim that, for those who can afford it, before long 70 will be the new 30. Whatever, we're all living lots longer, with added years and increased prosperity providing an unrivalled opportunity for those last decades. For many, if not most. Yet today's once golden baby boomers, those born from mid 1940s to mid 1960s and now the confident, affluent, demographically blessed young oldies, are likely to face a range of new troubles and hurdles in the next couple of decades as they seek to fill their final years. *Storytelling Can Change the World* provides an insight into the opportunities for reaching into those lives to influence and orchestrate a different, more satisfying, productive and constructive approach to the traditional image of a happy retirement.

When a story resonates closely with our audience's values and aspirations, amazing things become possible. Transformational stories told well have the knack of fixing themselves fast inside the brains of a receptive audience, settling there to liberate feelings, activate emotions, release passions and shape desires that all but compel our audience to act. Before you're even halfway through this book you'll be telling stories yourself more often, more confidently, more powerfully and more enjoyably.

And if you just aspire to be a better writer there should be some help and enjoyment in these pages for you, too.

> *'There are some parts of the human self that are not subject to the laws of time and space. And storytelling, the telling of, and the listening to, is one of those things.'*
> CARL JUNG, PSYCHIATRIST AND PSYCHOTHERAPIST

Entertainment or action? Why there are only two types of story

'How can this be?', I hear you ask, 'Surely there must be as many types of story as there are storytellers?'

True. But there's a big, important difference between stories that entertain and thrill, that leave a warm glow, provoke applause but where at their end the most we do is sit back and sigh in satisfaction, and stories that compel us to take action right now. So this seems a good time to introduce you to Caius and Marcellus, two characters who symbolise two quite different types of story.

Caius and Marcellus are heroes of ancient Rome beloved by the people, the city's star orators, best speakers by far in the Forum or on the floor of the Senate.

Caius is famed far and wide as the master of reasoned argument and logical thought. The people flock to hear him, for when he speaks Caius deploys words as precision instruments, each carefully crafted to complement the next, stringing his sentiments together in faultless flow so that the combined force of their sheer logic and rationality leads inexorably to his desired, inescapable conclusion. When Caius concludes his audience applauds long and loud. 'How wonderfully impressive,' they say. 'What a very fine speaker Caius is.'

Marcellus, by contrast, is renowned as the spinner of dreams and visions, master of passionate, powerful emotions and painter of word pictures. His prose thrills and animates, arouses high passions and deep ardour, makes hairs stand on end and lumps rise in throats. When Marcellus speaks the crowd is quickly roused to fever pitch. As his words fill the air the people leap to their feet shouting, 'Bravo! Hooray! Let us now march on Byzantium!' For Marcellus's passion and emotion have moved his listeners not to applause, but to action.

Both undeniably are the best there is, yet there's a big difference between these two. Symbolically, for this journey, Marcellus shall be our guide. For we don't want our stories merely to move our readers to applause. Rather, we want them to leap to their feet, passionate, angry, impelled and determined to make change happen and happen now. Much more than to applause, we want to move our audience to action. We don't want our stories to make people comfortable, because comfortable people tend to do nothing. If they're to move people to action your stories will most likely make some folk quite uncomfortable, and some others perhaps very uncomfortable indeed.

Stories that lead to action are no less varied or ancient than those that don't. They too fall into several distinct types – the hero legend, the sermon, photojournalism, the sales pitch, the blog, stories that raise money, or other forms of support, stories that unite an organisation, or galvanise it into action, stories from a soapbox, fables, parables, bedtime stories, reward stories, pep talks and even the summing up before judge and jury, to name just some of them… all stories where livelihoods and even lives can hang upon the eloquence and ability of the transformational storyteller.

> *'Until lions have their historians, tales of the hunt shall always glorify the hunter.'*
>
> AFRICAN PROVERB

Your story is all about its audience

Throughout the history of the promotional message the promoter has dictated the content based mostly on what he or she wishes to say rather than on what his or her audience would most like to hear. Which of course is not the same thing at all.

This isn't surprising. For the most part the promoters of goods, services and even good works don't see themselves as storytellers at all. They have an agenda, products to shift, students to teach, supporters or customers to recruit and donations to raise. The promoter of a product or proposition is on a mission and heaven help anyone or anything that gets in its way.

Transformational storytelling starts with the assumption that a story is all about its audience and what they want or are prepared to hear. The storyteller then structures his or her tale to have maximum impact and effect upon the listeners. It's the 90-degree shift, the storyteller's version of the poet Burns' famous invocation, to see ourselves as others see us. In transformational storytelling understanding this basic point pays, big time. Being right but not being heard equals being irrelevant.

It's possible to deploy a wide range of media and techniques to convey a campaigning message and tell a promotional story that will recruit people, money, or whatever else you need for your cause. How, why and when you can best do this is what I aim to cover in *Storytelling Can Change the World.*

Stories have influence

I've tried to lace this book with stories that will make your heart soar, your pulse race and your step spring. I've added tips to help you tell stories every bit as inspirational, every bit as engaging, every bit as influential. And because, for the most part, the stories we tell are true – they actually happened – you'll realise your stories do, really, possess the power not just to entertain, but to transform.

Stories are nice, enjoyable, fun. They can also be sad, sobering, shocking and stunning. Stories can be uplifting and depressing too, forgettable and unforgettable by turns. Stories are everywhere and uncountable. The transformational storyteller has to be a guardian of propriety, a prompt to social conscience and a window on what it is to be a human being.

For businesses, the transformational storyteller can be a key to accountability and corporate social engagement, the articulator of an enterprise's ethics, vision and values, an advocate of social purpose going hand-in-hand with profit-making. Yet don't please underestimate the storyteller's potential to make a big impact on any business's bottom line. In education also he or she can inject interest and engagement, so adding to the success of both teachers and students.

This book is all about you

It has a big purpose: to change the way you think about and tell your stories. And a great big fat point of view: that effective storytelling is the most useful social and business skill you can have. Storytelling can help you secure riches, status, success, approval and applause. And even if only little by little, storytellers *really can* change the world.

I realise this concept could be a bit contentious. But I'm an optimist and you have to give these things a go. If you believe, they usually work. If you think you can, or if you think you can't, you're right.

In 1992, I wrote a book called *Relationship Fundraising* that I thought should and could change the way fundraisers think about and communicate with their donors. At the time I didn't have any idea whether it would.

Yet to a surprising degree, it did. *Relationship Fundraising* has sold in every corner of the world and more than 22 years after its first appearance it's still selling respectably (though not enough for me to give up the day job). If I'm honest, while it changed attitudes fairly quickly it took its time to deeply change actions. And it's still a work in progress.

But it has made a difference.

At the time I could prove little of the big point of view that formed the spine of that book, but it just felt right – the idea that fundraisers would raise more money if they could be donor-focused and relationship-focused, rather than money and results-focused. If they were to concentrate more on the people sending the money than on the money they were sending I thought this would not only be more enjoyable and satisfying for all concerned, it would work better too, both for the donor and the cause and, so, for the fundraiser trying to serve both.

Then eight years after *Relationship Fundraising* first appeared a woman in Canada called Penelope Burk came along and through diligent and extensive research proved the principle right in almost every area. I've no reason to believe that the same thing will happen again and no doubt that once again I'll be challenged for the simplicity of my arguments and the naivety of my view. But it feels right all the same, so I'll give it a go.

At the end of each chapter in that book I told the story of an individual donor or a couple, 12 in all, to gently introduce a range of these people and their interests, issues, dreams and activities. These stories remain among the most appreciated and commented on parts of that book.

> *'Information and communication are often used interchangeably, but they signify quite different things. Information is giving out. Communication is getting through.'*
>
> SYDNEY J HARRIS, JOURNALIST

The truth, told well, really will change the world

It's a lousy world, so somebody should change it. And that might as well be us. Is there a wrong you yearn to see righted, a world you long to see? Almost certainly. If the revolutionary wave that will transform our world is ever to come to pass, it will need great storytellers to spread it.

This book is for a wide range of storytellers: agitators, fundraisers, campaigners, lobbyists, politicians, parents, mentors, evangelists and dreamers, to name but a few. It's for the inquisitive, the restless, the seldom satisfied. It's a book for business people who might want to make their products or services more accessible, to tell their tales more deeply and durably than in the average advertisement or press release. In short, it's a book for anyone who wants to change his or her own, or another person's, world.

This is also a book for those tired of blandness and imprecision in language, bored with the lazy, over-easy carelessness of expression that's exploded with the advent of instant electronic communication. It's a book for anyone looking for ways to do all modern media things better. It's intended to be a helpful, encouraging book for anyone who wants to write to make a difference and to do that job more effectively. It's an attitude guide for anyone who wants to get into real communication – to be not merely giving out, but actually getting through.

Information is giving out. Communication is getting through. Only one of these is useful. The other is simply a drain.

To a lucky few transformational storytelling seems to come naturally and some even appear hardly to have to work at it at all. For most of us, however, it requires application. Though, as it's usually fun, interesting and enlightening that should present no hardship. But please, remember the sage advice of the poet John Donne: that which is written with ease is invariably read with difficulty. In this endeavour, application pays.

The most sincere form of flattery

> *'Immature poets imitate; mature poets steal; bad poets deface what they take, and good poets make it into something better, or at least something different.'*
> T S ELIOT

> *'The secret to creativity is knowing how to hide your sources.'*
> ALBERT EINSTEIN

Precisely because storytelling is as old as dust and because I'm not hugely disposed to reinvent the wheel, I make absolutely no apology for quoting widely and frequently from the writing and findings of others as I assemble my case for effective transformational storytelling and how to do it. Indeed I've actively sought it out, so that you might have access to the best of thinking, rather than merely mine.

But risky though it is I have to disagree here with Einstein (though I'm sure his point was not meant to be taken literally). Where practical or when something is covered by copyright I've sought permission to quote and I've invariably acknowledged provenance wherever I can. Any errors or omissions are purely mine.

With those provisos I admit I'm a confessed, confirmed plagiarist and proud of it. Except perhaps when creating fiction, I advise any other writer to do likewise. As T S Eliot says, all writers are thieves. Only, some are better at it than others. Why trouble to think of your own big idea if you can pinch someone else's? Plagiarism is the most sincere form of flattery. Writers are like sparrows standing on the shoulders of eagles, so they can soar just a little bit higher. So by all means borrow, but acknowledge your source properly and always seek permission whenever practical, whether covered by copyright or not. Never pass off anything borrowed as your own. Add to your borrowings if you can to fit them to your context. Embellish if possible.

I'd go further. All writers should have an inspiration file close by them that they add to wisely and take from constantly.

Beware, handle stories with care

Some caution is called for when planning to tell transformational stories. The emotions that might be unleashed in the process are powerful and can be volatile, disturbing, invasive and unpredictable. They require deep sensitivity and careful handling from the storyteller if their use is to be appropriate.

I add this warning here in all seriousness. It's a powerful tool that you are seeking familiarity with. It deserves at all times to be handled with responsibility, sympathy and respect, just as if you were meeting each member of your audience in person, hoping to interest, impress and influence them but, above all, determined to be polite and nice to them, not to mislead them in any way.

Now, meet the author

I'm lucky enough to have spent most of my working life being paid to tell stories for a diverse range of organisations that all share an abiding dream. One way or another, they all want to change the world. Over nearly four decades I've worked to influence fundraisers and their supporters worldwide, telling stories for hundreds of great causes from Greenpeace, Amnesty, ActionAid, to NSPCC, Botton Village, Oxfam and a host of others. I've told stories about social workers rescuing children from abuse and refugees fleeing wars and disasters. I've advocated for adults living with learning disabilities and other special needs and described lifeboatmen saving sailors from stormy seas. I've told of campaigners in wet-suits shielding whales from the harpoons of evil whalers and of dedicated researchers poised on the brink of breakthroughs. While at it I've galvanised hordes of agitators, recruited legions of regular givers as committed donors and with their willing approval raised from them shed loads of money, always to make this world in ways large or small a better place for all.

Along the way I've had more fun than anyone has a right to in one life. I've served on several national and international non-profit boards and have run or at least sat at the top of some smallish but quite successful businesses too.

I should say right at the start of this book that while I use the term non-profit quite a lot, because internationally that's the current convention, I'm firmly with those who'd like to see that term change for good. Charities, universities, arts companies and other so-called non-profit organisations actually generate considerable profits usually very cost-effectively, though these enjoy a generally loftier purpose than those most other for-profit enterprises create. So I'd like to see the non-profit or not-for-profit sector renamed as the for-change sector or the social change sector, because that's what these organisations use their profits for. For change.

The thing about me is that most of all in my work I like telling stories the best. And whatever success I've had I put down to, in its broadest sense, telling stories passably well. Now as my working life comes to a close my ambition is to share my approach to and passion for storytelling with anyone who'll listen.

That, hopefully, includes you.

It's fitting to end this first chapter on the most important word in storytelling.

You.

CHAPTER'S END:
ACTIONS AND KEY MESSAGES

There's a world of difference between a story that leads to applause and a story that leads to action.

The five key stages of recruiting people to change the world are engagement, involvement, inspiration, influence and action.

Everyone can be a transformational storyteller.

Transformational storytelling offers many opportunities to make a difference.

The starting point of transformational storytelling is the audience.

Information is giving out. Communication is getting through. Never forget the difference.

The storyteller's task is to tell the truth and tell it well.

Plagiarism pays, though you have to do it right.

This book aims to change how you think about and tell your stories.

The most important word in storytelling is *you*.

TURNING POINT

Here's the story of an organisation that 'chunked up' effectively to find what they are *really* about and in the process told a story that captured the interests and imaginations of an entire city. For more on chunking and how to do it, see chapter 9.

Kristiansand creates 5,348 jobs in less than a month. But not for Norwegians.

Jobbskaper means job creator, in Norwegian. It's an inspirational idea from the Norwegian development aid agency Strømmestiftelsen (Strømme Foundation) and the title of their most ambitious campaign ever. And it's turning Kristiansand, Norway's fifth largest town, pink.

For years Strømme Foundation has led the way in small-scale microfinance schemes that provide revolving loans to farmers and other village-level entrepreneurs across the developing world, helping them to build a small business that will sustain their families, often from very little. Other organisations passionately promote micro-credit schemes, of course, and have been doing so for years. Worthy and commendable they are, sadly they seldom excite the imagination. Indeed, the problem with microfinance is that it's a great scheme, but dull.

Strømme sought to change all that, for good.

So with some help from their agency, Profundo, and a UK consultancy called Clayton Burnett, Strømme set out to give their micro-credit scheme a different focus and spin by telling the story of a much bigger dream. Instead of

the traditional concept of finding individual donors to sponsor single micro-finance schemes one at a time, the *Jobbskaper* idea would mobilise a whole city to create thousands of jobs in one single, focused campaign.

Kristiansand is famous as Norway's export port, with a long, proud tradition of entrepreneurial innovation. A micro-credit scheme, if you drill deeply enough into why it makes a difference, is essentially about creating jobs and livelihoods. Putting it like that, it suddenly becomes an important, urgent aspiration that everyone in Norway can relate to. So could Kristiansand, in one colourful, high-profile and time-limited campaign, create 10,000 real jobs and livelihoods for small-scale entrepreneurs at the far side of the world, while raising 6,000,000 kroner (£600,000) in the process?

With a population of just 80,000, that would call for 75 kroner each from every person in the city. A million dollar dream. But a dream that could just possibly come true or very near to it, if local people and businesses could be inspired and engaged in the right way, if the city's imagination and approval could be captured through a great story.

On a sunny late summer's day in September 2013 bright pink buildings began to appear all over Kristiansand. Pink balloons floated across the skyline and pink footballs appeared on the streets and in the parks. Newspapers and billboards carried pictures and stories announcing the plan, all with copious amounts of pink. A specially developed pink brochure was inserted into every mailbox. The mayor, in pink, made a moving announcement on local TV and radio. Wherever they were in Kritiansand that morning, no one could miss it. And new job creators began to be signed up in their hundreds. Within three weeks the campaign had produced over 5,000 jobs and was still going strong because the people could see that when they join *Jobbskaper* they are not simply doing revolving micro-credit, they are creating jobs so people can feed their families.

For Strømme Foundation *Jobbskaper* was the start of a very much more ambitious dream, to replicate the idea in every town and community across Norway. And as the first of these, the city of Kristiansand suddenly had something else to boast about – simply because Strømme Foundation had discovered a better way to tell their story.

Led by its mayor, Kristiansand goes pink for *Jobbskaper*.

2. Can storytelling really change the world?

'My daughter, Harley, has a physics teacher who tells fabulous stories. The kids think they are managing to get him off the point but there is always something hidden in the story that they quite often swallow without realising.'

KARIN WEATHERUP, WRITER

Imagine no more boring school lessons, no more tedious business presentations, no more dreary lectures at college and university, no more dull dinner parties and turgid social engagements. Imagine sermons, lectures and debates that are interesting, exciting, full of learning. Imagine working for and with people who make a difference, who interest and electrify, who inspire and entertain on a regular basis because they always tell a good story. Imagine if people everywhere could view their retirement not as a time of twilight and decline but as decades of opportunity for involvement and fulfilment, for changing the world.

Stories are the most digestible, memorable, enjoyable and shareable part of our common culture. Improved storytelling can change the world in some very substantial ways.

Quick wins at school

I hated school. Not the time outside school when I was mucking about with my pals and having fun – the rest of the time, when we had lessons or did homework, when I was supposed to be learning.

Despite spending long years at it I learned so little. When I look back on those dull, fruitless hours, days and weeks it was, obviously, a tragic waste.

Why couldn't it have been less boring?

Primary school was. I remember interesting stories that peppered our generally gentle lessons and had me enjoying learning. Then, from the ripe age of 11 it seemed to be assumed I'd outgrown stories. And boredom came in their stead.

The only bits of my schooling that I enjoyed and learned from were history, some geography and English literature. Now I love science and have a niggling sense that I might possibly have appreciated mathematics too – algebra, geometry and trigonometry were completely closed books to me. But back then my teachers simply had no idea how to make any parts of any subject relevant or interesting. No one tried to explain what they were for, or why they might be useful. Physics and chemistry were a succession of abstract principles and seemingly daft experiments with no clear explanation of purpose or meaning.

French was as bad. I was in the north of Scotland, miles from France. I didn't leave Scotland till I was 17. My father had fought in France as a 21-year-old and hated every moment of it. Other than that maybe I might have to do the same, why would I want to learn French? No one told me. I can see now of course – I was in my twenties before I went to France and fell instantly in love with everything about the place. Surely in five years my French teacher could have told me some stories that would have introduced me earlier to some of France's wonders, and encouraged me to want to learn the language at school?

Though why I might want to learn Latin largely eludes me still.

I'm not alone.

Professor Mark Lythgoe created and runs one of the largest medical imaging research facilities in Europe – the Centre for Advanced Biomedical Imaging at University College London – quite an achievement for someone who spectacularly failed his A levels and didn't go on to university.

Because he did so badly at school Mark's route into science was long and convoluted. On the BBC radio programme *The Life Scientific* he talked openly about this to presenter Jim Alkalili, explaining that when he was young his great love was disco and dancing and no one ever thought to connect his interests with what he might learn.

When Jim asked, 'What went wrong at school?', the professor replied, 'I just couldn't engage with the subjects I was being taught. I didn't understand how they would affect me and my friends and the life around me. I didn't find anyone who could bring these subjects to life for me. And then I became disinterested. My dad had to go into school to plead with the headmaster to keep me on in the sixth form, because I was doing so badly.'

Many share the professor's incomprehension and are equally let down by their education. Few though are able to turn things round as he did. It seems the key, frequently, is the presence, or absence, of someone in the role of teacher who can bring subjects to life. So many biographies of successful people hinge upon a favourite inspirational teacher who at a crucial, formative moment got through and left a lasting imprint on someone's life.

That opportunity must be why so many people choose to devote their life to teaching. The tragedy of our school system is that so few succeed more than superficially, or, perhaps more accurately, so many pupils miss out and fail to connect with that mentor who could draw out their interests and give their education life.

I remember being obliged at the age of about 12 or 13 to learn by rote passages from Chaucer's *Canterbury Tales*. The middle English he used is difficult for a modern English-speaking child to get to grips with. I had very little idea what it was about and my only abiding memory is that I hated it. Which is a shame. Later I learned Chaucer's *Tales* revolve around a medieval storytelling contest. And it's one of the earliest uses of the English vernacular, with its own fascinating history in terms of its evolution and influence down the ages. Contests in the art and craft of storytelling were regular events when it was written, with storytelling arguably the main entertainment of the time. Darn! I missed that. Teaching Chaucer still seems to be thriving in some areas while in decline in others. I suspect how it is told and taught may be playing a big part in this.

One thing I do remember fondly is our eccentric, elderly maths mistress telling us a sort of story that stuck and taught me and my school pals the difference between calculating the circumference of a circle and its surface area. She told this in the form of a poem in which

R = radius, D = diameter and pi (the number usually represented by the Greek letter π) is a mathematical constant that is the ratio of a circle's circumference to its diameter, approximately equal to 3.14159 (yeah, yawn!). Her poem went like this.

> *Twiddle-dee-dum, twiddle-dee-dee,*
> *A ring around the moon equals Pi D.*
> *But if you want a hole repaired,*
> *Remember the formula Pi R^2.*
>
> BETTY BAILEY, MATHEMATICS TEACHER, NAIRN ACADEMY

Thanks to the quirky way Miss Bailey taught it even all these years later I've remembered how to calculate a circle's surface area and its circumference. However, if you were to ask me how to work out a circle's diameter I'd have no idea. A tape measure, I guess.

Everyone remembers the basics of Archimedes' principle, that an irregular body will displace its own weight in water, because we were told the story of how Archimedes discovered this while musing on a problem in his bath. So excited was he by his discovery, he rushed out into the streets still naked shouting 'Eureka!' (I've found it!).

Who would forget that?

The problem that was taxing Archimedes at the time was how to calculate whether the gold in a crown made for the king of Syracuse had been mixed with inferior metal by a dishonest goldsmith. Archimedes couldn't melt it down without destroying it, but he realised, in his bath, that if he measured the weight of water it displaced that would give him its density while leaving the crown intact.

The story sticks, even though many of us remain a little hazy about the principle of physics that underpins it. Because, I'm sure, my science teacher didn't tell it well. I just remembered the bit about the guy jumping out of his bath.

Apparently Archimedes also tried to calculate the number of grains of sand it would take to fill the entire universe. While perhaps a challengingly large number, that too sounds as if it might have made a potentially instructive story.

The charming, apparently true story of Sir Isaac Newton's formulation of the theory of gravity when prompted by an apple falling from a tree, is another fine example. Newton was one of the most influential scientists of all time, yet it's the story of the falling apple that's remembered most. Curiously, many embellish the original myth by asserting that the apple landed on Newton's head. Whatever, it's helped millions grasp the concept of gravity.

Scientists wishing to explain the urgency of climate change might have fared better had they presented their warnings in the form of stories. Think of the lessons teachers could structure around, say, tales of trekking across the American prairies in the mid 1800s (rights violations, wiping out the buffalo, logistics planning, taking a risk, courage, enterprise, etc). Or from telling of Napoleon's, or Hitler's, marches on Moscow (blind ambition, inadequate planning, poor leadership, harsh climate, clothing and food supplies, morale and its maintenance, basic rules of warfare, etc).

I'm sure I was told no more than a handful of stories in secondary school. Yet they – and their attendant lessons – are what stuck.

Robert the Bruce and his spider was another. Fleeing after a heavy defeat Bruce hid in a cave, thinking he should give up. Above his head he spotted a spider swinging on its web, trying to gain a foothold on the wall above and failing time and again. Eventually, it swung far enough and made it. 'I can do no less,' swore Bruce, and so went on to become Scotland's king.

> *'I left school when I was 16. I didn't understand school and it didn't understand me but I grew up in a world of books and stories and lots of conversation round the dinner table. It seems to me that we have failed children in that we hardly even try to give them shared stories any more.'*
>
> BEEBAN KIDRON, DIRECTOR, *INREALLIFE*
> FROM *THE OBSERVER*, 8 SEPT 2013

I've no idea why monks on Lindisfarne Island should wish visiting parties of school kids to know that their illuminated gospels weigh 8.7 kilograms. But they learned long ago that to make that dull fact stick they had to say, 'That's the same as a full-grown badger.'

I remember being told that the accidental imprint of a key's image on paper led to Marie and Pierre Curie isolating radium and how America's first president discovered that sometimes it can pay to tell the truth. How easy it would be for teachers to tell similar tales to explain, say, the benefits of differential calculus, or the search for dark energy and dark matter, the Higgs boson, or of Hannu the Egyptian, the world's first ever explorer, or how life on earth started... Imagine if you have seven minutes to explain how the weather works, or to describe different cultures, or how different food in 50 years time might be from what your students ate in the last 24 hours...

Humphry Davy described science as better than magic, because science shows real marvels. Sir Charles Sherrington had a good go at making science interesting when he wrote his account of how the human eye is made, which he wrote before I'd even started school. For sheer wonderfulness I urge you to read this and the many other stories available free on the Online Story Bank (www.onlinestorybank.com).

It isn't as if we don't know how to present these things interestingly. They are intrinsically interesting. We just have to make that interest accessible. We could do that so easily just by telling stories. The current colourful crop of television programmes on scientific subjects tends to confirm this. The means they mainly use to make their points? They tell stories. Which isn't new. That august bedrock of science, the Royal Institution (founded 1799, slogan, 'science lives here') rather surprisingly tells its story briefly and well.

> *'From the very beginning the RI has been famous as a place to discover and discuss the world around us. There's still no better way to get caught up in science than to come to one of our events. They cover things as big as planets, and as small as our genes. They cover the stuff in the middle too, like art, your brain, climate change and beer. Almost anything in the universe – and, come to think of it, the universe itself – can be the topic for an RI event.'*
>
> FROM THE ROYAL INSTITUTION'S WEBSITE

I'd go to learn about that stuff, and gladly.

It's even possible to turn usually dry, dull statistics into visual, emotional stories that stretch and stimulate. If you have doubts or simply want to see exemplary teaching in action check out Hans Rosling's TED talk on *the best stats you've ever seen.*

Of course my problems at school were largely of my own making. I must have been a very trying pupil, uncooperative and uninterested. How my teachers must have despaired of me, my attention always wandering, staring out of the window most of the time. I could have worked harder, for sure.

I couldn't get out of school quick enough. I left at age 16 having decided that I hated learning and learning hated me.

The only exception was English. I got an A pass in my English Higher (Scottish equivalent of the English A levels). I know I only got that grade – one of just a handful in the whole school – because in the essay part of the exam I'd written a story about a lonely old man living in a big empty house on a windswept moor where he was visited at dead of night by a burglar. The old chap though didn't live entirely alone. He had as a companion a deaf, old, none-too-healthy Labrador on his last legs who wheezed, shuffled, slobbered and tried not to get in the way. I can't remember quite how the story panned out but the old dog saved his master at the crucial moment by scaring off the burglar just by being friendly.

It sounds hammy now, but was good enough to get me that A pass, the only time in my school career that I ever did well at anything.

Perhaps schools have changed since. I hope so. Still I'd bet there are thousands of youngsters up and down the land and across the world who could and would shine but are missing their potential because their teachers don't tell them the right stories in the right way. And as a consequence, what must we have missed, from them? From the simple absence of a convincing story, all sorts of potential is not being reached. So we should never underestimate what happens when we seek to inspire a student or a customer or a donor to do something so good she'll proudly tell others about it, for she in turn will be opening their eyes, spurring them on to higher aims and possibilities too. Then in turn they will do likewise, for others just like them. And this is how the world gets changed.

As far as I'm aware there are no exams or qualifications in storytelling.

Perhaps there should be. What a difference that would make...

Storytelling could even help young people not naturally inclined to sport. Though big and fit I also had no appetite for anything sporty. I was ungainly, I disliked being beaten. No one inspired or encouraged me so I didn't play.

If only I'd seen then what I saw during the 2012 Paralympic Games in London. The pride and talent, the emotion, tension, fears and passion that infused that event, the individual endeavour and achievement against seemingly overwhelming odds. Bingo, there's a story worth telling, one that even the most sport-averse imagination might respond to.

> *'If history were taught in the form of stories, it would never be forgotten.'*
>
> RUDYARD KIPLING, *THE COLLECTED WORKS*

The campaign for less boring higher education lectures

It isn't just secondary schools and their teachers who could illuminate their lessons with stories to help students achieve their dreams. University lecturers have been getting grief from several sources, including Wikipedia founder Jimmy Wales.

Wales recently achieved traction by telling the story of his academic education and its shortcomings.

> *'...from his own experience as a student, the traditional university lecture should have been condemned decades ago and replaced with an online video recording that can be stopped and started.'*
>
> SEAN COUGHLAN, BBC NEWS EDUCATION CORRESPONDENT, in an online article about Jimmy Wales' dissatisfaction with higher education

This isn't just about the coming tidal wave of online learning, fantastic though that might turn out to be. Nothing in technology seems likely to replace the individual, committed, qualified and well-equipped teacher. But technology, particularly film, might help those who are not natural storytellers to tell tales more easily without sacrificing effectiveness. If, like other teachers, university lecturers don't get more interesting their students will walk, because they now have other options.

> *'We're still not quite there. In university you're still likely to be in a large lecture hall with a very boring professor, and everyone knows it's not working very well. It's not even the best use of that professor's time or the audience's.'*
>
> JIMMY WALES

Perhaps ere long dull teachers will be replaced by a series of taped lectures for online learning. Let's hope then that the presenter of this series is a brilliant transformational storyteller, because young minds are too important to waste and their chances won't come again.

Banishing dull

In most subjects student attitudes to learning vary predictably from great, or at least OK, to awful, the absolute pits. Most opinions will be somewhere between, if having an opinion isn't itself too boring. Being bored is what students do. It's expected of them.

Business studies is often singled out, mostly because it's so dull. Yet business can't afford to be less than inspirational because it's desperate to attract the best brains, the most winning personalities, the most entrepreneurial attitudes.

Imagine if rather than ending up there because that's where the jobs are, more people were to flock to business careers because they found business inspiring, stimulating and exciting.

> *'I find business classes boring because all you do is regurgitate stuff that the professor and textbooks say and it's just inherently dry to me. No real analytical thinking and inane procedures, while science and*

> *engineering really tickle my brain so they seem interesting to me.'*
>
> STUDENT, WRITING ON ANSWERS.COM

Tickling brains seems a good idea. That's what storytelling is for. Though not everyone is put off by the seeming dryness of business.

> *Learning about photosynthesis never made me look at plants differently, but after studying business I began to instinctively analyse logo designs, coffee shop processes, shop window displays and more, just on trips into town. To study business at university seemed like the obvious decision.*
>
> STUDENT, *THE INDEPENDENT*, 23 NOVEMBER 2012

Proof that all subjects can be made interesting. Though no one should imagine there isn't more to be done.

> *'As fears grow over the economy, inspectors said a basic understanding of finance and how markets operate was "as important as... the laws of physics".*
>
> *'(Ofsted's report said) a third of lessons were "uninspiring" and students in half of schools and colleges failed to visit real businesses or take part in industry competitions to bring the subject to life.*
>
> *'Christine Gilbert, (Ofsted's) chief inspector, said: "Business teachers must be given the training they need to produce inspiring lessons".'*
>
> FROM *STUDENTS ILL-PREPARED FOR WORK AFTER BORING BUSINESS LESSONS* BY GRAEME PATON, EDUCATION EDITOR, *THE TELEGRAPH*, 25 NOV 2008

Business isn't intrinsically boring though many of its practitioners and advocates seem entrenched in the habit of making it appear so.

Storytelling could change that. Imagine the benefits if it did.

Stories inspire, encourage and unite

Companies can often seem like battlefields, with internal strife, silo mentalities, departments competing against each other and so on. Stories that build a common dream, illustrate shared targets and inspire aspirational potential outcomes, all can create durable organisational unity. A great story can encourage employees, customers and shareholders, give a clear vision of priorities and what work is about and enhance team spirit. It can add context, confidence and content to business communication and can be the glue that binds a dispirited, divided organisation together.

Take for instance new business goals. Obviously, it pays to improve employees' understanding of and support for new business targets and strategies. Yet few employers work at this, or realise how useful storytelling skills would be in helping spread enthusiasm where they need it most.

Stories can be used for closing sales, making proposals and pitches, technical explanations, briefings and cross-border presentations. They can introduce special events and a host of other activities all of which can build job satisfaction among employees.

Warren Buffett's eagerly anticipated annual letter to shareholders is a good example of how interesting business communication can be. His popular, perceptive and intelligent briefings, described by author Francesca Fenzi as, 'part economics manual, part philosophical musing and part conversation between friends', forms the meat and bones of opinion pieces from journalists and commentators everywhere. Mr Buffett is a great storyteller and a great spreader of stories too, well worth studying.

> *'This report, by its very length, defends itself against the risk of being read.'*
>
> WINSTON CHURCHILL

Good written communication is a commercial necessity

Some time after the end of the Second World War the British prime minister Winston Churchill sent a memo to his First Lord of the Admiralty saying, 'Pray state this day, on one side of a sheet of paper, how the Royal Navy is being adapted to meet the conditions of modern warfare.'

Concentrates the mind, doesn't it?

Churchill would be proud of the Plain English Campaign (motto, fighting for crystal-clear communications since 1979), which has helped many organisations with their documents, reports and publications by exposing nonsense, gobbledygook, jargon and misleading public information and awarding its crystal mark to documents that it deems well-written. Each year the campaign runs an award scheme to celebrate the best uses of written language and gives the Golden Bull awards to the most striking examples of how not to do it. A 2013 Golden Bull finalist was shortlisted for saying, 'The sale is very much in line with our ongoing focus on recycling capital out of assets at the appropriate time in the cycle in order to crystallise gains from higher value uses and redeploy into other profitable growth opportunities in our core markets.'

Organisations do sometimes communicate in the strangest ways. 'The submission of this document has failed due to departmental specific business logic in the Body tag. Your submission contains an unrecognised namespace.'

The winner of the Golden Bull award in 2013 was this effort by the University of Essex Centre for Psychoanalytic Studies, explaining one of their seminars: 'Between the unspeakable and the speculum: Poetry and Psychoanalysis. This paper will be a reflection on what endures and on the archaeology of utterance – an archaeology that is intimately connected to castration. As a Symbolic artefact poetry stands between the darkness of the unknowable – Freud's navel – and Lacan's mirror of semblance in which false architectures of the self, emerge as a parody of the truth.'

Yep, must be sure not to miss that. Such absurdities seem obvious with hindsight and of course their perpetrators should be taken outside and, at the very least, spoken to quite severely. But the basic problem most businesses have when they try to communicate is more insidious. So many seem incapable of writing about even the most colourful and potentially interesting subjects without sucking out the life or reducing them to the direfully dull.

Which, of course, is difficult to illustrate. Though a quick glance through most corporate waste-bins will quickly show that what I say is too often true.

Business is being choked by boring reports and tedious writing

Dull reports, tedious presentations, listless lectures, business books that line our shelves but are seldom read or referred to. All could be enlivened by better storytelling.

Business thrives when it crackles with energy, enthusiasm and ambition – not just to make money but to build something great. Invariably business works best when its drivers see that making money is the result, the outcome of a pioneering entrepreneurial endeavour, not the reason for it.

Instead nowadays business often chokes on its own output, swamping staff and customers with information, too seldom rewarding them with really imaginative communication.

Imagine what a difference it would make if that could change.

Businesses drown in dull reports. Mostly they're suffered under duress, ignored, half read or filed away after a superficial glance. Little is learned even from the few that are read. In many of the organisations I work with it has to be a report written exceptionally better than normal if I'm not to lose the will to live before I get halfway down page three. Often they drone on for 30 pages or more of tedium fatal to the information they seek to convey.

Really, this is serious.

Recently I met with the CEOs of two major international development charities. Midway through our meeting I ventured a heretical thought.

'Why,' I said, 'don't we banish all dull reports?'

There was a pause, laughter, then general agreement. If only we could…

But surely, that's not such an impossible dream. I ventured that reducing or removing impenetrable reports in international non-governmental organisations might be a really effective way to fight poverty. That suddenly didn't seem such a daft idea either.

Dismal, dull presentations

According to Toastmasters International, employees of countless companies around the world find themselves in career-defining speaking situations every day. Presentations like these often involve high stakes as their audiences are busy people with the power to influence careers. It's not just the usual death by PowerPoint. Now we can bump people off with webinars, Prezis, Google Hangouts and Skype sessions too.

Of course not all business presentations are bad, far from it. Loads of people in business are charismatic, engaging presenters, many of them brilliant. But lots are excruciatingly bad. And so, so many are downright dull. Far too few are schooled in storytelling. Many avoid the prospect of having to present whenever they can.

Fear of public speaking (glossophobia) tops the secret fears of people all over the world. In the global fears top ten, fear of public speaking comes ahead of fear of death, spiders, darkness, heights and all the rest, including apparently fear of being buried alive.

It really pays companies to work on the speaking skills of their employees and to realise that enhancing employees' storytelling skills is one of the surest ways of building speaker confidence. But good presentations, or rather not having to endure bad presentations, would also enhance everyone's job satisfaction. More job satisfaction improves performance and increased employee satisfaction will increase all business outcomes, including profit.

So storytelling can quickly add to the bottom line. Most employees are not indifferent; they want to make a difference; a positive contribution in their workplace. But so many miss a connection.

In his book *Practice What You Preach (*Free Business Press, 2003), David Maister shows that the most financially successful businesses do better than the rest on virtually every aspect of employee attitudes – on concepts such as commitment to clients, service quality, high standards, time-keeping, loyalty and employee development. As a result they're measurably more profitable. He also shows that employee attitudes actually drive financial results, not the other way around.

Presentations have to inject surprise, intrigue and interest. Great graphics, stunning illustrations and wonderful quotes all help but these things also frequently cloak bad content. The core is the story. What is this presentation telling me and why should I continue with it? How is it engaging me? What's the story?

It pays the presenter to inject drama and pace, to spice it up. Participation helps too. Online presentations now offer opportunities for interaction. Voting, on-screen comments, questions and answers, all are tools that the storytelling presenter has to master. So is telling jokes and getting the audience to relax.

That apart, it's worth remembering that of all the ingredients in our presentation – the words we use, tone of voice and body language – most important when it comes to getting listened to is our body language. Being able to radiate empathy and rapport is a skill that can be worked at and honed. Getting in the right mood before you start, standing properly, leaning forward, projecting your voice and a host of other things should be considered when deciding what will work best for your audience.

Perhaps that's why public speaking is so scary.

More opportunities for storytellers

Storytelling has equally important uses in other areas from child and parent bonding to therapy sessions in hospitals and clinics. The great hypnotherapist Milton Erickson, a major influence on the founding of neuro-linguistic programming (NLP), believed that the secret of his success was telling simple stories.

Storytelling has an unrivalled role in churches, social groups, clubs and gatherings. Stories figure large on websites and in all things Internet, of course. Television, radio and newspapers are naturally full of opportunities for the transformational storyteller. Though for sure they could do better, in these places professionals generally already tell stories often and well.

Advertising agencies have long understood the value of storytelling and many of the most durable campaigns feature ongoing stories that draw their audience in and help them to love the product. Remember Gold Blend coffee's series about two beautiful neighbours who kept calling on each other at odd moments of the day to borrow coffee? They had the nation on the edge of their seats wondering 'will they, won't they?' Few ads engage the nation so effectively nowadays. Oxo's ads featuring Philip and Katie were immensely popular in the 1980s and 90s because of their simple stories of mealtimes in this ideal family household, which somehow all managed to revolve around the gravy.

In the mid 1920s legendary direct mail copywriter John Caples penned an advertising campaign in a style that he called 'the first person story appeal', for the US School of Music. The headline, 'They Laughed When I Sat Down at the Piano. But When I Started to Play!' is perhaps one of the most effective as well as one of the most famous advertising headlines of all time. It's a story style that Caples honed and recycled over decades and it's still in use today promoting a range of products and propositions from hair restorer and mail order carpets to personal hygiene, health care and saving the environment.

Stories sell, no doubt about that. But they can do more, too.

According to Caples, more than half of all *Reader's Digest* articles – a non-fiction magazine – begin with an anecdote or a narrative of some kind. A story.

In Denmark 24 specially trained clowns from the organisation Hospitalsklovne (Hospital Clowns) cover the country visiting hospitals and entertaining very sick young children with a therapy that's often more powerful than medicine. They tell stories that make even the sickest children laugh. One seriously ill 11-year-old told his parents that a clown had visited him earlier in the day. 'I liked it,' he said, 'because the clown told me the truth. You and the doctors don't want to worry me so you tell me very little, that things are not so bad and that I'm getting better. And I know it's not true. The clown told me that however sick I am, I'm in the best place possible and they do some amazing things here. I liked that. I know I'm really sick. But now I know I'm in the best place to be.'

Angus the clown explains that sometimes children with cancer will stop eating because they get out of the habit. 'They're in constant pain,' he says, 'and sick with so many drugs they don't feel like eating.' So Angus makes up a story about food and the child's plumbing system, to stimulate their interest again.

'I can't take away their pain,' says Angus, 'But I can help change the situation, because humour helps people get better, especially little people with big imaginations.'

And Angus the clown should know, because he can blow a bubble right inside another, even bigger bubble. Of all the miracles that happen in hospitals, for very sick youngsters that may just be the best.

> *'That's what my mother always said, the time isn't right. It was never the right time. So, it was always the right time.'*
>
> PILAR, THE FLAMENCO DANCER, IN THE FILM *A LATE QUARTET,*

> *'All my life people have been telling me you can't think that, you can't do that. I've spent half my life doing things I can't do and thinking things I can't think.'*
>
> MICHAEL DEVITT, PROFESSOR OF PHILOSOPHY,
> CITY UNIVERSITY, NEW YORK

> *'Companies have no morality. But there are moral individuals within, and maybe we can change them.'*
>
> JOHN DOWD, AUSTRALIAN POLITICIAN
> AND HUMAN RIGHTS ACTIVIST

There you have it.

The time is now. We have to think differently and act differently. And we can stimulate and inspire change.

The information explosion

The information explosion has been commented upon since the 1960s. It's self-evident, doesn't seem to be slowing and most likely is gathering pace. Storytelling skills have to keep pace with and even overtake this explosion of information. It must be possible. We have to work at it.

Here's a scary statistic. According to a reliable source (well, OK, Wikipedia) in April 2006 the number of blogs worldwide was 35.3 million. That number has doubled about every six months and is still doubling even as I type. Apparently this is an example of the early stages of logistic growth, where growth is approximately exponential (proportional), since blogs are a recent innovation. As the number of blogs approaches the number of possible producers (in other words, the number of humans on the planet), saturation, we are assured, will occur, growth will decline and the number of blogs will eventually stabilise.

Imagine that. Growth will slow only when almost everyone in the world has a blog. Bloggers need to work at transformational storytelling more than most. If you've read a lot of blogs you'll know what I mean.

Not to mention email, Twitter, Facebook, LinkedIn and all that. Just imagine how much better a place the world would be if people asked themselves before using any of these things, 'How much better might this be if I tell a little story?'

The skill of communicating in 140 characters or less concentrates the mind, no doubt. Why are there not prizes for the best at these things, to encourage less mindless clutter and more useful communication? If Hemingway can write a story in six words we can tell ours concisely too. We can make these modern media work much better than, averagely, they do.

That said, the word limits that people set particularly for new media – for example, that these days no one will read a blog of more than 500 words – are mostly imaginary boundaries imposed in the notion that few nowadays have an attention span capable of coping with more words. I simply don't believe that. Your story should be as long as it needs to be, no longer, no shorter. If it's good enough, people will read, appreciate and learn from it, whatever the length. If it isn't, then it's still too long, whatever its length.

> *'My novels are just life, but with the boring bits snipped out.'*
>
> ELMORE LEONARD

The change enabler

If you weren't already there, by now I'm hoping you'll have come to appreciate that this tool, transformational storytelling, while both flexible and enjoyable, is also a powerful and effective device for influencing people for good.

Storytelling won't design change, neither will it lead it. It might shape it. It will make it happen.

Changing the world is a very egalitarian task. No one can do everything but everyone can do something. The job won't be done easily or soon so we're all in it together. It's good to feel a part of that. Seriously, if you are working in the voluntary sector, sometimes called the social change sector, it's a feeling that often is tangible, sustaining and frequently motivational and emotional. If you work in any other commercial area, imagine the impact you could have if you were to import voluntary sector commitment and enthusiasm into your workplace.

The change enabler. That could be **YOU**.

CHAPTER'S END:
ACTIONS AND KEY MESSAGES

Lessons often work best when told as stories, particularly with academic underachievers.

Business reports can be made much more readable, interesting and memorable with effective storytelling – which greatly aids the spread of useful information and can add significantly to any enterprise's bottom line.

Why storytelling is such a hot topic in commercial circles now. How great stories help build morale and unite your workforce, secure sales, develop brands and ensure job satisfaction.

How the world gets changed.

Storytelling helps sick kids get better and effective transformational storytellers to become change enablers.

Storytelling will neither design nor lead change, but it will shape it and make it happen.

Your story should be as long as it needs to be, no longer, no shorter.

You could be a change enabler.

TURNING POINT

I heard this story early in my career and have retold it often. It shows how we must not only tell the truth, we must also tell it in a way that our audience will find acceptable.

The king's portrait

Long ago, when a certain king required his portrait to be painted, he commissioned three painters each to try their different styles, the winner to be handsomely rewarded with gold. Unfortunately, by a second accident of birth this young king was severely crippled. One of his legs was shorter than the other, his back was bent and he was blind in one eye.

The first painter was absolutely honest and painted his king exactly as he was. The king was shocked and threw the artist in jail. The second painter portrayed his king as a dazzling Greek god. The king felt he was taking the mickey and had him deported.

The third artist painted a hunting scene – the king's favourite sport – in which his majesty was depicted with one foot on a tree stump (the shorter leg, naturally), his back was bent as he took aim and his blind eye was closed to fire his rifle.

The king was delighted, even though the painter had pictured him entirely faithfully, and the happy artist was duly awarded his bag of gold. The moral of the story is that you must tell the truth, but it helps if you can present it in an acceptable way.

Audiences react well if your story tells the truth as they like to see it.

3. The best sales opportunities you'll ever have

'Do good, have fun, make money. That's my mantra, in that order of priority. I try to do each of these, every day.'

KEVIN JOHNSON, PARTNER, INDEX VENTURES

Employers and employees are changing

Recently I attended a seminar where a high-powered business leader admitted to her audience that everyone working in her super-successful multi-national company is motivated by the potential to make a difference. So, she went on to say, the company's policy is to look for areas where their business interests align with making a social difference. Then, they offer their staff a chance to get involved. If their staff are having fun and doing good, she said, the business will thrive.

Wow! Such enlightened attitudes suggest the prospect of a new spirit of corporate social responsibility. Though, the idea may need some spreading. When I asked if I might quote her specifically on that, she was less than keen. Perhaps there's a growing realisation in boardrooms around the planet that doing good is good for staff and good for business, but there's still some reticence in confessing to the fact.

I'll have more to say about what people really want from work in chapter 6, which looks at meaning and fulfilment. But maybe doing good is not just good for staff, it's good for customers too.

The changing customer

Keith Weed, chief marketing officer at global household goods giant Unilever, recently claimed that use of the word 'consumer' is declining within his company as it seeks to identify new ways of initiating a more 'human' conversation with the people who buy its products.

Unilever is far from alone. Today every enterprise wants a better conversation with its customers. Making a sale is more likely now to come from serving than selling, from being inspiring and interesting rather than from interrupting or wearing down with high-pressure aggression, or distracting with flattery and gimmicks. Trouble is, most customers don't have much to say and have scant interest in having any kind of conversation with corporate entities, giants or otherwise. Our attention spans are short and shrinking, our interests too often shallow and superficial, our lives so busy and stretched we barely have time to text or talk to friends and family, far less anyone else. Or so it can seem. If these companies want to talk to us, they are going to have to find ways to win our attention that we will value, welcome and embrace.

Yet if these changing trends among employers, employees and customers could combine there might be a chance of going beyond profits with the corporate sector and doing some real good.

The changing world of work

Whether they will or not, for sure the world of work is changing rapidly and places of business now represent unrivalled opportunities for storytellers. Business has always involved great people making great differences, though invariably and inevitably with profit as the objective. Which is fine and, usually, healthy. Recently though the mood has changed. There's a new spirit abroad about openness, transparency and accountability and being a responsible part if not pillar of the community. There's a fresh appreciation of social usefulness and why it matters. Suddenly it seems that being useful and making a difference are things everyone wants to do – particularly at work.

The public's trust of a business is the key and issues such as integrity, probity and social impact have a new focus. So corporate social engagement makes more sense than ever. But businesses generally seem slow to see the writing on the wall. This should not deter us, though to be brutally honest you have to realise that the place they're starting from is shamefully low. Businesses are really mean – corporate philanthropy hovers below two per cent of all charitable giving whereas giving by individuals is somewhere above 80 per cent. Yet when organisations positively weave the good that they can do into the daily lives of their customers they find selling to them so much easier.

To close that gap, what's needed in business today is a realisation of vested interest, that there's a real opportunity here for all businesses, whatever their field.

Good can be good for business

Unilever is a company that's proud of being first. It claims to have produced the first black and white television ad, the first colour television ad in the UK and the first iAd (Apple's smartphone ad platform).

It's also big and growing. It has 14 €1 billion brands and they are planning to make that 20, then 30.

In an interview in *Marketing Week* Unilever's Keith Weed said, 'When I was a young marketer, I remember being jealous of retailers for having a direct interface with consumers, but now with mobile we [FMCG brands – fast moving consumer goods] can have that too. I think mobile is the most important thing because it's about direct connection.'

Mr Weed is right. Communication has changed radically and is still changing at what seems a gathering pace. And it's changing in the storyteller's favour.

> *'We use the term "consumer" less and less because it puts a label or a badge on people who are actually you, your mum, your sister and your friend... People are real people – they are not heads of hair charging around looking for shampoo solutions, or pairs of armpits looking to be deodorised.'*
>
> KEITH WEED, UNILEVER, TALKING IN *MARKETING WEEK*

Isn't that nice? I really like that. But is Unilever an odd exception, or a trendsetter? Is it for real, or just a cynical sales plot? How deep does this go? And is it getting deeper?

Unilever talks of its brands having purpose and depth, citing Persil's 'dirt is good' campaign as an example. Rather than simply telling people that Persil washes whiter they now seek to go further, to engage families in the experience of going out and getting dirty. This followed research commissioned by Persil's sister brand Omo and the Outside Play Foundation, which showed that children are playing outside less. A campaign was developed to highlight the importance of outside play and to inspire parents and children into action. Under the 'dirt is good' banner Unilever raises issues such as active child development and outdoor play, setting up advice and research programmes, going well beyond the selling of washing powders to encourage a much deeper relationship with their customer.

In Holland the Outside Play Foundation (OOPF) first targeted mothers of five to 12-year-olds to tell them about their research findings, then invited their children to register for details of safe, healthy outdoor pursuits. An amazing 270,000 kids registered with OOPF in Holland, clustered in 40,000 clubs. Think of the buying power of all those mums, now convinced that Omo cares about the quality and healthiness of their children's play.

Is this a symptom of a changing trend? Could telling stories about how our children can get fit while enjoying playtime help companies to engage with their customers? Of course it could. As involvement is the main purpose, it fits rather well. But what are the stories that a workforce might unite behind and who will tell them, how and when? In most enterprises these questions remain unanswered. The message though may be beginning to come through, even though the road to heaven is, as always, lined with convenient parking places.

Appreciation of the power of storytelling is spreading fast. Coca-Cola (slogan: refreshing the world, one story at a time) reckons the corporate website is dead. Inspired by the power of storytelling to cultivate engagement the company has launched the *Coca-Cola Journey* (www.coca-colacompany.com) as a highly visual, shareable digital magazine. The content on offer is themed around pop culture, social media, brand history, marketing campaigns, recipes, career advice and more, creating a site that – in their words, in a good way – is a far cry from the traditional corporate effort.

'We use storytelling to sell our chocolate every day,' says Shawn Askinosie, a small-scale fair-trade chocolate-maker from Springfield, Missouri, USA. On its packaging, website and other materials, most notable on the product wrappers, the company features a photo and story of the lead farmer whose cocoa beans were used to make the bar.

'The cocoa farmers are an integral part of our story,' explains Shawn. Their story also makes it clear to customers that Askinosie Chocolate pays higher than fair-trade rates for beans, compensates farmers fairly including profit-sharing and treats them like business partners instead of mere suppliers.

The result? According to Shawn, Askinosie's wholesale customer retention has improved by more than 30 per cent.

Stories encourage safety and sales

The international energy and health conglomerate Siemens is a well-known, readily-recognised company that touches a lot of people, day in, day out. But its customers usually can't see the technology that's behind the power they consume, the water, food and beverages they eat and drink, the buildings, transport and mining products they may use, or even the medical treatment they get. Siemens has technology behind the scenes in all these places and more.

So it makes sense for Siemens to employ a storyteller. Keith Ritchie, storytelling and marketing communications manager with Siemens in Australia, has been a senior manager with the company for several years. His job there has evolved into telling stories about the company's technology to make it more meaningful for people.

'To bring the technology to life we're getting our customers – ordinary, everyday people – to tell simple, heartfelt stories about how our brand has transformed their business or their lives. We might do this through a video or an integrated campaign. It's engaging for potential new customers because they stop and think, "if Siemen's technology helped that guy, how could they help me?"

Siemens uses storytelling internally as well. 'For example,' says Keith, 'we're trying to build a really strong safety culture because a lot of our people work in quite dangerous sites so we want to make sure they're safe.

'We're using storytelling as a mechanism to create that culture. Rather than just follow a set of rules, we want to change minds, so that people actually want to be safe. The best way to do that is to make an emotional connection through storytelling.

'One guy who volunteered to tell his story had lost an eye as a young apprentice. We interviewed him on video for a series called *This Is My Safety Story*. He talked authentically about losing his eye, so powerful messages got through because they were coming from an individual worker, not a manager telling you, "here's the rules you've got to follow to be safe". It makes workers stop and think, "Gee, I want to be safe. I don't want to lose an eye". It's a great example of how powerful authentic, emotional storytelling can be.'

> *'At Goldman Sachs, commitment to the communities in which we work and live has been an important part of our culture for more than a century. Recently our firm refocused its philanthropy to ensure it is based on discipline, innovation and a strategic approach over the long term. Interventions, whether in traditional non-profit work, public sector programmes or corporate philanthropy, are needed to more evenly spread the benefits of economic growth. So we have decided to focus our corporate engagement efforts on the agents of growth – entrepreneurs. More than just philanthropy, investment in an entrepreneur is self-sustaining. It has a compounding effect on local communities through economic growth and job creation.'*
>
> DINA POWELL, GLOBAL HEAD OF CORPORATE ENGAGEMENT, GOLDMAN SACHS

Corporate social responsibility is dead

Why is Goldman Sachs consistently a top five philanthropic giver among American enterprises? And isn't it interesting to hear them talking about 'more evenly spreading the benefits of growth'?

By-word for the ultra-rich and powerful, Goldman Sachs may seem to some an unlikely name to be leading a renaissance in corporate social engagement. But this firm is full of surprises and they've thought out their strategy thoroughly and well.

Goldman Sachs' people seek to make a difference through financial support, volunteering endeavours and partnerships with non-profit organisations around the world. The company describes its charitable support as philanthropic investments, claiming to adhere to four guiding principles that should:

- Align with the company's core business by focusing on economic growth and community engagement.
- Establish networks of non-profit and educational partners who have world-class expertise and experience.
- Be capable of rigorously measuring their results.
- Engage the time and talent of the people of Goldman Sachs at all levels of the firm.

The titles of Goldman Sachs' programmes tell their own stories, giving real-life meaning that shows the difference they and their people can make.

10,000 Women is a five-year, $100 million global initiative to help grow local economies and bring about greater shared prosperity by providing 10,000 underserved women entrepreneurs with a business and management education, access to mentors and networks and links to capital. Launched in March 2008, 10,000 Women is founded on research conducted by Goldman Sachs, the World Bank and others, which suggests that such an investment can have a significant impact on the growth of GDP.

10,000 Small Businesses is a $500 million investment to help small businesses in the United States create jobs and economic growth by providing entrepreneurs with a practical business education, access to capital and business support services. The programme is based on the broadly held view of leading experts that greater access to this combination of education, capital and support services best addresses barriers to growth.

Goldman Sachs Gives is a fund from which current and former Goldman Sachs partners can recommend grants to suitable non-profit organisations. In the past three years, nearly 10,000 grants totalling $570 million have supported organisations in 35 countries. The fund focuses on four strategic pillars: increasing educational opportunities, building and stabilising communities, honouring military service and veterans and increasing economic growth.

Community TeamWorks is a global volunteer initiative that allows Goldman Sachs' people to take a day out of the office to volunteer with local non-profit organisations. In 2012, more than 25,000 of their employees from 48 offices worldwide partnered with more than 950 non-profit organisations in a diverse array of community service projects.

The firm's vision for its philanthropy is to drive economic progress and sustainable growth for clients, investors and communities worldwide. Though all are clearly in line with the first of their guiding principles, above, the ultimate idea is, unsurprisingly, to make a positive difference.

And their staff and clients seem to love it. Whatever we may think of large, powerful corporate conglomerates, it's encouraging to see this kind of leadership from an enterprise such as Goldman Sachs. Hopefully other businesses will follow suit. It's perhaps over-optimistic to expect unselfish interest in changing the world from any busy, hard-pressed enterprise but we can hope for increased recognition of mutual self-interest, which in most cases will prove more robust and durable than mere philanthropy.

The days of corporate social responsibility (CSR) may be numbered as corporate involvement in giving isn't primarily about responsibility, it should always be about opportunity. So, long live the new Mecca of corporate social engagement (CSE) and the chance to raise some serious money for social good from the hitherto miserly corporate sector. Now that companies are beginning to show real interest in engagement strategies and to invest in CSE appropriately, this area should do well. As doing good aligns with what people want, it should be in every business's best interest to ensure this new mood has room and resources to thrive.

Kellogg's campaign to give a child a breakfast

These days commercial companies are just as likely to be found delivering the kind of social services more usually associated with a welfare charity. But if the people who need it can benefit, maybe that's no bad thing. And if the companies involved find that they too can prosper from telling the story of these campaigns they'll keep doing them and will come up with ever more creative opportunities for them too.

According to Kellogg's the cornflakes people, one in seven children in the UK and Ireland goes to school without breakfast every day. What's more, they say, it's getting worse. They claim that over half of teachers say the number of pupils starting school hungry is on the rise. Understandably, not eating breakfast affects how children learn, as they can't concentrate if their tummies are empty. If they turn up at all, hungry kids often play up in class and distract other pupils. And children who don't eat breakfast are more likely to get ill, missing the vital education they need to succeed.

For 15 years Kellogg's has been helping breakfast clubs all over the UK by providing breakfast to millions of children before they go to school. Now you might just conceivably detect a hint of self-interest in this. And why not? Obviously Kellogg's want to be seen as the breakfast people, to be front of mind when mums start seeing to it that their children start the day with a decent breakfast.

They already pay a fortune in advertising to try to plant that impression across society. The point is, if they tell the right stories, schemes like this could work better; could be the new shape of things to come. These days sales growth is more likely to come from helping than persuading, from listening rather than interrupting. So you're increasingly likely to find a company running this kind of campaign rather than upping its advertising or adding to its opportunities for hard sell.

Through the Give a Child a Breakfast campaign, Kellogg's is

currently working with a number of other groups and charities to beat child poverty and put a stop to children going hungry. Through the thousands of breakfast clubs they fund Kellogg's target now is to donate two million breakfasts to children in need.

That can't be a bad thing, can it, for Kellogg's or the kids? Of course it's possible for companies to tell stories to cover up bad things as much as to spread good things, and we should always be wary of that and punish it appropriately wherever we find it.

But maybe if this campaign succeeds others will follow and Kellogg's will start to think beyond just selling their traditional breakfast cereals to the benefits of giving the nation's children a healthy, nutritious start to their day. Which might lead to more emphasis on what's good for kids rather than what's sugary and sweet.

I'd be inclined to think that rather a good thing too. Millions of parents, wherever they may be, I'm sure would rush to agree.

All kinds of organisations use storytelling to change their world

And in all kind of ways too. There are lots of good reasons why companies should take storytelling seriously and lots of good ways that they can use it, not just in their corporate social engagement strategies but in a range of other areas too. Some of these will be covered in coming chapters.

Someone recently likened the Internet to a vast ungovernable country that will have an impact on the daily lives of everyone on the planet. The most powerful tool for social change ever invented is the mobile smartphone. Because they're hand held and ubiquitous mobile telephones have had more impact on the fight against poverty than all of the charities and all their handouts, all of the development aid and official interventions and all the strategies, plans and budgets of the entire aid business put together.

It's way beyond the scope or purpose of this book to predict or analyse the changes that are coming, but it seems likely from the gathering pace of technology that change will feature even more in the next few decades than it did in the past.

Great. Change adds excitement and opportunity so should be understood early then grasped enthusiastically. But some things remain the same whatever else is changing around us. The fundamentals of storytelling will stay the same and however busy and self-absorbed people get they'll always respond to politeness, consideration, good manners and timeliness.

So when people say to you that it's OK to address senior business chiefs as Ron, or Pete, or Betty, or whatever the name is, because you're writing via email and everyone uses first names in emails, don't believe them, any more than when they tell you that your customers don't demand good grammar, or politeness along with prompt, considerate service.

The best sales opportunity of all

This is so important. Believe me. Read and act on this.This opportunity revolves around something that's regularly neglected or badly executed and often omitted altogether. Something that down the ages people have begrudged, scrimped on, avoided if they could. Something businesses of all types and sizes often regard as a chore, an inescapable evil or an after-thought at best.

Yet it's something so universal, so unarguable and so potentially valuable you have to wonder what planet all those who ignore or skimp it are on.

I'm talking about the process of saying, or sending, or by any means conveying a simple thank you. And perhaps adding to it some words of welcome or even congratulation. And offering appropriate feedback too. Fundraising charities do this kind of thing all the time but even they are only just coming to realise its full potential.

> *'Anyone who doesn't thank a donor properly is an idiot as well as rude.'*
>
> JO HABIB, *TINY ESSENTIALS OF RAISING MONEY FROM FOUNDATIONS AND TRUSTS*

What Jo says, of course, applies equally to customers, staff, students, patients, campaigners, lobbyists and listeners just as much as to charity donors. From an early age most of us have had drummed into us by a succession of older relatives that it's the height of bad manners not to show proper appreciation of every gift or consideration. But look at how business is conducted almost anywhere in the world and you'd think we'd all but forgotten this human fundamental entirely.

It's also idiotic because saying thank you, welcome, well done or congratulations is the best sales opportunity of them all, bar none. Everyone, everywhere, appreciates being appreciated. If you want loyalty, enthusiasm, commitment, say welcome, thank you and well done, nicely.

'But,' I hear communicators saying regularly, 'our customers don't want us to waste our – or rather, their – money sending them a thank you that they don't really need.'

Of course they don't. That's simply because you haven't explained to them how valuable to you and useful to them that seemingly unnecessary thank you really is. And saying thank you is the first stage of effective feedback. So it's the first step in securing repeat business.

Charities pay a heavy price for allowing their publics, who generally are not stupid, to remain ignorant of the realities of how they work. Take for example that old bugbear for fundraisers: administration costs. For decades charities have colluded in allowing the public to imagine that their enterprises can be run on thin air and that anything spent on admin is by definition a bad thing. How foolish. Obviously the opposite is true – you wouldn't want to give your donation to a charity that isn't properly administered, because in that case nothing would get through to the cause. Of course prudent and well-managed administration is worth paying for.

To justify saying thank you, a simple statement is all you need.

Dear Mrs Generous,

Thank you for your gift, which is already making a difference. Just so you know, it's our policy here at Panda Survival Trust to always acknowledge every donation, for three good reasons.

1. So you can be sure your gift has been safely received and applied as you intended.

2. Because we can use the opportunity to show you the impact your support has, the difference it makes to the welfare of pandas everywhere.

3. And because we consider it not just basic politeness, but also one of our best, most mutually useful opportunities to connect with you, our valued supporter.

From the last 27 years working with our supporters to help pandas we've learned that when our donors – just like you – see the difference their support is making they find it very encouraging. When our donors are happy it encourages them to continue their support. So you'll see, sending a simple thank you and brief update is neither costly nor a chore for us. On the contrary, we love to do it, and it's one of the very best investments we can make to ensure long-term support for the pandas from people like you.

On behalf of all of us, thank you for your generous gifts. They're much appreciated, because they make possible everything we do.

With best wishes, etc.

Something like that: simple, unfussy, sincere. Anyone offended by that is likely to be offended whatever you send. What's more, the chance to say all of those things opens up the best opportunity for storytelling that'll ever come your way. Amid all the advice in chapter 9 there's a stack of useful information about how to thank and welcome properly.

Commercial companies seem to appreciate the value of a timely thank you, particularly those working online. But many could make more of the opening this provides.

Imagine the opportunities you'll have to tell a donor or customer what a difference their recent gift or purchase has made, or about something new and exciting that's happening in the area that interests him, or her. Imagine telling them a short, emotional story at this time that will make their hair stand on end – how children everywhere are learning to play safely and healthily thanks to their favourite detergent. Or how entrepreneurs in some of the poorest parts of the planet are learning new business skills from their investment manager.

Telling stories quickly and well soon after their initial contact with you is neither a chore nor an inconvenience, it's an unparalleled chance to build customer relationships that can work for any enterprise committed to enhancing the customer experience.

Any business concerned to get the most out of its thank you, welcome, congratulations and feedback strategy should put these tasks firmly in the hands of a transformational emotional storyteller.

CD Baby, a service for musicians and songwriters, is one company that gets this. Perhaps tongue in cheek and more than just a teensy bit over the top, at least in some markets, see opposite for how they say thank you to their customers.

Many commercial entities are good at acknowledging orders and confirming transactions, particularly electronically, but few are as good as they could be at making their customers feel special. Many are prompt, then spoil things by overtly soliciting a further sale. Charities, paradoxically, have the perfect opportunity for creating a great opening to the relationship they want to foster with each and every customer, yet few are good at making the most of it. If you're not a charity, what might your enterprise, cause, or mission be able to offer at the initial contact in your relationships, to get things off to a flying start? What's your equivalent of the opportunity to say thank you, welcome or well done?

Thanks for your order with CD Baby!

Your CD has been gently taken from our CD Baby shelves with sterilized contamination-free gloves and placed onto a satin pillow. A team of 50 employees inspected your CD and polished it to make sure it was in the best possible condition before mailing. Our world-renowned packing specialist lit a local artisan candle and a hush fell over the crowd as he put your CD into the finest gold-lined box that money can buy. We all had a wonderful celebration afterwards and the whole party marched down the street to the post office where the entire town of Portland waved 'bon voyage!' to your package, on its way to you, in our private CD Baby jet on this day.

We hope you had a wonderful time shopping at CD Baby. In commemoration, we have placed your picture on our wall as 'Customer of the Year.' We're all exhausted but can't wait for you to come back to CD Baby.

Thank you, thank you, thank you! Sigh... We miss you already. We'll be right here at www.cdbaby.com, patiently awaiting your return.

It's undeniable that some people, particularly the British, are inclined to be shy and reserved about being thanked and rather than being thrilled (to external appearances, at least – they may be pleased as punch on the inside) can instead get bashful and embarrassed.

So an alternative strategy may be called for. And may even work better anyway.

'Congratulations!' 'Well done, you've just done something wonderful... brilliant.' 'Thanks. You can now look forward to making a real difference. What you did today is nothing short of revolutionary.'

You get the picture. There's no percentage in underplaying your customer's achievements. But equally, don't over claim. Be sincere. We want to make their day with a story that will surprise and impress them with all the amazing things they've just done and the impact it's had, what a difference it's made. If we get the congratulating right, donors and customers will thank us for giving them the opportunity to do that good thing they just did.

Here's a fine example. Once when I ordered a new car I got a letter all the way from Germany that described my car on its journey through the factory, being built to my specification with my name on it. It painted a lovely picture of fastidious *lederhosen*-clad carmakers eager to please me, their new customer, an image that stayed for years (and helped me come to terms with the high cost of that car).

Get this process right and you'll have a strategy that will engage customers in dialogue, secure their second and subsequent purchases, give brilliant feedback and build trust, confidence and commitment. It will open doors for closer bonding and further initiatives, develop opportunities for telephone contact and meetings, focus your programme of regular communications and form the foundations of all the relationship-building you could ever need.

Feedback is the magic ingredient...

Let me tell you about what a great thing you just did. About what a difference you made when you wrote to your MP, about the extra efforts we're making to get your holiday just right, about what we did when you told us how you use our product. Let me tell you about the changes we're going to make since getting so many great suggestions from that survey you just completed, or after you shared your travel experiences, reviewed that concert, rated that restaurant. Congratulations on your recent gift, that special purchase, your decision to get involved. Welcome, come in and take a seat, make yourself comfortable.

...but speed is the essence

Organisations get between people all the time. They block stories and stifle conversation. Invariably, they and their systems slow things down.

It really pays to get back quickly, while the emotion is still swirling,

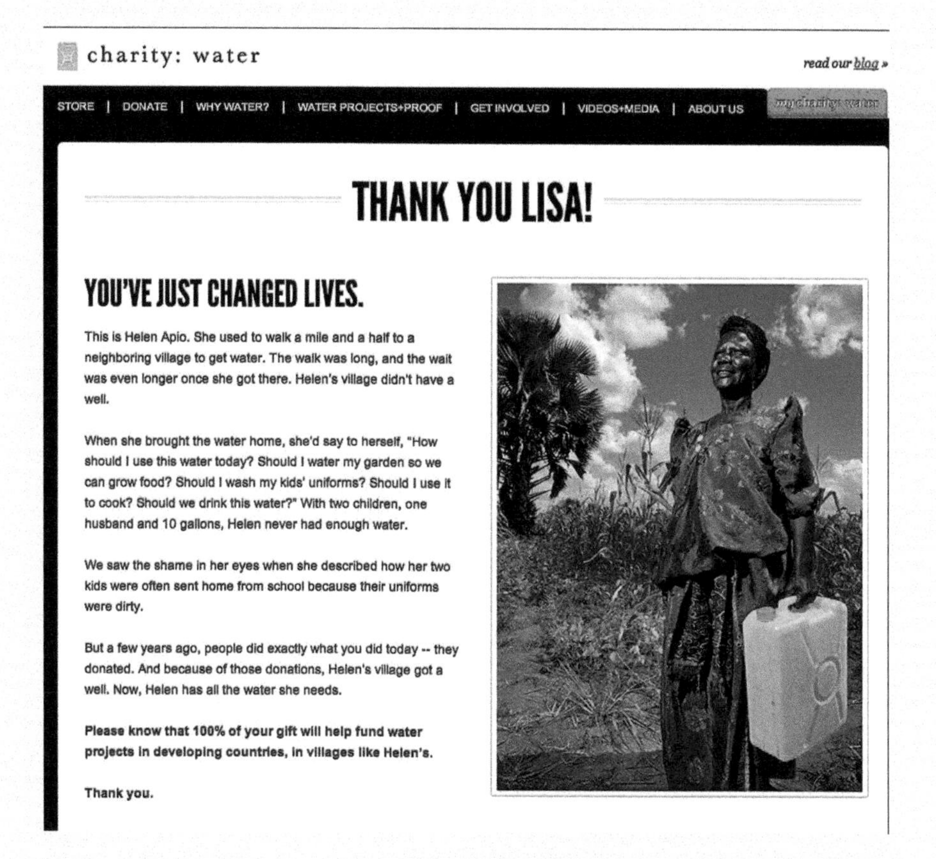

CHARITY: WATER IS AN ORGANISATION WELL WORTH FOLLOWING, IF ONLY BECAUSE IT THANKS ITS SUPPORTERS CREATIVELY AND WELL.

while the iron is hot, the action is front of mind, the anticipation is high.

Delay and the moment is lost, the world turns, the feeling has to be recreated. But of course all our organisations delay all the time, responding when it suits them and not when it's most likely to influence their customers.

Understanding the need and reward cycle

The need and reward cycle is a neat device used by some storytellers to remind them of the link between feedback and relationship-building and, more importantly, of the imperative to get back to the customer, student or donor very quickly after their purchase, or enrolment, or after their gift is received – in hours, not days. For fundraisers it's based on the two most common questions in any donor's mind – did I make a difference and what's in it for me?

The graphic opposite illustrates what should happen when a donor makes a gift or someone decides to get involved in any action. It can apply equally to anyone purchasing a service, joining a customer care scheme, or signing up to be part of an online special interest group. It can be anywhere where the transaction involves an intangible product, offer or service rather than the purchase of something that, when it arrives in the post, provides its own justification and reassurance just by being there.

You tell your story, launch your appeal, get your message out by whatever means. Your customer responds quickly because your story was urgent and important and it's inspired and excited them. You now need to get back equally quickly, as close to instantly as possible, before that interest and enthusiasm has any chance to go off the boil.

This is where the vast majority of 'change the world' enterprises get things spectacularly wrong. They think once they've got the order, or the interest, or the gift, it's OK to leave it days or even weeks before they get back to their customer.

Wrong! Obviously.

The need and reward cycle shows they all should respond much more quickly, reassuringly and effectively.

'Did my gift, or order, or action, make a difference?'

This question arises instantly the action is taken and needs to be answered fully and swiftly or the doubt will nag away, or your

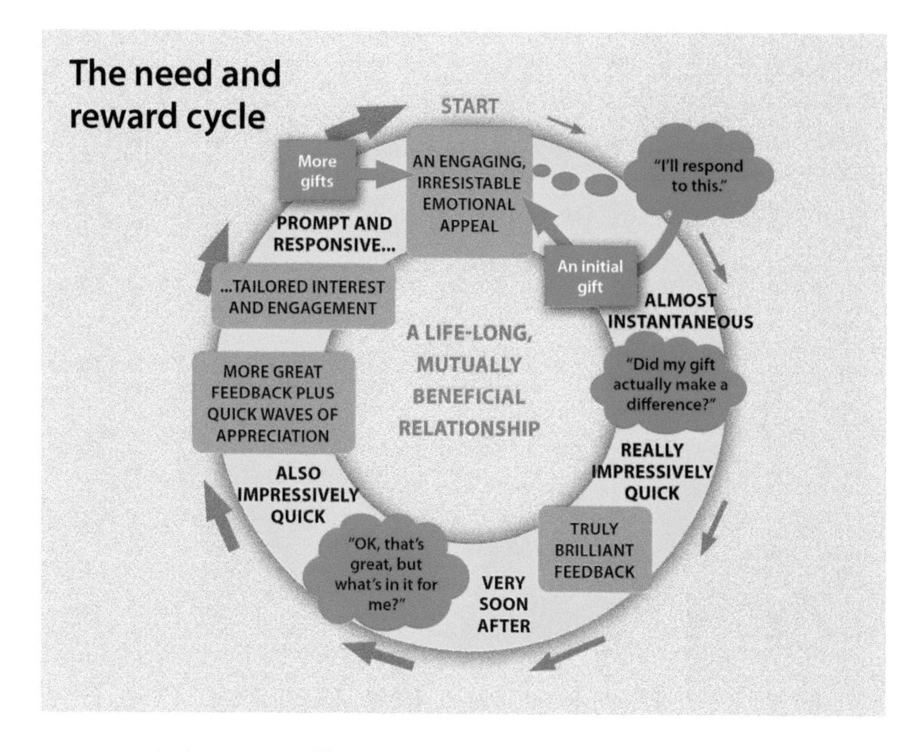

customer's interest will wane and his or her attention will move elsewhere.

The customer's second question, 'what's in it for me?' comes simultaneously or mere moments later and may not even register consciously, but it's powerful and important all the same.

Other questions may follow swiftly. 'Did I do the right thing?' 'Have they got my order?' 'What happens next?' And so on.

All will be resolved by effective, quick feedback.

Electronic communication makes it possible, even easy for us to respond much more quickly these days. Mobile phones are particularly brilliant for it. How much speed with efficiency matters you'll know yourself from the last time that you had an order confirmed promptly and well. The key point is that the responses must be quick as well as good. Hours, not days.

The need and reward cycle shows that we need to keep the emotion and urgency of our story in our customers' minds right through subsequent interactions. We have to keep that close-to-instant momentum going as long as we can while acknowledging, confirming, thanking, congratulating and welcoming. Then on a varied, regular, ongoing basis we should provide the most brilliant feedback our storytelling powers can summon.

Then you'll have a happy, fulfilled customer who will stay with you for the long term, through thick and thin.

Five secrets of sales success

'Girl Scout Cookies!'Girl Scout Cookies! GIRL SCOUT COOOOOOKIES!'

The cry was yelled from the park area of the Greenbelt as I took a walk during my lunch break. I had no intention of buying as I walked past the table of screaming Girl Scouts who were selling their sweet treats. But that all changed in an instant.

A young Girl Scout started walking next to me.

'Excuse me, maam,' she said politely. 'How would you like to get an extra-special greeting from your family when you get home tonight? Of course I knew what she was getting at, but her original approach stopped me in my tracks. I replied, 'I'd love to get an extra-special greeting tonight.'

Kayla introduced herself and asked if she could show me the different ways I could earn that special welcome. She walked me back to the table and pointed to the Peanut Butter Sandwich, Shortbread, and everybody's favourite, Thin Mints.

I said, 'I'll take the Thin Mints'.

'Great!' she replied. 'What other type would you like?'

'Okay, I'll take the peanut butter, too, but that's all.

How much are they?'

'Seven dollars for both.'

To see if they offered a volume discount, I asked, 'How about six dollars?'

'Sorry,' she replied. 'Seven dollars is our best price.'

I gave her the money and finished my walk. I then realised how impressed I was with her sales technique. Here are the sales principles that Kayla had already mastered:

1. **Go where the customers are. Look for potential clients where there is a high chance of finding qualified potential customers.**
2. **Shoot with a rifle, not a shotgun. Kayla targeted me individually by speaking directly to me, so was able to land the sale.**
3. **Get attention by describing the benefits. Your customers/clients are always thinking, what's in it for me?**
4. **Always sell UP. Once a customer commits to buying, always try to earn add-on sales.**
5. **Don't negotiate price after the sale is made.**

FROM *THE BEST SALES PITCH EVER: FIVE KEY THINGS ALL SALES PEOPLE SHOULD INSTINCTIVELY DO* EXECUTIVE TRAINING RESOURCES INC, IDAHO FALLS, USA

A few more reasons why businesses should tell their stories quickly

- Attention spans seem to be shortening, though probably only as a function of too much choice rather than anything evolutionary. No doubt these days companies and brands have to tell their stories effectively very quickly.

- Thanks to Twitter we now have to learn to tell our stories in 140 characters or less.

- Stories can be told in a photo (or two). Apparently more photographs have been taken in the past year than in all the rest of human history. People seem to want to photograph everything and nothing. Hand-held devices are undoubtedly changing the way we think and how we socialise and will probably change the way we tell stories too.

- A report from digital marketing specialists Econsultancy points out that despite a widespread understanding among marketers of the need to build long-term loyalty only a small percentage of companies are truly committed to relationship marketing strategies. The second annual 'Cross Channel Marketing Report' found that 'many businesses are failing to move beyond a campaign-centric marketing mindset rooted in new customer acquisition'. In other words, once they've gone to the trouble and expense of recruiting new customers, businesses fail to keep them because they haven't got the storytelling bit right.

- For short stories the focus will be increasingly on film. Though there's so much rubbish film around, those who get it right really fly. Short, smart, subtle, original films can spread like wildfire, sending stories around the world.

Big business these days seems to be getting away with murder – tax avoidance, corporate corruption, massive undeserved bonuses and self-serving profligacy on a scale as never before. Yet despite or perhaps even because of this reckless excess, more and more people want to work for and be associated with enterprises that aim high, make a difference, are part of the solution, not part of the problem.

As a transformational storyteller you can unite people behind common standards, aims and dreams, doing things differently but doing them properly, valuing the people you are telling stories to and treating them right.

The paradox is that in the future this approach will pay.

> *'Sometimes one finds what one is not looking for.'*
>
> SIR ALEXANDER FLEMING, DISCOVERER OF PENICILLIN

CHAPTER'S END:
ACTIONS AND KEY MESSAGES

Companies can prosper when they serve rather than sell – how the corporate sector is slowly waking up to a new paradigm.

How businesses now view their customers and their corporate social responsibilities. And where storytelling fits into the kind of relationships companies now seek to create.

How storytelling builds interest, trust, confidence and value.

A shared vested interest in corporate social engagement can make selling much easier, for all kinds of enterprise.

Why your company should give away some of its money. And how to do it wisely.

Why it pays to offer customers a chance to make a difference and how saying thank you, welcome, or congratulations provides the best opportunity to cement a relationship with them.

How to say thank you and welcome nicely and why anyone who doesn't thank a customer properly is an idiot, as well as rude.

Some helpful examples.

Why prompt, effective feedback really matters and why, if you wish to prosper, you'll want to get very good it.

How to understand the need and reward cycle and make it work for you, your product, service or cause.

The best sales pitch ever – five key things all sales people should do.

Why being quick is so very important.

TURNING POINT

The diagnosis of multiple sclerosis can seem like a death sentence. Despite promising scientific advances, many feel that the dream of launching an appeal to raise enough money to fund research that might finally put an end to the scourge of MS should not be articulated, for fear of raising expectations.
Possibly. But Kate Hely-Hutchinson's pitch to the trustees of the MS Society in the UK is a good place to start the process of changing that...

End MS in our lifetimes

Thank you all for coming to listen to what I have to say today. My name is Kate Hely-Hutchinson. I have a dream, a realisable dream, which I want to share with you today. This dream came to me through one person, my husband and father to my three children, Nick. He is the bravest man I know. He has multiple sclerosis, along with 100,000 others in the UK alone. Seven more are diagnosed daily. They are why I am here today.

Four months ago, with 40 or so others, Nick and I attended an MS Society evening and listened to MS sufferers and scientists speak passionately of the tragedy that is MS and the groundswell of research coming to the fore.

What seemed like a distant dream when we arrived became a possible dream when we left.

With the right level of funding MS can be stopped in our lifetimes. This is an irresistible proposition. A major step change in fundraising at your MS Society is needed.

The message is clear, the message is simple. End multiple sclerosis within our lifetimes. What an unbelievable, extraordinary, once-in-a-lifetime opportunity for a charity such as the MS Society and you, the trustees, to rise to this challenge.

Look at the progress that has been made in research over the last 20 years, with relatively little funding. The MS Society has played a significant role in this. Only 26 years ago the celebrated cellist Jacqueline Du Pré died aged 42, at the prime of her life. Then there were no effective drugs for managing the disease. She and many tens of thousands died with no hope. Imagine what could be achieved with a step change in funding now there is so much real hope and real belief. The MS Society has an excellent reputation and trust in the field of research. If you couple this with a large body of research scientists crying out, 'The time is now,' for a significant step change in funding, an end to MS is in sight.

It is time to think step change. It is time to think big. This should not be difficult for the MS Society because it has always punched above its weight. It gives the feeling of being a bigger charity than it is. Use this to your advantage. Make it the biggest, most influential charity in the field.

How much is needed you ask? How can it be done? How much will it cost?

The hard work of the how has been done. The scale of fundraising is best achieved through a campaign. The formula is tried and tested. Your core income will grow dramatically and the charity's profile will soar. The excitement and passion of the appeal will energise the MS community, your membership will expand like never before, you will not look back. Be bold, be brave, end MS.

This is what my 18-year-old daughter wrote about living with MS.

> *'He stood so proudly, so confidently, so blissfully unaware. Things couldn't be more different now. My dad used to soar over me like a shield. Now, I am his. The spontaneity has gone, replaced with times of doubt and despair. But he has hope. He has belief that he will walk again.'*

You owe Nick, our family and 100,000 other families like us. You must have belief. The alternative is unthinkable, the fallout from MS too profound, the exclusion, depression, isolation, desperation, family break-up...

The long-term aspiration of all charities is ultimately not to be needed. You the trustees have the opportunity to do what some charities couldn't even imagine.

End MS and end it now.

4. The story of the story

'The world is shaped by two things — stories told and the memories they leave behind.'

VERA NAZARIAN, *DREAMS OF THE COMPASS ROSE*

'To hell with facts! We need stories!'

KEN KESEY, AUTHOR OF *ONE FLEW OVER THE CUCKOO'S NEST*

The natural way we learn and teach

In the beginning was the word. And the word was spread about and around and all over the place by the telling and retelling of stories. Long, long before the invention of printing presses, moving picture shows, TV screens, computers and social media, if ever anyone wanted to influence anyone else about anything at all what we did was, we told a story.

It's what we humans do. Telling stories is how we learn and how we pass that learning on.

And what a rich, vast and varied tradition those stories encompass. Remember the treasury of tales you were told as a child? How great were they, how formative and influential? Storytelling is an integral part of our lives. The stories we tell are the measure of us and our values, of what we believe matters most. Throughout their adolescence I was constantly telling and re-telling tales of my misspent youth to my sons, Joe and Charlie, usually to groans and grimaces indicating varying degrees of tolerance. But they learned a lot, I'm sure, from tales of my adolescent experiences, if only that their Scottish relatives have a strange sense of humour and that growing up nowadays, though perhaps measurably safer, less austere and less strict, might at times also be less fun. And while I regaled them, as they were listening and their characters and values were forming, I had the chance to get through to them some of the things that I thought would matter most, to them.

The storyteller in most cultures is the focal point for his or her society. Words assembled and deployed as stories told with power and passion can promote peace and postpone war, or they can spread dissent, discord and discontent. They can provoke laughter or anger, inspire fear or warmth, spread hatred or love. Stories turn, transport, tantalise and transform. Words precisely arranged form one of our most powerful tools for change. How we use them is in our stories. Our stories define who and how we are.

> *'History will be kind to me, for I intend to write it.'*
> WINSTON CHURCHILL

> *'History is just one damned thing after another.'*
> ARNOLD TOYNBEE

It's no surprise that stories so evidently deserve our greatest respect and consideration. Rather, it's wholly incomprehensible that we do not give the story more attention than we do and elevate it and the craft of its telling to the status of fine arts. Should we aspire to be very good at this thing called storytelling? Of course we should. The wonder is that it isn't our prime priority.

Just as anyone can be a storyteller, anytime can be story time and anywhere too. Since the world was young stories have been carved, scratched, painted, printed, inked, or engraved on wood, rocks, stones, walls, tusks, teeth, pots, parchments, leaves, papyrus, skins, silk, cloth... Now they're mostly printed on paper though also recorded on film and tape. Or they've just been memorised and retold by heart. Whatever, stories are valued, refined and kept to be handed down as the record of what our society is and stands for.

Stories have always changed opinions and social direction. Our history dramatically and clearly shows the ability stories have to influence the turn of events. The very word 'history' is mostly made up of story. The stimulus and impact of the Bible, the Torah, the Qur'an, the writings of Confucius, the sacred Hindu epics the *Mahabharata* and *Ramayana, the Book of Mormon, the Tao Te Ching* and other religious texts are impossible to measure or even estimate. The stories woven through these texts have shaped our world and just about anyone who's ever lived in it. Wishing to surely and soundly convince their readers, the writers of religious texts almost invariably set out their teachings in the form of stories, because when it comes to influencing and convincing, well-told stories work.

> *'After nourishment, shelter and companionship, stories are the thing we need most in the world.'*
>
> PHILIP PULLMAN, AUTHOR OF *HIS DARK MATERIALS*

> *'Religion is the ultimate expression of story's dominion over the human mind... Sacred fiction has dominated human experience like nothing else.'*
>
> JONATHAN GOTTSCHALL, *THE STORYTELLING ANIMAL*

For an increasingly influential modern-day format consider today's TED talks, those short Internet-based films of lectures as 'ideas worth spreading' in technology, entertainment and design.

A fine example from TED is the story of architect Diébédo Francis Kéré from the tiny, impoverished village of Gando in Burkina Faso, West Africa. At the age of seven Francis was lucky enough to be given the chance of an education, which meant he had to leave his family and friends to live with an uncle in a distant big city. Years later he returned as a qualified architect with visions of a new kind of sustainable building using only locally-available materials and the sustained, collective labour of everyone in the village, all working together to create buildings that would transform life for the entire community. For an example of innovative rural development as it should be, you'll love to see and hear Francis telling his story on TED at www.ted.com/talks/diebedo_francis_kere_how_to_build_with_clay_and_community.html.

By 2012 more than a billion views of TED talks had been logged and it's growing all the time. With TED talks the medium may be new but the method is as old as dirt. TED gives ordinary folk a platform. It's like

Speaker's Corner in London's Hyde Park, brought up to date. If you want to make a point, inform opinion, start a movement, launch a campaign then give a lecture on TED. But you'd better be good. You'd better be an accomplished emotional storyteller.

Another storytelling site worth visiting is www.themoth.org/stories. There will be many more.

Everyone is a storyteller; everywhere is their stage.

Everyone knows a good story when they hear one. Though what makes a story good, well, that's a different story. And a single story's influence can sometimes be enormous.

Stories line the ether; they stick in our subconscious as well as our conscious minds. They're all around us, making up perhaps the richest, most entertaining, instructive and absorbing element of the fabric of our lives. Not quite as essential as food, water and the air we breathe they're not far behind. Stories have been told forever, whenever and wherever people gather, by day or night, in fields, streets and houses, round firesides, in marketplaces and ale houses, in church and chapel among priests and parsons, in dens of depravity to thieves and vagabonds, wherever people come together and have any time at all to fill. Stories spin spells, build consensus, inspire imaginations, bind relationships, break hearts, entertain, amuse, spread fun, love, misery and mischief.

Of course storytelling pre-writing wasn't entirely oral and isn't now. More often than not stories are accompanied by gestures, exclamations and other body language from grotesque expressions and exaggerations, arm-waving, over-acting and other unseemly accompaniments, even silence. A pregnant pause can be a powerful comment. It is no accident of evolution that the almost infinite repertoire of human expression, hands, arms, eyes, lips, mouth, stance, dress and appearance all lend themselves splendidly to storytelling.

And that's just the teensiest tip of it. If this were the right place and we had time and space for it – which we don't – I could try to tell you about how stories started, how they developed and spread, about how stories and their telling became so central to all our lives. I could tell how travellers' tales have produced the superstars of their age, from Marco Polo to David Attenborough. I could introduce you to the chunky, testosterone-filled warriors who throng the hero myths and legends. I could have a go at describing the Icelandic sagas, that vast literary phenomenon chronicling nearly 50 epic tales from Iceland in the tenth and eleventh centuries. Just one of these, the *Groenlendinga*, tells of Erik the Red's son Leif Eriksen sailing to the Americas 500 years before Columbus. And I could aspire to thrill you with tales from the Australian aboriginal people's dreamtime.

Since prehistory the role of the storyteller in the aboriginal dreamtime has been central to the identity of his or her society. The tribe's storytellers act as custodians of maybe 20 or 30 stories each and with these inform and educate the young people, thereby preserving the culture and identity of their community. They guard the lore that governs not just the land but every part of it: the water, the air, the environment, the universe and the stars. Their stories, added to by each successive storyteller as they're handed down from one generation to the next, evolve into the history and culture of the community by constant retelling. All transformational storytellers today could aspire to something like that.

How stories shape us

As long ago as 1726 *Gulliver's Travels* by Jonathan Swift was described as, 'universally read, from the cabinet council to the nursery'. Swift's book, an early and complex political satire, is considered by many to be the prototype of science fiction and a forerunner of the modern novel (*Robinson Crusoe*, by Daniel Defoe, came out five years earlier and is considered by many to be the earliest work of realistic fiction). Rather weirdly, in *Gulliver* Swift refers to the two moons of Mars about 150 years before their actual discovery, detailing their orbits with startling accuracy.

The Woman in White by Wilkie Collins (1859) is widely believed to be the first ever work of detective mystery fiction, establishing what must be one of the best loved and most ubiquitous of literary genres.

In *The Seven Pillars of Wisdom* T E Lawrence (Lawrence of Arabia) initially set out to define in a scholarly way the main religious systems of the world through a focus on the seven great cities of the Middle East, though later his book evolved into an autobiographical account of his adventures in the Arab revolt of 1917. In an act of monumental absent-mindedness and misfortune Lawrence lost the manuscript for his great work when he misplaced his briefcase while changing trains at Reading railway station in southern England (you couldn't make this up, could you?). National newspapers alerted the public to the loss of the 'hero's manuscript', but to no avail: the draft remained lost. He had kept no notes. Backing up onto a hard disc was of course unheard of, back then. So writing from memory he recreated the lost work (it's this more than anything that has earned the man my undying admiration). Though heavy going it had some enthusiastic followers. In a private letter to Britain's prime minister Stanley Baldwin, George Bernard Shaw wrote of it: 'The Work is a masterpiece, one of the few very best of its kind in the world.'

From the time of Herodotus, the father of history (c. 484 – 425 BC), historians have documented our past and drawn conclusions to shape and form our future, although chroniclers of popular legends are reported as predating even him. The followers of Jesus, when recounting the sway their master held among the populace, wrote of his power to spin parables, stories that captured the popular imagination while making an even more popular point.

But...it's just a story!

For sure stories have frequently turned the tide of history. Whether they lastingly shape many minds or just one very important mind, stories can change the world and a surprising number of works have done just that. I've already mentioned the most obvious of these, the Bible, the Qur'an and other sacred stories too.

In his *Life of Alexander* the Greek historian Plutarch explained that Alexander the Great was by nature a lover of learning and reading. He considered Homer's epic poem *The Iliad* to be the last word in military art, so took an edition everywhere he went, sleeping with it under his pillow, next to his dagger. It was study of *The Iliad* that gave Alexander his thirst for conquest and impelled him to carry his gory campaigns to all corners of the known earth. Those invasive adventures, which so reshaped the world, might have been very different but for Homer and his *Iliad*.

Homer's other epic poem, *The Odyssey*, is also something of a world-changer through its influence on other poets and storytellers and its depiction of issues concerning women and servants as well as fighting men. Both epics had a massive impact upon Greek culture, which went on in turn to influence the emergence of subsequent civilisations. Virgil's *Aeneid,* inspired by Homer's Odyssey, is considered the Roman equivalent and it in turn profoundly influenced many other works, notably Dante's *Inferno.*

Endless adaptations of Charles Dickens' *A Christmas Carol* (1843) are largely responsible for how we celebrate Christmas. Until this short tale achieved mega-popularity Christmas as a festival was generally considered no big deal. Then along came the story of Scrooge with its carol singing, presents, turkey dinners and stuffing and this has grown inexorably into the over-long commercialised ritual that we indulge in today. Whether Dickens did us a favour or not is a moot point.

Through her poignant personal diary with its first-hand accounts of growing up while hiding in the attic the young Anne Frank introduced successive generations of fellow teenagers to the onset of adolescence and the true horrors of the Nazis. Her personal narrative imprints indelibly upon young minds an enduring sense of outrage and abhorrence at the wrongs done to her and millions like her. In so doing the forever-young Anne has shaped the values and beliefs of successive generations, thereby reducing the chance of such a holocaust ever occurring again.

Such can be the reach of storytelling, even in a secret diary.

Books from an array of authors helped spur and spread the feminist movement and thinking around the world. Simone de Beauvoir, whose best-known book *The Second Sex* created its own wave of social change, credits the early French writer Christine de Pizan (1364 – c. 1430), the author of *Le Livre de la Cité des Dames* (The Book of the City of Ladies) and *Epître au Dieu d'Amour* (Epistle to the God of Love) as the first woman to write about the relationship between the sexes and first too to denounce misogyny. Hundreds of feminist writers have followed in her footsteps, blazing a bright though seldom uncontroversial trail as they went.

Edward Bulwer-Lytton's 1835 novel, *Rienzi,* about a heroic Roman tribune of that name, became an opera by Wagner, first performed in 1842. Listening to this opera one evening at the turn of the twentieth century, according to Jonathan Gottshall, was a young man who was so inspired he walked the streets through the night wrestling with his emotions before concluding that he would lead the German people '... out of servitude to the heights of freedom.' Adolf Hitler often spoke of his *Rienzi* epiphany, once telling a friend, 'At that hour it all began.'

World-changing, obviously, though not for the better and the tale anyway has been disputed, though the original manuscript for Wagner's opera, now lost, was apparently with Hitler throughout his final days in the Berlin bunker.

Attempting to list unambiguously world-changing books quickly becomes an onerous task and it would be next to impossible to settle upon a fixed canon of literature that has shaped Western social and cultural development down the ages. Though many books from Plato's *Republic* to Chaucer's *Canterbury Tales* and Karl Marx's *Das Kapital* to Mao Zedong's *Little Red Book* have obviously had profound influence, to list and catalogue them is beyond my brief and competence, so I've merely skimmed the surface. Television and radio in their turn have also played huge roles in spreading change, exposing prejudices, exploding myths and liberalising attitudes. Stories are living things, constantly evolving and forever changing us, too.

But there can be no doubt that stories transform history. And more than any other human construct they shape the people who tell them, as well as those who listen and are inspired to act.

The story paradox: happy endings and endless discord

We spend a lot of our time immersed in stories. According to the TV ratings company Nielsen the average American watches about 34 hours of television each week, which adds up to 73 days out of every year. Other countries won't be far behind. So, over the course of his or her lifetime the average person can expect to spend more than a decade in front of a TV screen. Most of that will be given over to stories. Then there's books, newspapers, cinema, online, jokes...

We all like happy endings, of course. We want to be happy always, to avoid unhappiness whenever we can. And we like neat solutions, nice feelings and tidy outcomes. So why is it that stories are almost always about problems, conflict and trouble?

The basic ingredients of stories are rather odd. It's said that almost all stories everywhere feature a hero figure struggling to overcome trouble, wrestling with and resolving a problem to get to his or her happy ending, safely home. This construct was defined in 1949 by Joseph Campbell in *The Hero with a Thousand Faces* as the monomyth, a term he borrowed from James Joyce's *Ulysses*. Reviewing tales from different times and regions Campbell found a core story with repeating patterns and shared fundamental structures and stages – the flight from disaster, the wandering, troubled hero's epic search for a lost treasure or a new home. Tolkein's *Lord of the Rings*, written before Campbell's definition, is a good example of the monomyth, the basic components of which were already over a thousand years old when Virgil told it as *The Aeneid* around the time of Jesus's birth. It was just as popular in 1972 when Richard Adams wrote *Watership Down*. Many film-makers still today study Campbell's book and the monomyth's influence can be seen in films such as *Star Wars* and several Disney epics. Some consolation, hopefully, for any writer who imagined authenticity was everything.

Others claim that hard-wired into every human that ever lived is the need to respond to the seven basic story types – the quest, the voyage and homecoming, rags to riches, rebirth/salvation, comedy, tragedy and vanquishing the monster. All involve a hero.

The thornier the predicament faced by the hero, says Jonathan Gottschall, the more we like the story. The hero gets his or her desires in the end, but usually at a cost and meanwhile we are kept at the edge of our seats. Stories without threat and conflict are dull and generally, ignored.

The paradox is that people seem to thrive on tales about things that, in real life, we'd find so calamitous.

Bad news, dramas and disagreements

By the time he or she reaches adulthood the average American child will have seen 200,000 violent acts on television alone and witnessed something like 40,000 killings. Yet fiction generally is very moral. When bad guys kill, that's wrong. When good guys kill it's with justification, usually as a last resort and often with reluctance and regret. Such generalisations of course are only loose, vague guidelines. The storyteller is always free to improvise and invent.

Undeniably our newspapers and televisions are packed with bad news stories, dramas and disagreements. The news media give far more coverage to the world's problems than to what's going right. Movies overflow with tragedies, disasters, conflicts and strife. Fairytales and nursery rhymes are chock-full of the stuff of nightmares – death, disease, disfigurement and disaster – and these are mirrored in the way children play. Almost invariably the stories children tell themselves, even from an early age, are pretty grim.

The first nursery rhymes date back to the fourteenth century. Though disguised as children's entertainment they were often laced with secret messages and meaning. Such was their popularity and catchiness they've endured to this day and seem set to last for centuries more.

Many of the traditional nursery rhymes we grew up with are just nonsense rhymes to amuse children though others have hidden, sinister meanings more suited to adult horror stories, or record political or religious turmoil, lessons for daily life, scandals and gossip, convey warnings or common-sense wisdom.

The macabre sense of humour in some have been so ingrained in us since childhood we hardly notice that babies are falling from trees, winsome wenches are held captive, or live animals are being cooked. It's only when you listen closely to the actual words of these infectious rhymes that you appreciate their dark, disturbing absurdity or the hidden lesson within.

Humpty Dumpty tells of the loss of a great canon in the English Civil War, *Baa Baa Black Sheep* is a political satire about a tax on the wool industry in 1770, *Jack and Jill* may illustrate the beheading of the king and queen after the French revolution, or it could be a cautionary tale to warn young women of the dangers of extra-marital relationships. *Mary, Mary Quite Contrary* references Bloody Mary, the Catholic queen and the numbers of protestants she killed (the same Mary who wielded the carving knife in *Three Blind Mice*). *Goosey Goosey Gander* is all about what happens if you don't say your prayers. Many of these are just fun while others are durable, effective stories told initially by transformational storytellers.

'One of the most adventurous things left to us is to go to bed. For no one can lay a hand on our dreams.'

E V LUCAS, HUMORIST, ESSAYIST, PLAYWRIGHT

Dreaming of a deeper meaning

Our dreams too are filled with bad stuff. Those who've looked into these things conclude that most of our dreams are about bad things happening: threats, worries, anxieties and danger. Sigmund Freud believed that children sleep more soundly and deeply than adults and described dreams as the disguised fulfilment of a repressed infantile wish. Long thought to be prophetic and of heavenly origin the earliest insight into dreams comes from the *Epic of Gilgamesh,* one of the oldest surviving pieces of literature, from Mesopotamia in 2700 BC. Among other things, it suggests that dreams are the gods' way of announcing their plans to the people.

Freud observed that everyone dreams and that some of our dreams are connected to what has happened to us in our waking lives, hence we all have a notion that dreams must mean something. Dreams are a product of our own minds, so no matter how weird or alien, they're a part of us, therefore must be able to tell us about ourselves.

> *'Do not keep children to their studies by compulsion but by play.'*
>
> PLATO

> *'Play is often talked about as if it were a relief from serious learning. But for children play is serious learning. Play is really the work of childhood.'*
>
> FRED ROGERS, AMERICAN SONGWRITER AND TELEVISION HOST.

Though scientists have long studied dreams the jury's still out on them – it's not yet fully understood why all human people and animals too dream as we do. Many now believe that dreams are merely the meaningless effect of random nerve firings during REM (rapid eye movement) sleep, with the function of getting rid of nervous tension accumulated during the day. Some claim dreams are the brain filing away aspects of what happened during our day. Others are sure that dreams – night stories – shape our minds and profoundly influence how we develop and how we behave. Whatever, dreams obviously are a good source of stories.

According to Jonathan Gottschall in *The Storytelling Animal,* dreamland is rife with emotional and physical peril, far more threatening than the average person's waking world. Even sex dreams are laced with anxiety and regret. We dream, says Gottschall, in a vivid, story-like way for around two hours each night, which in a normal lifespan works out at about six years of our lives spent non-stop in dreaming. The average person, he reckons, goes through around five threatening episodes each night in his or her dreams. The most common dream for all adults involves being chased or attacked. Other universal themes, says Gottschall, are falling from a great height, drowning, being lost or trapped, being naked in public, getting injured or sick, dying and being caught in a disaster.

So though a curious paradox, perhaps it's unsurprising that most stories are about danger and trouble, with happiness coming, if it comes at all, only at the end.

Religious stories have had such impact and popularity down the ages because they aspire to answer the big questions that have obsessed our species since the beginnings of time. How did I get here? Why am I here? How will I die? What will happen to me after I'm dead? What's the meaning of life? Such questions are universally consistent across races, cultures and individuals, social status, age, the sexes and intellectual abilities.

The happy ending we humans ultimately seek from our religious stories is salvation, absolution, eternal life, or at least a safe solution. Religious stories abound with dos and don'ts, death and disaster, threats of damnation and eternal hell-fire, self-denial and chastisement. All are designed to keep us fearful, obedient, struggling and still worshiping, even if only because it's sensible to play safe. They're not always stories that give instant easy answers though, rather they keep their adherents anxious, questioning, striving, reminding them that until they die, they remain unsaved.

Perhaps such questions are unanswerable, definitively. Philosophers down the ages have sought solutions in the pursuit of knowledge, happiness, pleasure, liberty and freedom from fear. No single answer seems entirely convincing except, perhaps, an unquestioning devotion to some kind of god, a leap of faith that many people simply cannot make. Those seeking to provide such answers, whether prophets or charlatans, have for the most part chosen to promote their points through stories.

So storytellers seem set to continue fulfilling the useful function of exploring, analysing and spreading thought on all of our species' important issues. There's no sense that the importance of religious stories will diminish any time soon. While religious observance and respect may be declining in much of Europe, in most parts of the world the major organised religions are adding converts faster than they're losing them.

For storytellers today this all adds up to a massive opportunity and a powerful responsibility. However this world of ours might develop in future, storytelling will play a part no less profound and valuable than it has always played. And with modern media and communications methods, all sorts of enterprises and individuals can turn this powerfully to their advantage.

CHAPTER'S END:
ACTIONS AND KEY MESSAGES

How the story has influenced events down the ages.
What history is.

Storytelling predates almost all other forms of communication.

From Alexander the Great to Hitler and Lawrence of Arabia to Anne Frank, how stories have changed the world by spreading ideas, influencing opinions and shaping social direction.

Tales of calamity and why we thrive on them. On hidden messages and meanings.

The stuff of dreams and why everyone likes a happy ending.

Why religious stories have such power.

Why stories matter as much now as ever, if not more so.

PART TWO

Making the difference

TURNING POINT

This story's from the 1950s, before television came to my home town. To my memory, growing up in the Scottish Highlands, the world then was in black and white. I was six years old, all cardigan, balaclava and short trousers, socks round my ankles, football in the street, jumpers for goalposts, that kind of thing.

Fundraising is fudge

Back then my mother volunteered as area secretary for the national childcare charity Dr Barnardo's Homes. It was her job to dish out their distinctive 'cottage' collecting boxes to as many households as would take them, then after a suitable interval collect in the money.

She did it for the orphans and the unhappy children. She was big-hearted, my mum. Twice a year she'd run an ad in the local paper and all the kids from miles around would come to our house clutching their distinctive Barnardo's boxes to have their contents totted up. It was my job to count the coppers and odd thruppeny bits into shilling piles. Lots of money! I loved it.

But even back then there were many other worthwhile causes all competing for home collectors. So my mother hit upon a genius idea. She offered each kid bringing in a box a piece of her home-made fudge as reward.

Now my mum made the world's best fudge. Word spread and soon kids were queuing round the corner clutching their colourful boxes ready for emptying. I was worked twice as hard at the totting up so I thought, a piece of fudge for you for bringing in the box, a piece of fudge for me, for counting it.

It was only fair.

My mother grew to be one of the top fundraisers in Scotland for Dr Barnardo's Homes. I grew to be a rather large child, from too much fudge.

But it was here that I learned the value of reciprocity. The more you give, the more you get too. And it's surprising just how many opportunities there are for fundraisers and storytellers to give as well as get. If nothing else, the fundraiser should always leave the donor with a good story of what their support will achieve.

5. Understanding your audience

'If we don't understand them, how can we expect them to understand us?'
DAVID OGILVY

Knowing whom we're talking to and the precise effects that our stories are achieving are obviously vital to the transformational storyteller. The task of understanding our audiences, though, gets more difficult every day.

Too much information, not enough stories

We live in the age of information overload. These days it seems like information is infinite, as if every printer and portal on the planet is stuck on spewing the stuff out. Yet, while no one ever tires of entertainment, engagement and involvement, almost nobody wants more information. Rather, they all search out nuggets of relevant content, they revel in intrigue, drama and amusing anecdotes and invariably they all enjoy a good story.

Look at what's around. Note what you enjoy listening to or like to read. It's the stories, right? They're when you learn most too, aren't they?

Of course all writers have to communicate information but they need to do it succinctly and at lightning speed. It's something people who put on TV shows and make films take almost for granted, what screenwriter David Mamet referred to as 'cramming a shitload of information into a little bit of time'. Mamet famously told his scriptwriters on the TV series *The Unit*, 'The audience will not tune in to watch information. You wouldn't, I wouldn't. No one would or will. The audience will only tune in and stay tuned to watch drama.'

This is great advice. Imagine what a difference there would be in, for example, the written or verbal output of, say health agencies, charities, government departments, or most businesses, if this guidance were taken literally and acted upon.

David Mamet described drama as the hero's quest to overcome the things that prevent him or her from achieving a specific goal. So the writer, for every scene, has to ask three questions.

- Who wants what?
- What happens if s/he doesn't get it?
- Why now?

How the writer answers these questions will show if the scene is dramatic or not. There is no magic fairy dust, Mamet went on to say, that will transform a boring or merely informative scene and make it dramatic. If it's not dramatically written it won't be dramatically acted.

That's good to know, for all storytellers. Drama, of course, is the key to entertainment. It can also be the key to action.

> *'People will not be bored in print. They may listen politely at a dinner table to boasts and personalities, life history, etc. But in print they choose their own companions, their own subjects. They want to be amused or benefited.'*
>
> CLAUDE C HOPKINS, *SCIENTIFIC ADVERTISING*

Our audience is individual, all different yet all the same

Of course all storytellers have to approach their audiences as a collection of individuals all with varied interests, expectations and potential outcomes. I like this little vignette from negotiator Gavin Kennedy, which illustrates the point.

Imagine, he says in his book *Essential Negotiation*, an old wooden chair for sale in the window of a second-hand shop, with a price tag of $15.00. You pass by and look at a pile of books on the shelf outside, while thinking about it. A middle-aged woman stops and looks at the chair. She's thinking it would suit her student son's new apartment as a bedside chair for his alarm clock, because he's not very good at getting up early. And it would double as a clothes rack for his shirts as his room at home is always untidy. A young girl, perhaps a drama student, looks at it and considers its possibilities as a stage prop. A bearded, serious type inspects it, checking underneath the seat, evaluating its potential as the fourth of a set of three he already has at home. An antiques dealer recognises it as an example of the work of Joshua Prendergast, the early twentieth century art deco legend. Meanwhile the seller may be indifferent to whether or not he sells the chair, or may be short of cash and eager to get whatever he can for it.

And so on. Gavin's point is that this shows well how a single object can have a range of values for different people in varying situations. It demonstrates equally well how individually members of your audience will approach the story you're telling. They may see it in a different light, influenced by their individual circumstances to give it a meaning or interpretation some distance from the one you hoped to convey.

Yet all your listeners are in many ways all the same too. The insurance industry – described by Winston Churchill as 'the magic of averages' – is built upon it. People as a mass behave with actuarial predictability. They have more or less similar influences and respond to pretty much the same stimuli. They laugh, cry, get angry, afraid, or elated by the same ideas and images and by the variety of buttons that the transformational storyteller presses. They all respond to the same emotions, the same generalisations, the same jokes, the same needs, wants and desires. Or not. Nothing in life is ever certain and what goes with a wow in Wandsworth or Wichita can die a death in Doncaster or Des Moines, no doubt. So success is seldom guaranteed. But we can comfortably assume, with some precision, that when a story works well with some people it'll work with others too.

What makes people the same is that they are all so very different.

Why does everyone everywhere support the Lifeboats?

There's a salutary lesson for storytellers in why the Lifeboats (the Royal National Lifeboat Institution) is one of Britain's largest, most popular and most respected charities.

Non-profit organisations generally under-invest in really understanding their donors, their customers, so they can get ever better at supplying what the donor wants (the main secret of success, whoever your audience, whatever your task). Here, adapted from my earlier book *The Zen of Fundraising* (Jossey-Bass Inc, 2006), is one dramatic example of how it pays to get this right.

Britain is a seafaring nation with a long and proud nautical tradition. The United Kingdom's third biggest non-profit, the Royal National Lifeboat Institution (RNLI), has as its mission saving the lives of those in peril on the sea. With over 200 coastal stations dotted around the country it boasts the largest private fleet in the world. Specially designed and constructed lifeboats are manned by volunteer lifeboatmen and women who launch their tiny craft into stormy waters at any time of the day or night, to provide a round-the-coast, round-the-clock emergency rescue service that is the envy of the world. For years this ancient, august institution firmly believed that this mission was the main, even sole, reason why such a high proportion of the British people hold this cause so close to their hearts and give it such large sums with such regular reliability. This must be, they assumed, because of the nearly 2,000 lives that the RNLI saves, year after year.

But it isn't so, as RNLI quite recently learned to its great profit. The real reason why donors support RNLI in their droves is fundamentally different. But RNLI learned about this only when they took the bold step of investing in research. They'd been in existence for more than 150 years before they got around to asking their supporters why they support the Lifeboats. During all that time RNLI had quite the wrong idea about why their supporters give.

This research among RNLI's supporters showed convincingly that, while no one objects to it, saving lives at sea is not what inspires donors to support this famous organisation. Not at all. Windsurfers swept accidentally out to sea? Serves them right. Rich yacht owners who get into trouble in high seas? Who cares? Drunken Soviet sailors who fall overboard in a force nine gale? Throw them back!

What the research showed so convincingly was that donors and would-be donors don't give to RNLI because they feel sympathy or concern for those many souls who get into trouble on the high seas. No. They give because they are thrilled, inspired and in awe of the heroism, courage and self-sacrifice of the volunteer lifeboat crews who at risk of their own lives launch themselves in all weathers into untold dangers to save people they don't even know.

That's why these people give. It's a powerful motivation much different from concern to save lives at sea. Donors love and admire heroes and will give what they can to help them. Ask Greenpeace, Médecins sans Frontières (Doctors without Borders), Amnesty International, the cancer nurses, the international development agencies and a host of others.

Do you imagine that this realisation made any great difference to how RNLI goes about its business of raising funds? You bet. The difference is crucial. This simple understanding transformed RNLI's fundraising beyond measure. How they did it is another story, which I'll relay on page 130. But all storytellers can learn from their example of the extraordinary value and benefits that can derive from *really* knowing your donors, or customers.

Knowing which story to tell people can make a massive difference to just about any organisation, enterprise, cause, or individual with a similarly detailed tale to tell. It'll pay all social change campaigners to realise the importance of good market knowledge and to appreciate that if they are really to understand their supporters, or customers they should invest sensibly in sustained, relevant research. Those that don't, make an often spectacularly false economy. They condemn their organisations to be permanent victims of the curse of assumptions, wrongly anticipating their supporters' true feelings because they simply didn't know any better.

Transformational storytellers shouldn't make similar mistakes.

Funnily enough, it isn't about money

Prompted by the story above, this seems a good place to introduce another lesson charity fundraisers have learned about their donors and what they will and won't respond to. Oxymoronic though it might seem, fundraising isn't about money, it's about work that urgently needs doing. Money is the means to an end, not the end itself. 'Where will we find the love?' is always more powerful than 'where will we find the money?'

- Fundraisers and like-minded others shouldn't focus on the money, instead they should focus on the people who're sending it.

- The promotion of any cause, even when it involves mass marketing, is still about one individual talking, or writing, to another about something they both care deeply about.

- It's about inspiring people, one by one, to believe they can make a difference, then helping them to make it.

- It's not about securing a quick single gift or action, it's about building sustainable, mutually beneficial, long-term relationships that deliver *lifetime value* to both donor *and* cause.

- It's certainly not about irritating the donor with repeated, disconnected asking. Instead, through their storytelling, fundraisers should seek to cultivate a thought process in the donor that goes something like this:

  Talk to me about something I care about.

  Interest me in what you're doing about it.

  Show me that I could make a difference too.

  Introduce me to the joy of giving.

  Take me through what we've achieved together.

  Let me revel comfortably in that a while.

  Later, remind me about it and give me similar opportunities that recreate and add to the original excitement.

Always treat your audience with respect

Commercial organisations often don't. Charities (in essence, just a different kind of commercial organisation) can be even worse. It's not just basic politeness and doing the right thing, it's sound business practice to be polite and considerate at all times and it's much more fun and satisfying too. When I tell stories, write letters, or plan any communication I always have just one individual reader in mind who I want to get my message to. Most often, it's my mother. And I wouldn't ever do anything that might upset or offend my mum.

Yet often our organisations have systems and structures that stand in the way of natural good manners. Take charitable donors who for one reason or other (mostly an avoidable one) have stopped giving to a once-favoured cause. Invariably, charities refer to these former supporters as lapsed donors. It sounds quaintly biblical, like 'fallen women'. How dare they lapse, these people? I mean, would you want to live next door to a lapsed donor? Or allow your daughter to go out with one?

If we refer to people in unflattering terms we'll also write about them, or for them, in unflattering ways, or think about them in that way too. I once worked with a very fine organisation, full of very nice people who entirely unthinkingly referred to some of their best customers in the most disparaging ways. They had segments on their database that they described as *the leftovers, the residue, the sediment* and *the dead pool.*

Enough said, I hope.

When brevity is best

These days you have to capture people's attention very fast so, even if you're planning to tell them a long story, you need to start with a beautifully boiled-down opener to stop them and draw them in. Mostly we write too many words and add too much detail and diversion. So the storyteller has to learn both to practise brevity and to kill his, or her, babies.

Stories can be surprisingly short, indeed are often the more powerful and penetrating for being so. As George Bernard Shaw is famous for saying, 'I apologise for sending such a long letter. I didn't have time to write a shorter one.' Or was it Oscar Wilde? No one really seems sure.

Try writing slogans and jingles for a living and you'll soon know what whoever it was meant. When Ernest Shackleton sought to recruit intrepid adventurers for his polar expeditions he told a short story in a lineage advertisement that, apparently, had eager, aspiring explorers queuing around the corner and down the street. As it happens responses from the ad (figures of hundreds and even 5,000 respondents have been asserted) and even its very provenance as written or placed by Shackleton himself have been disputed. But whatever, it makes an agreeable story. The spirit of adventure is not dead. Hoorah!

Harrison. No. 34 Baker st.
EDWARD HUGHES, 41 Fish st.

MEN WANTED
for hazardous journey. small wages, bitter cold, long months of complete darkness, constant danger. Safe return doubtful, honor and recognition in event of success.
Ernest Shackleton 4 Burlington st.

MEN—Neat-appearing young men of pleasing personality, between ages of

I'm not sure it would have worked as well today, as a tweet, but perhaps it might, if Shackleton had managed to keep it relevant and interesting while condensing it to under 140 characters or less. Most tweets fail.

Though not always true (direct mail letters are a consistent exception, see page 114), in transformational storytelling I'm sure that generally it's sound advice to say less, to be brief. Cutting copy improves it, most of the time.

Ernest Hemingway was famously set the task of writing a book in just six words and claimed it the most difficult book to write. The result – though again perhaps apocryphal – is now famous and the only book I remember from start to finish.

FOR SALE.
BABY'S SHOES.
NEVER WORN.

ERNEST HEMINGWAY, A BOOK IN SIX WORDS

A brilliant, moving orator, Abraham Lincoln's most famous speech is the Gettysburg Address, delivered several months after the battle of the same name. In it he defined and espoused the principles of human equality set out in the US Declaration of Independence so powerfully that his words are remembered as some of the most significant in American history. Yet Lincoln's oration that day was merely the supporting act, the main speaker at the event was Senator Edward Everett, former governor of Massachusetts, a famous orator himself. He delivered from memory a two-hour oration on the battle and history has duly forgotten almost every word of it. Lincoln, on the other hand, delivered just 272 of the most important words ever spoken, which have since become part of the cultural upbringing of every American schoolchild. Later Senator Everett wrote to Lincoln, 'I wish that I could flatter myself that I had come as near to the central idea of the occasion in two hours as you did in two minutes.'

Indeed, sometimes brevity and simplicity are best. My business partner Alan Clayton is fond of a mantra that cleverly uses ten words, none of which is longer than two letters and still says something sensible and complete.

'If it is to be,' he says, 'it is up to me.'

As evidence that short is best you may have come across the following.

Pythagoras' theorem:	24 words.
Archimedes' principle:	25 words.
The Lord's prayer:	65 words.
Gettysburg address:	272 words.
Ten commandments:	313 words.
US Declaration of Independence:	1,309 words.
European regulations on the sale of cabbages:	26,911 words.

Sadly the statistic about regulations on cabbages isn't quite accurate. Or rather, is entirely inaccurate. Still the point it makes is no less valid. We all need to work at saying less, but better.

Long stories vs short

How long should a story be? If it's interesting and well told the only answer worth offering is: as long as it needs to be. For an email header, very short is best. For direct mail, four or even six pages may be needed to do the job right.

> *'Short-copy ads set in poster style and containing only a few words or a slogan are usually used by advertisers unable to trace the direct results from their advertisements.'*
>
> JOHN CAPLES, *TESTED ADVERTISING METHODS*

As the legendary Mr Caples shows, those who measure response quickly learn that, more often than not, long copy works best for their ads and direct mail letters. The theory is that once drawn into the story the writer can take his or her time to properly develop the offer and set out its benefits. Length of course is directly related to relevance. Copy that is too long bores readers. Copy that's too short fails to inform, and often, fails to sell. The storyteller's task is to judge it just right.

When using a picture that really does say a thousand words it's often possible for the writer to cut description accordingly. On occasions the best advice is to say nothing at all, except to let the image tell the tale for you.

What's important is not how long or short your story is, but that you never waste a word.

> *'Chinese warriors in the nineteenth century would carry a lamp when attacking at night, to give the enemy a sporting chance.'*
>
> NORMAN LEWIS, TRAVEL WRITER, FROM *SEMI-INVISIBLE MAN*

How to find your angle, style, content…

Getting the right angle for your story is important. When trying to persuade people in public washrooms to wash their hands it's been shown that asking, 'Is the person next to you washing their hands?' is a more powerful inducement to hand-washing than simply saying, 'Now wash your hands'. This, presumably, is because people are more concerned about what others think of them than what they might get away with themselves.

Almost any story can be adapted to the points you want to make. Early in my career I came to believe that many non-profit fundraisers and campaigners were neglecting to master the basics of their trade because they were distracted by the many shiny, fashionable new things around, by pursuing the latest hot idea rather than what really matters. While seeking a simple way to get this across I came upon the following story from a perhaps unlikely source, which I quickly embroidered into an effective lesson for would-be world-changers.

... and to stay 15 minutes ahead

We are – most of us – from a generation reared on stories, images and visions of invasions from outer space. *Star Wars, Star Trek, Alien, The War of the Worlds,* these tales of extraterrestrials always revolve around the notion of visitors from space light years in advance of us, scientific streets ahead, with minds immeasurably superior to ours. The instant these superior beings arrive they set about quelling we puny earthlings into submission with their fabulous heat-rays, stun-guns, phasers or similar death-dealing machines, succeeding rather easily because they're so far ahead.

But the American comedian Woody Allen had a vision of a different kind of space invader. He foresaw invading aliens not as light years ahead, but just 15 minutes ahead.

These space beings, Woody believed, would be 15 minutes ahead in *everything*. They'd always be first in the queue at the supermarket checkout, first to grab the last available drier at the launderette, first to predict the winner of the 3.30 at Epsom, or the World Series, the Superbowl, FA Cup, or whatever. Though just 15 minutes ahead these infuriating extraterrestrials would always be in front, constantly pipping us at the post, thereby ensuring that whatever we might try to do they would always win. So total world domination would be easy.

There's a parallel here for storytellers and any other kind of communicator. It's increasingly difficult these days to get really significantly ahead of the field and almost impossible to be light years ahead. But you can still win, consistently, by being just 15 minutes ahead. If you can be just a little ahead of your competitors that's all you'll need in these rapidly changing times to ensure all the success you could possibly wish.

So, I'd then advise my audiences to be constantly on the lookout for ways to put their organisation 15 minutes ahead. This, I told them, more often than not involved not aiming for the stars, miles out of reach as they are, but reaching down to gather up all the small but collectively significant near-to-hand and achievable ideas and opportunities that they'll find swimming around their feet, day in and day out.

This story and the images I used around it worked rather well, as you can imagine. They were instrumental in getting these perhaps unpalatable messages through.

CHAPTER'S END: ACTIONS AND KEY MESSAGES

Why almost nobody wants more information.

Where to learn how to communicate succinctly at lightning speed.

Reciprocity pays. Why would-be influencers always seek to give something, even if it's just telling a great story.

Research is vital. If we don't understand our audience we can't expect them to understand us.

The danger of boring people and why drama matters more than information. How to use drama to create excitement and action.

Why benefits matter.

The importance of treating people as individuals and why, as a mass, people behave predictably even when, individually, they may surprise you.

Understanding true motivations. Why everyone supports Britain's favourite charity and how you can copy it.

The benefits of treating people with respect and thinking about them in the right way.

Short versus long copy and how to make sure you never waste a word.

How to find your angle, style and content, while staying 15 minutes ahead.

TURNING POINT

The message below arrived one day in the charity's office, unannounced. It shows how an innocent question asked from politeness – 'how are you doing?' – can release a flood of emotions and a new personal resolve. Training in the telemarketing company concerned, R Fundraising of Dunfermline, Scotland, revolves around building rapport through storytelling.

A letter in praise of telemarketing without a script

Hi, I lost my partner in August this year after an eight-month battle with cancer. She sadly died in hospital before we had time to request the Macmillan home cancer support service.

A few weeks after her funeral I answered the phone at home – it was a lady from Macmillan who asked if I would be willing to accept a collection box for donations. I agreed to, stating that I had recently lost my partner. The lady said she was very sorry to hear this, then to my amazement asked me how I was coping and whether there was anything I needed any help with.

I had spent countless hours in doctors' surgeries and many different wards of various hospitals and departments, talking to medical staff about my partner, and I realised that this was the first time that anyone had asked me how I was.

You are a remarkable group of people and I would like you to know that I am coping very well, thank you, by doing anything I can to raise money for Macmillan. The phone call made me realise that just because my partner has gone does not mean my fight against this terrible disease has to be over.

I am happy for you to use my story in any way you wish if you feel it could encourage others, either in their own battles, or to continue to donate to Macmillan afterwards. No need to reply unless you really wish to. Thank you very much again.

Signed,
A donor

6. Adding purpose and fulfilment

'We make a living by what we get.
We make a life by what we give.'

WINSTON CHURCHILL

What most people really want

Business people are well advised to heed the wisdom in Churchill's words. There's always been profits to be had from feeding people's appetite for what they want. Now, we have the means to understand and answer those needs deep, deep down. It's here that transformational storytelling really comes into its own.

Report after report confirms that people want to make a difference in their lives – not just to survive, thrive, or merely enjoy themselves, but to tangibly influence something for the better.

So, just like you and me, really.

A research project in the USA funded by the MacArthur Foundation in 2012, Net Impact's Talent Report *What Workers Want*, reveals that employees who say they have the opportunity to make a direct social and environmental impact through their job report higher satisfaction levels than those who don't. Employees who say they can make an impact through their work report greater satisfaction than those who can't by a ratio of two to one. Two-thirds of graduating university students report that being able to make a difference through their job is a priority, so much so that 45 per cent of students claim they would even accept being paid significantly less to do so. Seventy per cent of college students say 'having a job where they can make an impact on causes and issues that matter to them' is very important.

No surprises here then. Scratch the skin of any optimistic, balanced young person and you'll quickly get to a rich seam of pent-up idealism just yearning to find expression. That describes us, doesn't it? Equip people like us as transformational storytellers and there's no limit to the difference we might make.

If you can't make a difference at work – and many jobs allow limited scope for it – then the next best thing is to make a difference outside of it. One way or another, the opportunity to make a meaningful difference in life really matters.

> *'Never doubt that a small group of committed people can change the world. It is the only thing that ever has.'*
> MARGARET MEAD

Margaret Mead was an American anthropologist and this, I am sure, is the most durable and perhaps most perceptive thing she ever said. She was so, so right. I have kept those words of hers close to my heart for most of my working life and they've guided and influenced me more than most. What a great debt I owe her and what a wonderful thing she did, in telling me that.

To paraphrase Ms Mead, never doubt that a small group of committed, brilliant storytellers can change the world. They'll do it much more quickly and certainly if they are equipped to be transformational storytellers. Everyone wants to change the world, even if most don't immediately realise that to succeed, they first have to change themselves. With almost equal foresight Margaret Mead also said, 'what people say, what people do, and what they say they do are entirely different things'. That, in itself, seems worth changing.

The progress paradox

Anyone aspiring to change anything these days is obliged to operate in a business and social environment that itself is changing rapidly and constantly. Some of the consequences of this are surprising and will open up opportunities hitherto not even guessed at for those who would change the world. Massive technological upheavals are already leading to hitherto undreamed-of chances for the would-be social change agent, the change warrior, wherever he or she might work. (I coined the phrase 'change warrior' to describe the kind of people I think we need to be encouraging in our organisations and enterprises. I describe them more fully in the final chapter of this book. Though, I don't wish to encourage belligerence, just a modicum of swashbuckling brio.)

Like all opportunities, we have to spot these undreamed-of chances in time and exploit them to the full. The progress paradox, I submit, is one of these.

Progress, it seems, might not be making our species happier. These days our society's unease may not be coming, as it traditionally has, from endemic poverty, from people having to go without, so much as from prosperity, our being increasingly able to go 'with'. General affluence, it appears, does not automatically arrive in the company of general contentment. It's in the most affluent societies that one finds the longest queues outside the psychiatrists' doors. Affluent people in a rush are most likely to head that queue. And the stress these time-poor rich people feel is more likely to come not from the speed of social change but rather from the feeling of powerlessness to do anything positive to influence things. So change warriors might be just the people to solve the biggest of their perceived problems.

According to a feature in *Newsweek* a few years back, as living standards improve people don't necessarily feel the benefits. Although folk like us now averagely start work later in life, work fewer hours each week, are retiring earlier (well, some still are) and in reality have oodles more time than our ancestors, we persist in feeling time-poor. Obesity is as large a health risk for the affluent as going hungry is for the poor and, like poverty in the developing world, it's growing in our society. Instead of more money making us happier, griping apparently rises with income.

It's a world turned, apparently, on its head.

It seems more and more people find that with increasing affluence comes a decreasing sense of fulfilment. Maybe as we cease to need to worry about basic survival, other issues of purpose and fulfilment crowd in upon us. Particularly, it's in the most unequal societies that one finds the most discontent. Employers should be recognising and responding to this even if politicians don't. In order to spread happiness and contentment for all, the case for some redistribution of resources is a strong one.

Look! Storytellers can offer meaning…

Could this be an opportunity for social change-makers? I think so; it could be a great one. Given the proven track record of social causes, their variety, character and the urgent nature of the needs they aim to meet, who could offer fulfilment and meaning in life for those without it better than those who want to change the world?

This opportunity is not exclusive to the voluntary sector. There's opportunity here too for entrepreneurs, employers, relationship managers and customer service people, to name but a few. Perhaps in this new progress paradigm, storytellers could expand their role. If significant sections of society face a problem that stems from their growing affluence, maybe we're just the folk to relieve them of it.

And if time too is in short supply then we can make everything very easy for them as well as appealing and interesting. If the meaning of life is becoming increasingly incomprehensible, or out of reach for many, cannot advocates for social change like you and me and the causes, issues and propositions we promote or work for, help many people find the answers they seek? If we tell them the right stories in the right way at the right time, they'll flock to us.

Think about it. What could be more appropriate for well-heeled people in a hurry than inspirational storytellers prepared to make it easy for them to find worthwhile and interesting homes for reasonable amounts of their surplus money without any pressure or hassle? And with a lot of fun, satisfaction and rewarding feedback thrown in for them, in return. We could become *the* people to turn to when the pressures of modern affluence become too much to bear.

This might be a better role for the corporate engager, educator, campaigner, lobbyist, fundraiser, or change warrior than that which he or she currently enjoys. She or he could become a provider of fulfilment for busy people, spinning stories of propositions, products and opportunities through which they can make a real difference in their society, in the wider world and for themselves.

Types of tale

There are numerous types of story deliberately crafted to make people think, then act. Here are some of the more interesting ones.

Stories of hero figures.

The heroes of legend and the super-heroes of the comic books abound and all inspire us to action, to the noblest of human emotions. Today's equivalents are not only the cancer-care nurses, the hero-medics of Médecins sans Frontières, or Greenpeace's wet-suit clad adventurers, they're also other more unlikely heroes – the business high-flyer, the entrepreneur, the inspirational teacher and the company role model.

We all respond to heroes and all admire bravery, cleverness and self-sacrifice. Good triumphs over evil, one person telling another about a wrong that needs righting and saying, 'We must do something about this. We can make a difference.'

It would take a lot, you might think, to persuade anyone to rise up in rebellion or lay down his or her life, just by telling a story. Yet few tools are more effective than the hero story or hero myth at inspiring young men and women to take up arms, to put their lives on the line for their family, friends, country, or even, at times, for people they haven't met and will never know. Or for an idea, an ideal, or a belief. Since storytelling began, tales of the righteous hero sacrificing for the common good have inspired such actions.

In a survey in several countries for *Marie Claire* magazine it turns out that the figure women most fancy everywhere is not the politician or the rich businessman, nor is it even the social change agent or the transformational storyteller. It's the fireman. Particularly if he's just rescued a small child. Médecins sans Frontières is regularly voted by readers as the most popular charity, thanks to tales of handsome, brave doctors.

The anecdote about the Lifeboats in chapter 5 shows this perfectly, as a key to the importance of understanding your audience.

Bedtime stories

These don't necessarily involve the promise of reward but they're no less action oriented just because their ultimate objective is to get the little darlings off to sleep. Well, going to sleep is an action of sorts, is it not? Peace, contentment and a satisfactory ending all aid the process, so bedtime storytelling is invariably a good training ground for transformational storytelling.

Stories as a promise of reward

'If you get into bed and settle down, now, I will tell you a story...' As sleep usually follows with this one too this, not unlike other bedtime stories, tends to result more in the absence of action than its presence. But the promise of a reward in your story is powerful and valuable. The anticipation of satisfaction settles your audience and gives you the floor. Deny your audience an agreeable outcome and they'll soon let you know.

Nursery tales

These have been referenced already, on page 97. Given their history as spreaders of instructive messages there seems potential for the modern-day storyteller in the medium of nursery tales.

Fables and parables

The parable is a well-recognised device from ancient times, a story with a moral or instructive twist or principle. Told in prose or verse its purpose is to provoke change, to use simple analogy to prompt deeper thinking and a different way. It was Jesus's parables more than anything that helped the early Christian church to take root around the world, long before the populace had access to books. Remember the Good Samaritan, who crossed the road to help his traditional enemy and left money at the inn to ensure his upkeep. How great it would be if the world were more often reminded of that.

Equally ancient, fables follow the same form and function but use the anthropomorphising of animals or inanimate objects, rather than tales of people, to make their points. As we grew, Aesop made a powerful imprint in our consciousness with, among others, his fable of the dog with a bone crossing the bridge. Looking down the greedy dog saw only his own image looking up, clutching the bone in his jaws. Thinking he was seeing another dog with an even juicier mouthful he opened his jaws to grab the second bone and his own fell into the river and was lost.

The moral is simple, the lesson profound. It pays not to be too greedy.

Speeches and sermons

Usually, though not always, sermons exhort action from their listeners, even if it's only a negative one, as in 'go forth and sin no more'. Martin

Luther King's speeches always seemed to be sermons and none the less powerful or effective for it. Other speeches unquestionably have changed the world, though not always for the better. Often their impact's been such that they've become the stuff of legend, featuring orators from Cicero and Demosthenes to Hitler and Churchill, with scores more in-between (almost always, but not invariably, men), all credited with turning the course of history on a well-phrased, well-structured, well-delivered speech.

The sales pitch

A detailed 'how to' for sales pitching would take more chapters than we have space for in this book. Yet without doubt effective sales people too are transformational storytellers. Sales people depend on overcoming resistance, surmounting barriers, gaining trust and confidence, on their ability to paint pictures, capture imaginations and quickly, neatly, get to the point. Whether delivered in person, by letter, over the phone or by other less personal media, sales people rely on every trick and technique required of the transformational storyteller. Though not, it has to be said, always in a good cause.

Blogs

All sorts of people blog on all sorts of issues for all sorts of reasons and it's a universal compulsion that as yet shows no sign of slowing. If they're to get any better will depend on how well-versed their authors become in the fundamentals of effective storytelling.

Stories that raise money

Usually for a social purpose, a worthwhile cause, a job that needs doing and in some way improves society and makes the world a better place. Fundraising for good causes now is a massive industry, but one that rightly prides itself on its value to society, on its rich tradition, on its daily devotion to making a difference. Fundraising, at its heart, is all about emotional, transformational storytelling.

Stories from the soapbox

Tub-thumping tales told on street corners and in parks to campaign for the conversion of passers-by to some form or other of political, personal, or social change.

The improving tract

These were forerunners perhaps of the tweet or facebook post – short, strident messages designed to change a life rather than merely fill an empty one.

Pep talks

Team coaches excel at this. Anyone who's ever been two-nil down at half time in a cup final knows the power and potential of the pep talk. 'Go get, em, champs!'

Summing up in court

Presenting the case for the defence or the prosecution, persuading a judge or jury to convict the accused or to let him off has to be one of the most difficult challenges any storyteller can face. It's among the hardest forms of oratory because few audiences are more inclined to be prejudiced or partial. The person summing-up usually has no script to cling to, must marshal complex arguments in his or her head, must hold the attentions of a sometimes hostile or indifferent audience with only the facts of the case and the emotions of the situation as aids. He or she is subject to frequent interruptions that must be respected and often has to wear some fairly weird clothing to boot. It's a bit like storytelling in the pub on a Friday night, wearing a suit and tie.

> *'A great video can be many different things as long as it sticks to the framework of telling a great story, showing action and informing viewers. That's the recipe for a successful video.'*
>
> JESSICA MASON, *YOUTUBE FOR GOOD*

> *'Of all of our inventions for mass communication, pictures still speak the most universally understood language.'*
>
> WALT DISNEY

Visual storytelling

Given Disney's self-evident advice above it's quickly clear that stories told using photography, illustration, film, or video enhanced by music, sound, or voice tracks aren't so much a distinct section on their own, they're more ingredients you leave out of your stories at your peril. It's rare that the voice of the narrator stands as an island, entire of itself. Good visuals almost invariably improve not just your ability to tell a story but your audience's enjoyment of it and their ability to take it in and remember it. The effective transformational storyteller usually has to work with images, sound and vision too.

> *'When I came back to London and tried to talk to people about some of the horrors I had seen I realised most people really didn't want to know. I became determined to change that. As a foreign correspondent I see my job as a storyteller, giving voice to those who have none and trying to get the attention of those back home reading the paper over their breakfast cereal.'*
>
> CHRISTINA LAMB, FOREIGN AFFAIRS CORRESPONDENT, *THE SUNDAY TIMES*

Photojournalism

Photojournalism has an illustrious track record as an agent of change. In its golden age, the 1930s to the 1950s, upmarket, glossy journals such as *Picture Post, Life* and *Paris Match* made household-name heroes of individual photographers including Robert Capa, Margaret Bourke-White and Henri Cartier-Bresson. Bourke-White was the first female war correspondent. Their lenses took readers directly to where the story was, into the action on the spot and up to the minute, telling stories as a detached witness, reporters working only in image, telling their stories in pictures and captions.

Journalism

In all its formats journalism provides endless scope for transformational storytelling. Of late there's been an explosion of media generally with an obvious shift towards the electronic. So the range of outlets and column inches that daily have to be filled, both printed and electronic, grows and grows, though outside of the best-established organs fine writing – particularly in great stories – is still a hard-to-find exception. So opportunities for the transformational storyteller remain good.

This, of course, is a far from finite list. There are other types of story that change the world. Anecdotes, apologues, romances, myths, legends, folklore and ghost stories, all have their place. Even writing captions can be transformational. Jokes, perhaps not all that surprisingly, are a powerful format for storytelling, with comedians often among the most incisive and perceptive of opinion formers. For all, one thing is sure: the challenges for the would-be transformational storyteller are many, varied and complex. So in coming chapters we'll consider some of the tips and techniques that are around to help you.

On doing without

In the search for fulfilment and the meaning of life it sometimes pays us to consider those who can get by with really very little.

Like many people I'm somewhat disillusioned with the so-called technological advances of recent years and the questionable benefits they've brought. But the wonder of modern gadgetry and gimmickry is how good you feel when you do without them. This reminds me of the story of the rabbi and the poor man who lived in one small room with his wife and three children.

'I can't stand it!' wailed the man. 'What can I do?' The rabbi told him to get a dog. The dog barked at the children and messed up the floor. Then the rabbi suggested he get some hens. The dog chased the hens, which frightened the baby. 'Get a goat' insisted the rabbi. And so on, until the rabbi added a horse and the whole thing became completely impossible. 'Now, get rid of them all,' said the rabbi, 'and tell me how you feel.' 'It's wonderful!' cried the man in gratitude. 'There's just me and the wife and the children. And we have the whole room to ourselves.'

Possibly the gadget we really need is the one that we can programme to get rid of all the others.

All progress may indeed be in the hands of unreasonable people, but it seems to me that the rest of us should reserve a healthy scepticism for all changes and, supposed, advances. To underline this point let me end with a wee story from a perhaps unlikely source, which at first glance appears to contradict my earlier remarks about the opportunities offered by the remorseless march of change.

'Advances – what advances? The number of hours women devote to housework has not changed since 1930, despite all the vacuum cleaners, washer/dryers, trash compactors, garbage disposals, wash-and-wear fabrics. Why does it still take as long to clean the house as it did in 1930?

'It's because there haven't been any advances. Yet 30,000 years ago when men were doing cave paintings at Lascaux, they worked just 20 hours a week and the rest of the time they could play, or sleep, or do whatever they wanted.'

IAN MALCOLM, THE MATHEMATICIAN IN MICHAEL CRICHTON'S *JURASSIC PARK*

Evidence perhaps that in reality we have made no progress whatsoever. But I suspect that 30,000 years ago, while the men had all that time to play, sleep, or whatever, the women still had to spend just as long doing the housework. *Plus ça change.*

CHAPTER'S END: ACTIONS AND KEY MESSAGES

The only thing that has ever changed the world and why it's so powerful.

To change anything you first have to change yourself.

Appreciate the impact your stories might have on others, particularly if you get your story through at a vulnerable time.

People everywhere want to make a difference in every aspect of their daily lives, but particularly at work. It'll pay you to seek out the many ways you add meaning and fulfilment to busy lives when you tell your stories.

Study the progress paradox, as the time could be just right for transformational storytellers to help people find their interest, purpose, or the chance to do something worthwhile.

People can change. They can be reached and interested. But some things never change.

TURNING POINT

This is the tale of a classic piece of communication from an organisation that now knows its audience, inside out, and knows just how valuable that knowledge is.

Finding the image that's just right

A few pages back I told how Britain's most respected charity, the Royal National Lifeboat Institution, learned the true reason why their millions of supporters all give to them so willingly. At the time many in the charity were shocked and surprised to learn that donors don't dig deep to help sailors in distress, they give so generously because they're inspired by the brave volunteer lifeboat crews who at all times of the day or night in the worst of weathers will launch their fragile craft upon savage seas to save people they'll probably never know.

Did this insight change RNLI's fundraising? You bet it did. If heroes are what the public wants, it wasn't difficult or remotely off message for the charity to give them heroes, in spades. The advertisement below is a direct result.

Stained with the passage of time and the spills of age the face staring out at the reader from this single sheet insert has lost nothing of its strength and power to impress. This simple direct proposition is one of the classic fundraising offers of all time and the image is essential to it. It has to be a bearded face. Though there are lifeboat women, tests show it's a rugged bearded male face that generates maximum response. And he has to look bedraggled, as if he's just been washed in by those 30-foot waves.

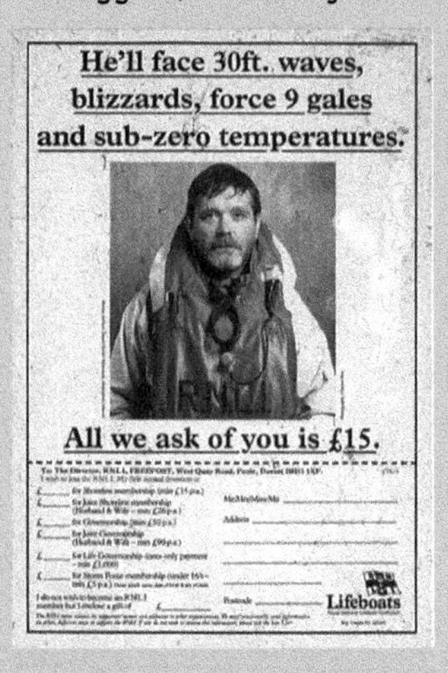

In the mid 1990s my agency in London took these photographs of real lifeboatmen and tested their effectiveness in press inserts. Legend has it that in the studio, unbeknown to them, a young assistant with a bucket of cold water was waiting behind a screen. Just before the photo was taken, at a signal from the photographer the wee chap would step out and toss the contents of his bucket over the startled coxswain who, drenched, stepped back in shock and at that precise moment the photo was taken. Only then was the image just right.

And
now for
something
that will
really
make a
difference ...

7. A life-stage fairytale: how Beryl and Clive found the meaning of life.

'The market for something to believe in is infinite.'
HUGH MACLEOD, *@GAPINGVOID*

Fifty-nine-year-old Clive Broomhead is only half listening to the radio. He's doing the housework, a chore set to occupy most of his morning. This may be because his heart's not in it, or perhaps he's just not very good at it. Or maybe it's because Beryl, Clive's wife of 35 years, keeps adding fresh tasks so he's no sooner finished one thing than it's on to the next. Beryl is a hard taskmistress.

Clive is doing the hoovering. In the background, from the radio, a succession of interviews are coming at him live from the revellers then thronging Glastonbury, Britain's premier outdoor music festival. For Clive this is deep background, particularly with the hoover on. So he's only vaguely aware of the interviewer's increasingly desperate attempts to glean conversational gems from a succession of drop-ins to the festival's radio tent. Beryl is elbow deep in suds in the kitchen, so not listening to the radio at all.

Then as Clive paused in his hoovering to release some jammed paper a curious phrase from one of the interviewees cut through to his subconscious and stopped him in his tracks. He rubbed his ears in disbelief. Next moment Beryl's usually restrained, taciturn husband was waggling his radio under her nose while waving his other hand wildly in the air. Something was up.

'Did you hear that Beryl? Did you hear *that*?' Clive had turned the hoover off, to facilitate matters.

Of course she hadn't. Beryl glowered up at her husband as if finally he'd lost the plot.

'Eh?'

'From Glastonbury! The old Druid! I nearly missed it... What he said...'

'Did you know,' said Beryl, trying to be calm and reasonable, 'that the first Glastonbury was held in 1970, the day after Jimi Hendrix died?'

'Eh? What? No. No! That's not the point. Just listen...'

Across the airwaves from deepest Somerset the interview was still in mid flow, though the interviewer was struggling to keep up with what seemed to be a voluble, evidently eccentric interviewee.

'He's a hippy Beryl. The old bloke he's talking to. No, he's a Druid. Really. Listen!' shouted Clive. 'He says he's found the meaning of life.'

'What are you on about? The meaning of life?'

'Yes, yes, listen, you cloth-eared bint. Just listen!'

As Beryl focused reluctantly on what was going on she caught the interviewer's breathless, high-pitched description of what the aging Druid was at that instant pulling from the folds of his robe, the faded old bottle battered by time and tide, stained by sun and salt water that was being squeezed out from under the old man's clothing and plonked on the table before him. It was an ordinary, empty bottle of domestic bleach.

'He's a charlatan!' Beryl whispered.

'Hush,' Clive replied.

'Yes,' the old Druid was intoning with relish. 'Indeed sir yes, I do know the meaning of life. I read it, here, on the back of this bottle of bleach. The meaning of life. Read it! *Read it*!'

Clive and Beryl could picture the interviewer's expression as hesitatingly, as if translating the inscription on a sacred scroll, he read from the faded, cracked label and couldn't quite believe his words,

'Stand upright, in a cool place.'

There was a pause.

'That's it?'

'There,' said the old Druid. 'Told you, din't I? There you have it. The meaning of life! That's all I ever want to do. Stand upright, in a cool place.'

There was another embarrassed pause.

'Mad old bugger,' announced Beryl.

More silence. Suddenly, determinedly, her husband switched off the radio and stood before her as one transported, lost in thought.

'No, Beryl, he's right'

Clive spoke slowly, with conviction, as if he'd just undergone an epiphany. 'He's one hundred per cent right Beryl, as it happens. That's it. That's all I want to do, too. Stand upright, in a cool place.'

'Clive, darling,' Beryl exclaimed. 'Have you lost your marbles?'

'Not at all, Beryl. No, I mean it. It's time we changed the wallpaper of our lives. Time we stopped fussing around and stood upright. And did cool things. Time we weren't always only thinking of ourselves and doing things selfishly for the family, for us. Not cure cancer or anything. But do something useful, make a difference. That sort of thing.

'I'm not bonkers Beryl, not a bit. It's like we've been rushing headlong these last 30 years, doing what we have to do because we have to do it. Now, maybe, could we change it all round and do what we *want* to do instead? I mean, the meaning of life. Why not?'

Beryl's dismay softened, just a bit. She thought to herself, maybe Clive is right. Then she had a startling realisation – as long as we can keep our comfy lifestyle I could be with you in this, Clive old chap. Really, I could.'

But she kept it to herself. What she said was, 'Come off it Clive, we can't afford to stand upright, in a cool place, or any other place, with our outgoings, in these recessionary times. How would we pay for all this, "what we want to do"?'

That's when the Life-Stage Fairy intervened. Because she felt she had to. And she changed Beryl and Clive's lives forever.

When planets align

The market for something to believe in really is infinite. Everybody wants to change the world. Most of us would like to reorder our own lives too. The trouble is, nobody wants to change themselves. Change is uncomfortable, difficult, disruptive and distracting. Our days are full enough and we just don't have room to cope with the upheaval of change.

Mañana, mañana, we say, and put off inconvenient things until another time. But another time never quite arrives.

Except, that is, on ultra-special occasions, when we find within ourselves the power to confront change head on and make it happen. Or, more likely, when we reach any of a small number of significant milestones in our lives, when change becomes more easily achievable, more practical, even on some occasions unavoidable. Though very rare, such times come to almost everyone. To some, however, more reliably and more convincingly than others.

These are the life-stage moments. They're singular, precious and few.

Life-stage moments occur throughout our lives. When we leave our parents' home, change career, become parents, or when our children leave home. For most people a life-stage moment comes when they retire. Some manage it earlier. Some never manage it at all. The most incredible, most wonderful, most valuable thing about such times is the capacity they have to enable each of us to make a massive difference to our own lives and the lives of others.

Beryl and Clive Broomhead were perched on the verge of a well-deserved, comfortable, not to say stress- and anxiety-free, retirement.

It's at times like this when folk like Beryl and Clive are most likely to be visited by that curious phenomenon, the Life-Stage Fairy.

Bear with me, please, this is a fairytale.

She, of course, only ever intervenes in earthly affairs when someone needs the kind of celestial intercession only she can make. Her aim is to help anyone she can to find their way through a bewildering transition, to emerge at the other side confident, competent and relaxed in an important new role: world-changer.

It's for people like these and the opportunities they provide that we tell stories, to help them change the world. And stories – whether you believe in fairies or not – can work their magic at any time.

So here goes.

Once upon a time, in a land near at hand and not at all long, long ago there lived a happily married couple. Clive, an honest shoe-mender, and Beryl, his wife, a high-flying international investment banker.

Clive and Beryl were very happy together. They lived comfortably in an elegant, spacious house in a well-served, tree-lined suburb of the capital with their two academically bright though dull and gangly sons, their three plain but accomplished daughters, a superior cat called Cosmo and a mangy, flea-bitten pooch called Eric.

As soon as she discovered that at last this fortunate pair had stumbled upon the meaning of life, the Life-Stage Fairy sprinkled magic stardust over the daily domestic routines that defined their busy lives.

And then *everything* changed.

'You, Beryl and Clive Broomhead,' she explained, 'are now approaching that very special time of your lives: the golden years. Soon your children will fly the nest, your pets are on their last legs, your mortgage has been paid in full, your parents have passed on, your pension funds are about to kick in and several chunky insurance policies are soon to mature, all conveniently just when work pressures for both of you, such as they are, are about to reduce considerably.'

Beryl and Clive reflected on this. Comfortable though life now was, it hadn't always been a bed of roses. For the best part of two decades they'd laboured to make their way and pay the bills. They'd scrimped, sacrificed and struggled to raise, feed, train and please their brood of dependants. Throughout those challenging, hectic years Clive and Beryl had little time, money or inclination for anything other than merely surviving.

But they were still very happy. Well, fairly. True, as the years passed the struggles had slowed and the sacrificing and scrimping lessened too. Until today they'd never noticed that life for them had become really rather agreeable. In this their lives differed but little from those of a substantial part of the human population, when they too reach 'a certain age'.

'From now on,' the fairy announced, 'no more doing what you have to do. Life has changed, there's no going back. Now, you can do what you want to do.'

She then informed them that imminently they would be transformed into PINKs – pension + income + no kids. It was a moment of earth-shattering insight. They'd soon have time on their hands and money to spend to match their unfulfilled ambitions.

Clive and Beryl were delighted.

'Is this the meaning of life?' Clive asked, in disbelief.

'You just wait,' said Beryl. 'The world will now beat a path to our door.' Clive looked worried. 'We'd better start building barricades,' he said.

'Why?' exclaimed the Life-Stage Fairy.

'Why, to keep out the cadgers, that's why,' snorted Beryl. 'The opportunists, the rogues, anxious to part us from our assets. Financial investment advisers, hucksters, charlatans, charity fundraisers and their likes, who'll soon surround us and besiege us with blandishments, flattery, subterfuge and enticements to separate us from our hard-earned dosh, to impoverish us as we enrich everyone else.'

'Crikey no!' exclaimed Clive, aghast. 'Not charity fundraisers! For goodness sakes, not them.'

'Oh, come on you pair, it won't be so bad,' said the LSF. 'Get used to it. Be glad. You've got disposable income. And time. Suck it up why don't you? The world now will be your lobster. But, ... there's just one condition attached.'

'What's that?' asked Beryl and Clive in unison.

'Have fun by all means. Party, party, party. But the condition for being allowed to live long enough to enjoy this new life-stage is...

you have a new duty, to act wisely and unselfishly. Some of the time, with at least some of your new-found wealth, you have to do some things that will make the world a better place.

'What kind of things?' asked Beryl and Clive fearfully.

'Ah, that,' said the fairy, 'remains to be seen. Think about the old Druid and standing upright in a cool place. The beauty of that part of this life-stage is, it's entirely up to you.'

'You mean,' said Clive, 'we should maybe make a plan, should consider how to fill the next three decades of our now comfortable, time-rich but not entirely meaningless lives? We should work out a way to leave a lasting legacy, while having fun?'

'Yep. That's about the shape of it.'

Thanks to the Life-Stage Fairy and some fortuitous retirement planning, a magic carpet of opportunities began to unfold before the Broomheads' startled eyes. Clive and Beryl were all set to become...donors.

Or, maybe not. The thing is, they have the choice.

They could if they wished dabble in politics, or the arts. Or they could opt to kick up their heels and spend their money on a seemingly endless succession of good times. They could travel and see the world, sail the seas, be kidnapped by Somali pirates, or trek the Hindu Kush, that sort of thing.

They were, it seemed, set to live happily ever after.

The Life-Stage Fairy then made an admission followed by a dire warning.

'You did have a bit of a point, back there Beryl, when you were going on about the cadgers,' she confessed. 'As soon as you pass 60, it's true, a procession of sales people, lifestyle gurus and others of good intent but often suspect practices will arrive on your doorstep. They exist solely to target the likes of you two; they'll buzz around with urgent appeals, proposals, scripts and other inducements, all designed to part you as quickly as possible from what will soon become a rapidly diminishing pile.'

At this Beryl and Clive fell to bickering over the challenges and opportunities of their new lives, so the Life-Stage Fairy took her leave. Her parting shot from outside their window was, 'Just remember, Beryl and Clive, that despite all this, things aren't so bad. Some of these people will engage and inspire you, will help you to open doors to a cornucopia of good things that you can do, now, to help yourself and the rest of the world too. You may even make new friends.

'You can rejoice, Beryl and Clive,' she announced as she unfolded her wings and readied her broomstick for a swift departure, 'for at this point, into this frenzy of hard-selling, over-information and excessive asking there will appear a shining knight or, even, a shining damsel, rushing to the rescue, to see you alright.'

And saying this, the Life-Stage Fairy turned to...you!

Yes. That's right, dear reader. She was describing *you*.

At that moment Beryl and Clive too looked up, to see you, sitting there on the sidelines, looking in. As the Life-Stage Fairy explains your role in things, all three are regarding you with eager anticipation.

The Life-Stage Fairy knows you want to be different and distinctive, that you're a storyteller with a plan, way above the rest. She's confident that you'll reach into Clive and Beryl's lives in a responsible, caring way. That you'll excite their interests and their imaginations, inspire their altruism, free their inhibitions and, generally, give their lives the meaning, fulfilment and the joy of living and giving that they so urgently seek.

That's the Life-Stage Fairy's mission.

Beryl and Clive Broomhead and hundreds of thousands of life-stage enhanced prospects just like them are waiting, now, just for you. And what's the most effective way for you to get through to them?

Why, of course, with *stories*!

Fairytales have meaning too

Beryl and Clive, like millions of couples and individuals and even groups like them, will be determined to enjoy this new stage in life. Soon planning for fulfilling, productive years post-work and pre-decline will become the norm. People will prepare earlier for this, the time of their lives, and budget for it. They'll aspire to make the most of life as the scramble starts to take advantage of the potential opportunities offered by a decade or two of active retirement. Marketers of every shape and style will love this group and shower attentions upon them. So smart storytellers will get in there quick with their inspirational causes and claims.

Beryl and Clive won't be a soft touch. They'll be unresponsive to waffle, superficiality or empty offers. They'll look for sensitive, considerate, interesting engagement. So stories will often get through where direct requests won't.

Even before they leave their jobs for the bliss of retirement Beryl and Clive may be of additional interest to you, the transformational storyteller. If say, through Beryl, you were to aspire to influence her international company on the positive rewards of corporate social engagement. Or to pique their curiosity as to how valuable storytelling might be in boosting company morale, or to have a go at uniting every employee behind the new strategy, or improving the messaging, appeal and presentation of a range of financial services.

Clive too might be excited by your enthusiasm if your stories, spun well, could influence him in his role as school governor. You might encourage him to persuade the teachers at his school to improve storytelling in the classroom, thereby benefiting successive generations of students who now might find their lessons much more interesting and memorable.

Unlike most fairytales, the value in these opportunities is real enough, for sure. That's what encouraged the writing of this book, and its aim to present you with all you need to know about telling stories to help Beryl, Clive and their likes to change their – and your – world.

CHAPTER'S END: ACTIONS AND KEY MESSAGES

The value of the hero figure. And how to present her, or him.

Never forget that the market for something to believe in is infinite.

Find and appreciate the real meaning of life. Though perhaps equally unexpected, it's not, as proposed by the computer in *The Hitchhiker's Guide to the Galaxy*, the number 42.

How to identify the key life-stage moments and prepare your messages accordingly.

Some groups will be more attractive to transformational storytellers than others. How to recognise them and respond to their changing circumstances while capitalising on their desire to change the world.

People of a certain age want to have fun with the hard-won fruits from their years of working and saving, soon to be coming their way. But, they'll also want meaning, fulfilment, new challenges and opportunities, thrills, spills and adventure. Transformational storytellers can help give them all that.

PART THREE

Brilliant emotional storytelling

TURNING POINT

Sunday was the Lord's day so off I'd go in my kilt and tweed jacket to the kirk for a generous helping of hellfire, brimstone and the kind of stern, wrathful god-fearing that only Scottish Presbyterians can dish up. It was at the kirk that I met the Lord's sister and learned from her a lesson that's lasted.

The Lord's sister explains the joys of earmarking

Potentially transformational stories told weekly from the towering pulpit to a dwindling, though still sinful, congregation indelibly burned a succession of scary images into my young, impressionable mind. Most were lost opportunities not just for me but for the other sinners too, I'm sure. Our minister wasn't a great storyteller. Invariably his dull rantings would float unscrutinised way over my head. I'd yawn uncontrollably, survey the serried backs of heads before me, read and reread the roll of honour celebrating our glorious dead, suck a pan drop (a mint sweetie) and then faint. I fainted a lot. My uncle Gavin would carry me outside for fresh air and, later, would reward me with a cigarette for getting him a break from it too.

We were used to it. It was the Scottish way. Stern elders saw to it that young people were brought up properly to fear God and do their duty.

Most fearsome of all the elders at my kirk was the Lady Mary Mackintosh. She was no ordinary woman, so fiercely religious she was known to all as the Lord's sister. Her brother was Lord Mackintosh the clan chief, but all knew only too well that her true Lord was a higher, much more fearsome being.

The Lord's sister was a devoted fundraiser for the Leprosy Mission and she soon apprenticed me to the cause. Leprosy, she dinned into me, numbs and kills the nerves so you can't feel pain, thus you burn your extremities and lose first your digits, then your limbs. It sounded unspeakable. Leprosy among the distant heathen was a scourge of biblical proportions but it had been discovered that a course of sulphides could cure it. 'You, young man,' she commanded, 'will raise money by collecting sixpences around the town, door to door, to buy sulphides and so save the infected.'

Then she did a curious thing. She gave me a handful of plastic vials. 'Each of these,' she said, 'will accommodate 25 sixpences. Precisely. Twelve shillings and sixpence, that's all it takes to buy a course of sulphides that will cure leprosy, once and for all. Leave one at each house for the people therein to fill and return.'

There was no room for doubt. From the Lord's sister I learned about the power of earmarking – designating the destiny of your donation before you give it – and creating a tangible, clearly-priced product that your audience can visualise and will want to buy. This was to prove extremely useful to me, in years to come.

Enough sixpences to treat leprosy.

8. The truth, told well

'Don't start by writing. Start by feeling. Feel, and feel passionately and the emotion you feel will come through the spaces in between the words.'

INDRA SINHA

Inspiring people to change the world

Booker prize shortlisted author Indra Sinha knows how to move his readers to action. In the mid 1980s and early 1990s he wrote the much-celebrated, now revered Amnesty International long-copy press advertisements (see page 14 for their resurrection in recent times) that are credited with changing the face of political campaigning and fundraising in Margaret Thatcher's Britain. These passionate tirades recruited floods of new donors for Amnesty at a profit, an achievement almost unheard of in those days and even less likely now, using a medium that, generally, was felt to be in decline. Yet more than 20 years later Indra Sinha is still telling stories successfully in a similar way for other causes including the Bhopal Medical Appeal, which he co-founded. It's worth learning a few of his techniques.

For most of his working life Indra Sinha was by trade a top-flight advertising agency creative director. He's a transformational storyteller by instinct and his approach has much to offer others who would emulate his art. The following extract on writing from the heart is taken from an article originally written for Indian creative directors, *The Last Word*. It is published in full on the Showcase of Fundraising Innovation and Inspiration. (www.sofii.org), as are most of Indra's ads.

To write for and from the heart involves breaking the basic rules by which most modern advertising is conducted.

A direct-marketing guru once told me that every campaign he did played on one of just three motivations – fear, greed, or sex. His work was predictable and his guru-hood rested on response rates of less than one percent. It is far more effective to give up overworked formulae, stop trying to manipulate people and speak directly to the reader's moral sensibility. Some of our Amnesty ads had response rates of 450 per cent. For every pound they cost, they raised £4.50, a staggeringly good result – ask any fundraiser. And they recruited new donors in their thousands.

Ask yourself before tackling any new brief: how can I find a way to do this that will be genuinely valuable to people?

Devise campaigns that commit your client to positive social action. A paint-maker could be coaxed into a campaign to clean up a dirty city. An air-conditioning giant might well be persuaded to take on the problem of air pollution. (I once got an oil company to spend a lot of money cleaning up rivers.)

If you have a client with murky secrets, propose a strategy of apparent openness. This may seem like a cynical PR play, but once light and air start getting inside it's difficult to reverse the process. A particularly nasty company could be permitted to make extravagant claims, for which they can later be called to account.

Advertising can often pave the way for reform. Commit the client to certain aims and courses of action. You'll be surprised how often you will end up effectively creating company policy. Once it has been said in public they can be held to it.

It is sometimes possible to use the budget of one unpleasant company to expose and embarrass another. I know these tactics work because I and like-minded friends have used them for years.

Find ways to involve the public in your work. Be a voice for the real feelings of ordinary people: their anger, frustrations, despair, hope. Work with them. Speak out on issues that need airing – corruption, specific injustices. You don't need to be deadly serious. Use humour, mockery and satire to make your point. Such campaigns are generally very popular. They produce happy clients as well as getting good work done and you can run them for anything from pickles to banks.

Give as much time as you can to worthwhile causes that need help and cannot afford to pay for it.

If you can do nothing else, make people laugh.

You can't do these things with every brief. Often, opportunities are there, but hard to spot, like moths camouflaged against bark. Hunt them out. Strong copywriters make their own chances.

Most of what you do will hardly seem to make a difference, but once in a while, you will create an almighty impact. Finally if, given the vastness of the problem, guerrilla action by a few individuals seems futile, remember what Peter Benenson, the founder of Amnesty International, once said:

'It is better to light one candle than curse the darkness.'

Stirring stuff. That last quote, variously attributed also to Gandhi, Churchill and Confucius, is a beacon for the transformational storyteller, a thought well worth cherishing, even displaying above your desk.

In London recently the SOFII Foundation held an event for campaigning fundraisers who want to change the world. Before 300 of their peers 21 young aspiring storytellers presented a campaign they envied, under the heading *I Wish I'd Thought of That*. From the comments received afterwards, the organisers compiled the following broad consensus summarising the key ingredients of the 21 chosen campaigns.

- Keep it simple.
- Tell the truth and tell it well...
- ...with integrity, empathy, sincerity and conviction.
- Spin an emotional spell. Let the strength of your story carry the case.
- Don't just think outside the box, throw the box away.
- Avoid the temptation to be clever. The clever thing is to be real.
- And gritty. Expose itch, supply scratch.
- Get angry. Write with fury and feeling.
- Be bold. Think big.
- Don't hesitate to ask.

'The truth, told well'

I came upon this slogan not long after my return from Africa, following the incident I've called *the worst tourist in the world* (see page 190). It is the catchphrase of the advertising agency group McCann-Erickson, and how I wish it were the motto of all transformational storytellers everywhere. The truth, told well. That's all we should aspire to, to win the hearts and minds of our audiences.

'True' is a good adjective to attribute to people. People aspire to be true to a cause, to a mission, to a vision, to a dream. It's a good sentiment to work into your writing. Psychology professor Jen Shang has discovered in her research that people describe a 'moral' person or a 'good' person using primarily nine adjectives: *caring, compassionate, friendly, fair, generous, hard-working, helpful, honest, kind*. A good addition to that list might be 'true'.

The emotion words

Although the total of words around to express them are nigh limitless there really is only a handful of terms that describe the emotions that govern all human behaviour and play such significant roles in our individual and collective evolution. Wikipedia lists 72 'emotion' words from 'affection' to 'zest' and as their list encompasses so many great things for the storyteller to work with I've included them all, below. Most commentators prefer far fewer for their shortlists of key 'emotion words', six or seven seeming to be optimum. Often their lists don't agree.

> **Affection, anger, angst, anguish, annoyance, anxiety, apathy, arousal, awe, boredom, confidence, contempt, contentment, courage, curiosity, depression, despair, desire, disappointment, disgust, distrust, dread, ecstasy, embarrassment, envy, euphoria, excitement, fear, frustration, gratitude, grief, guilt, happiness, hatred, hope, horror, hostility, hurt, hysteria, indifference, interest, jealousy, joy, loathing, loneliness, love, lust, outrage, panic, passion, pity, pleasure, pride, rage, regret, relief, remorse, sadness, satisfaction, self-confidence, shame, shock, shyness, sorrow, suffering, surprise, terror, trust, wonder, worry, zeal and zest.**
>
> WIKIPEDIA, THE ONLINE ENCYCLOPEDIA

The basic emotions are described as anger, contempt, fear, disgust, happiness, sadness and surprise. When writers venture to suggest their list of super-powerful emotion words these seven, plus perhaps greed, guilt, elation, love, and maybe a few others, crop up time and again. Some also include the actions that generate emotions – flattery, exclusivity, salvation, release. Others say only two emotions really matter: fear and loneliness. Fear is widely acknowledged as the most powerful emotion of them all.

As author Seth Godin put it, knowing there are only a few keys on the keyboard doesn't make it easier to write a pop hit or a great novel. But it's a good place to start. So this might be a list worth keeping by you, so you can check that each story you produce uses a few of the emotion words, at least. When the right stories are told in the right way we get a Pavlovian reaction to certain causes, dreams and aspirations. Get behind these and success is assured.

The moody leader

My business partner Alan Clayton is bipolar, so for most of his life he's had to cope with dramatic mood swings, from manic euphoria to deep depression. Mostly, he manages pretty well and our business prospers in the process, because as his mood moves his creativity rises from merely exceptional to frequent brilliance. Creative people know well the necessity of managing their moods so employ a variety of means, legal and otherwise, to cultivate the right mental temperament or disposition that for them generates the most exceptional creativity. As well as being one of the most creative, effective individuals I've ever worked with, Alan is leader of several successful businesses and an internationally recognised inspirational speaker and storyteller.

Rather obviously, one person's mood can affect another's, very significantly. No doubt, an individual can alter the mood of an entire team, audience, or conference. At a football match, if one person starts singing, soon other voices will join in till they become a throng. Like or loathe her, Margaret Thatcher's mood could transform everyone in her political party. Freddie Mercury, Bruce Springsteen and others could change the mood of a packed stadium just with a shouted phrase or by strumming a few chords. When she refused to give up her seat on that bus in Montgomery, Alabama in 1955, Rosa Parks changed the mood of a whole people. Political leaders work hard to excel at such things. Gandhi, Lincoln, Churchill and Hitler, when they spoke, could change the mood of an entire nation.

Churchill and Hitler are interesting as nowadays they'd both be identified as bipolar or, as it was previously called, manic depressive. Only Hitler, however, was diagnosed. Churchill may or may not have diagnosed himself as depressive but he certainly self-medicated by drinking large amounts of alcohol on a daily basis.

Hitler it seems was a massive hypochondriac. His personal physician, Dr Morell, considered his leader to be afflicted with so many medical ailments that he prescribed immense doses of drugs for daily consumption, including a range of amphetamines so vast they must have left the Fuehrer on a permanent high. Cocaine, caffeine, morphine, strychnine and many other potent drugs formed part of his daily diet. Which may explain Hitler's frequent outbursts of rage and the extreme mania he evinced in his public presentations.

Churchill, by contrast, always sounded determined but calm to the point of gloomy, promising us nothing but blood, toil, tears and sweat plus long months of struggle and suffering.

It's interesting to think what might have happened if either or both had managed their moods differently.

A highly creative brilliant communicator excels at times of change. When everything's steady and settled, an efficient but stable manager or administrator will be better for the job, whatever it is.

Emotions, moods and feelings clearly affect and govern our lives, day in and day out. And there's still much to learn in this vastly complex field. For this book I'll restrict my focus to how emotional storytelling helps us get our messages through, and makes them stick.

Emotion vs intellect: making the emotional case

The human brain is by an as yet immeasurably large margin the most complex organism in all of history, creation and evolution. Categorising, describing and understanding it is fraught with difficulties and almost any attempt will be a considerable simplification, so subject to heavy qualification at the very least. Yet, we have learned many useful things about the brain.

A popular way of looking at the human brain is as two distinct hemispheres: the left brain, seat of rational thoughts and logical organisation and the right brain, home of creativity and all the emotions. In the parable of Caius and Marcellus, from chapter 1, Caius would be an example of left-brain thinking, Marcellus of right-brain. As both hemispheres contribute to both sets of processes it's a gross simplification, but one that has some uses.

Emotions are many times more powerful than logic. In their book *Switch* authors Chip and Dan Heath tell the story of the mahout and the elephant. The mahout, the rider, represents the logical, rational side of our brain, the elephant the emotional, passionate side. When the mahout wants to go one way and the elephant wants to go another, it's the elephant, of course, who's inevitably going to get his way.

So it is with emotion versus logic. The point is, if we would be effective transformational storytellers we must study and understand our emotions and make them work for us effectively, as they so evidently can.

An emotion is the body giving the brain a signal of what to do right now. It's feeling becoming an action. Like Pavlov's dog we react immediately and automatically, which can be dangerous. So our species has developed logical thought, a fear response that follows almost instantly, causing us to pause and take stock, to ask ourselves, is this wise? This is useful as it warns us to think things through before following the reaction prompted by emotion. It often prevents us from doing something rash. As they grow and professionalise, organisations tend to over-emphasise this pause and over-rationalise it, thus sucking out the emotions. This is almost invariably a mistake. Best to keep the logical part of our case short, clear and unarguable, so that our audience accepts it and is reassured by it, leaving us and them to focus on the far more powerful emotional impulses to do what needs to be done.

Emotional storytellers often ignore logic altogether yet their stories are none the worse for it.

Songwriters, though generally unconstrained by any need to be logical, excel at emotional storytelling and their medium lends itself perfectly to telling stories. Bruce Springsteen springs to mind – a self-confessed moderate guitar player with a limited vocal range, his songs tell stirring stories in the most unforgettable way. There are many others, from Kenny Rogers to Leonard Cohen and Dusty Springfield, just to mention a few.

'When the drinks finally hit her
she said, "I'm no quitter,
but I finally quit livin' on dreams.
I'm hungry for laughter and here ever after
I'm after whatever the other life brings."

'In the mirror I saw him and I closely watched him
I thought how he looked out of place.
He came to the woman who sat there beside me
He had a strange look on his face.

'Now his big hands were calloused, he looked like a
mountain.
For a minute I thought, I was dead
But he started shakin' his big heart was breakin'
And he turned to the woman and said.

'"You picked a fine time to leave me, Lucille.
With four hungry children and crops in the field
I've had some bad times, lived through some sad times
But this time the hurtin' won't heal
You picked a fine time to leave me, Lucille." '

KENNY ROGERS, FROM *LUCILLE*

'Morning came
and then came noon,
Dinner time a scalpel blade,
lay beside my silver spoon.

'Some girls wander by mistake,
into the mess that scalpels make.
Are you the teachers of my heart?'
'We teach old hearts to break.'

LEONARD COHEN, FROM *TEACHERS*

> *'I'd have been the shadow of your shadow, if it could have kept me by your side.'*
>
> DUSTY SPRINGFIELD, FROM *IF YOU GO AWAY*

Storytellers could aspire to making their best stories as recognisable and as socially significant as the best songs. Imagine if we could do that, or even get a bit close. All that schmaltzy stuff about limitless, undying love, pools of sorrow, waves of joy from just around the corner to the edge of the universe. It might all add up to changing the world, for someone.

Not sentimental, really quite practical

Copywriter Karin Weatherup has helped many national and international causes to really reach their readers. Here are some things she's learned about telling the stories of three very different causes to mothers and grandmothers.

Womankind – woman to woman

'A woman supporting the charity said to me, "Supporting Womankind is like being able to help another woman across my garden fence, except I'm not where she is."

'Her comment struck me. I found it was true of lots of the women I spoke to. They saw helping a woman facing domestic violence or forced marriage as like helping a neighbour – a woman-to-woman thing – except that the woman was in Ethiopia, or Somalia.'

Barnardo's –tackling those challenging teenagers

'Convention says that older people are scared of teenagers, so you shouldn't ask them to help teenagers. It's safer to stick to little children and disabled children.

'So we asked 20 supporters aged 65+ what they really thought of teenagers. Every one raised the issue that they feel so very sad for teenagers nowadays. Whereas they had often experienced material poverty growing up, these donors felt that the emotional poverty so many teenagers face today – no guidance, not feeling loved, dealing with big feelings on their own – was infinitely more difficult to cope with. All had enormous empathy with teenagers. Some had experienced difficult teenage years themselves and were grateful for someone outside the family having taken an interest in them. Most had raised their own teenagers and seen how vulnerable they can be; some had seen their own kids, or friends of their kids, go off the rails and need huge support.'

Feed the Children – identifying with mothers

In war-torn Bosnia Feed the Children had a specific remit from the UN High Commission for Refugees to help mothers with young babies.

'Before we started working with them their appeals were about helping the child. I moved to making it more a mother-to-mother thing, because having just had my daughter, Harley, I realised the ache mothers have to protect their children; that it was a very powerful feeling to trigger in other women. The idea that a woman couldn't protect her children was unbearable, to think how she must feel. I remember some battles as people who didn't have kids tried to swing it back to the children, but I was stubborn and the whole baby box for Bosnia appeal was "from one mother to another", from one parent to another. The card we included in the mailing, for people to write a message to be popped into a baby box, showed that this "from one mother to another" message had resonated with the audience's own experience of motherhood.

'Cards came from grandmothers, mothers, some dads... all aimed at the mothers trying desperately to look after their kids in camps, bombed-out houses, etc.'

The story of Feed the Children's baby box can be found at www.sofii.org/case-study/feed-the-childrens-baby-box

Understanding the emotional brain

There are many books that delve in detail into the workings of the mind and the indispensable, still imperfectly understood significance of the emotional brain. Though life would be dull indeed without emotions, it's a heavy, impenetrable subject and the scary – or exciting – thing is how little we know for sure. If you have trouble sleeping these books can help. So finding what matters most for storytellers is far from easy and there's a lot still to uncover. Three books I recommend are *Descartes' Error*, by António Damásio (Vintage Books, 2006), *The Emotional Brain,* by Joseph LeDoux (Phoenix, 1999) and the *Rough Guide to the Brain* by Barry J Gibb, (Rough Guides, 2012).

What are emotions?

Here are a few insights culled from various books about the brain.

- Emotions are a biological function of the nervous system. Most emotional activity occurs subconsciously.
- So emotions happen to us. They're not ours to command.
- Yet it's emotion, much more than reason, that drives our actions.
- Emotions are hard to fake.
- Thinking and feeling are not the same thing.
- Until recently emotions were seen by scientists as 'too complex'.
- Most research on the emotional brain has been done on animals.
- A strong emotional experience stays and influences later behaviour.
- We still have much to learn about how the brain responds to stories.

It strikes me that the penultimate point above is really important – a breakthrough of four-star importance. For me, this was the biggest finding from the hours I spent wrestling with these tomes – the realisation that there is potential for some kind of emotional imprint inside our brains that can be recalled later at will, or prompted involuntarily by a carefully planted signal or stimulus. Imagine! If a strong emotional experience stays and influences later behaviour this could have huge implications for emotional storytellers. It explains why some campaigns and causes resonate so powerfully with our publics and how the emotions associated with them can be reawakened instantaneously by words and pictures, often from the slenderest suggestion. Could this be why certain images influence us so powerfully, for example, the eyes of a child awaiting sponsorship? Or the queues of starving children, such as those filmed and described so movingly by Mohamed Amin and Michael Buerk at the time of the

Ethiopian emergency in the mid 1980s, which led to the phenomenon of Band Aid/Live Aid? Or that extraordinary final scene in the final episode of the hit BBC television series *Blackadder*, when the funniest programme on our screens suddenly was not funny at all?

The cast of *Blackadder* waits for the whistle.

Going over the top

If you've not seen the series I apologise, but I also envy you because you're in for a treat. All four series in the *Blackadder* saga are priceless. But the final scene of the final episode is a curious departure because all of a sudden the atmosphere changes and in an instant the audience that earlier was laughing heartily is suddenly fearful, nervous, terrified and finally reduced to tears.

It happens as the last survivors of the cast that had entertained us for so long assemble in a trench in some unnamed section of the Western Front, for the final push. For successive generations similar scenes have become a shared emotional memory in the aftermath of that bloodbath known as The Great War. Quietly but indelibly they've been imprinted in our minds. Grey men huddled together in the pre-dawn silence, the damp muddy walls, the ghostly no-man's land, the blank, hopeless faces, the terrible wait for that inescapable whistle, the clatter up ladders and the sickening lurch up and over amid falling comrades as bullets cut into bodies and shells explode all around. Going over the top. Unspeakable hell. We can't help but picture it, imagine it, live it. It's the awful anticipation of that whistle that's burned most vividly into the memories of those who were not there, that and the futility, the inevitability, the pointless waste. As Lieutenant George turned to Captain Blackadder to say, 'Golly cap, I'm scared,' that emotional memory kicked in and the entire watching nation was transported in an instant to a quite different emotional place. Thanks to the near universal power of that memory simply, skilfully and wordlessly conveyed in the climax of that final episode from the *Blackadder* comedy series, viewers everywhere could see just how poignant, tragic and suddenly unfunny that final scene was.

Such is the power of imprinting emotional memories.

In future all transformational storytellers will study the workings of the emotional brain and will reap rich rewards if they can unravel any of its many secrets.

There's a danger of course that the emotional storyteller will be seen as manipulative. We want to get our points across but we have to manage the emotions we deploy sensitively and responsibly. Ask any gambler and he or she will tell you about how machines manipulate the human mind with fun sounds, free spins and small payouts. Consider the difference between 'I lost' (a problem-free gambler) and 'I almost won' (a potential gambling addict). The human mind can be entirely susceptible to differences that are very slight. We should try to understand this. Appealing to the emotions is not something to be taken on lightly.

Chocolate moments

Hormones are chemicals released by a cell, a gland, or an organ in one part of the body that affect cells in other parts of the organism. Neurotransmitters are chemicals that are used to relay, amplify and modulate electrical signals between a neuron and another cell.

Neurotransmitters and hormones are emitted from different places but for practical purposes can be thought of in the same way. Some hormones are also referred to as neurotransmitters. Small wonder this subject's confusing and little understood. But, we've got to start somewhere. If I'm honest, don't look for serious science here. I'm just trying to focus on how I use this stuff, to tell better stories.

Both neurotransmitters and hormones affect cells and so influence our feelings and behaviour. In essence, they are chemical messengers that transport signals from one part of our body to another, through our cells. Though different, for convenience I'm going to group them together. Most hormones are natural but there are synthetic chemical compounds that can act like hormones too.

Hormones and neurotransmitters affect the body by stimulating or inhibiting growth, influencing moods, cell development or regression, activation or inhibition of the immune system, regulation of the metabolism, management of hunger cravings (warning of the need for food) and so on. They prepare the body for mating, fighting, fleeing and other important activities, sexual arousal, control of the reproductive cycle and preparation of the body for a new phase of life, such as puberty, parenting, or the menopause. Thus, hormones and neurotransmitters are pretty important.

Neurotransmitters include seratonin, peptide, glutamate, and dopamine. Hormones include oxytocin, cholesterol, adrenalin, oestrogen (estrogen), testosterone, insulin and many others. Many hormones are used as medicines to treat specific conditions and, importantly, to alter moods and even minds.

Again it's beyond the scope of this book and the intellect of its author to go into detail on these wonders and new things are being learned about them all the time. But a few observations are worth making.

Ninety per cent of the body's seratonin is produced in the stomach. As seratonin is a main influencer of happiness and well-being, it's entirely accurate to refer to gut feelings, though the phrase predates by many years any understanding of the scientific basis for the term.

Chocolate is the only food that contains seratonin naturally. Of course. It's supposedly also one of a very small number of foods thought to produce adrenalin, the hormone and neurotransmitter that increases heart and respiration rates. Seems logical, doesn't it? Fright has a similar effect.

Oxytocin is known as the love hormone and is even marketed as a nasal spray. It's also believed to influence our propensity to be generous. So, if you want to attract a new lover or recruit a potential major benefactor (or both), perhaps the secret is to find your prospect in an unguarded moment and spray some oxytocin up his or her nose.

Maybe not. Effective storytelling should be able to produce similar effects and won't lead to trouble with the law.

Six questions to ask before you start your story…

- Is it about the reader, rather than about your cause, case, objective or, heaven forbid, organisation?
- Is it interesting, surprising, unexpected?
- Is it believable? Real? Accessible?
- Is it a good, gripping story? One person, talking to another?
- Is it simple, visual, memorable and friendly?
- Does it *truly* grab the emotions?

…and the world-changer's seven most powerful words

All you have to do is use them wisely and often.

You, now, together, free, new, because, thanks (or thank you. Or even, congratulations, well done).

Effective storytelling is all in the mind

'First capture their hearts and minds, then their wallets will follow.' So my first fundraising mentor, Harold Sumption, architect of Oxfam and an early pioneer of mail order direct marketing in the UK, was fond of saying. What Harold meant was, people need an emotionally compelling reason to engage, then they'll seek to reinforce their emotional impulse with a logical justification to give. After that, persuasion is easy. (Equally, prospects can use an emotional reaction to construct a barrier to action that is nigh impossible to shift.)

Of course Harold's advice was sound and applies just as well to all kinds of storytelling.

But we know emotions don't live in the heart. It's just a pump. Emotions, like thoughts, are formed in the mind, the brain, where they will be imprinted and retained like slumbering giants, ready for future activation, to gush out productively or destructively, far more powerful and irresistible than logic.

The big question is, though emotions tend to happen to us, can we learn to influence and control our emotions and the emotions of others? Of course we can. One way is by telling emotional stories.

Remember your fears and anxieties growing up. Watch your own children navigate their teenage years and feel your emotions surging as you take on their vulnerability, anxieties and fears. Imagine that lonely fear your son or daughter had, of losing their mum to breast cancer.

It might pay us to look further into how the human brain works, to see if anything of value might emerge for transformational storytellers. I've found a cornucopia of usable treasures as well as a potential Pandora's box. For, as we all know, a little knowledge in careless or inexpert hands can be a dangerous thing. Yet in the process of ploughing through some wearisome tomes I've unearthed troves of fascinating insights, such as the startling tale of Phineas Gage. While working to build the American railroad, Gage was victim of a terrible accident when an exploding metal rod ripped a two-inch tunnel diagonally through his head, tearing away his pre-frontal lobe. Amazingly he survived to live a further 13 years, physically recovered but remarkably changed in character and behaviour. Though it took scientists many years to realise it, Phineas Gage was living proof that though brain and mind are connected they are not single entities. Instead the brain is made of several different compartments all with distinct and separate, though connected, functions.

The instructive story of Phineas Gage is told in detail at www.theonlinestorybank.com. In reading up about such things I think I've stumbled onto a few nuggets of real gold.

The main 'controllers' of emotional memories in our brains are the amygdala and the hippocampus (we have two of each, reflecting the hemispheric nature of the brain). The hippocampus plays a major role in the forming and storing of memories whereas the amygdala is the controller of our emotions.

Again, this is something of a simplification. Their roles, interconnectedness and relationship with other parts of the brain are still imperfectly understood. And not just by me.

The amygdala and hippocampus are found side by side in their respective hemispheres and seem to work together. In his blog American storyteller Tom Ahern picked up on the amygdala.

'The amygdala is all about fear. It's our species' onboard warning system. It tries to make you notice the things that are new in your environment.

'To the amygdala, new represents opportunity. Opportunity to survive. Opportunity to thrive. Your amygdala's radar asks the same two questions over and over: will it kill me, can I eat it? It notices the new and dismisses the familiar ... because anything new in the environment could be a potential threat. Or a meal.

'Tell me something I don't know? My amygdala tells me to pay attention. Tell me something I already know? My amygdala says I can safely ignore it.'

How many transformational storytellers are aware of, far less studying, their readers' amygdalae? Or of the hippocampus and its importance in the laying down and retrieval of emotional memories? Maybe we don't need to know such things, but for sure it's an area we should watch because there's much still to learn about the mysterious brain.

The functions of the amygdala seem to centre around the fight or flight responses. Fear, anxiety, arousal, hyper-vigilance – all seem to be housed in or at least influenced by those tiny, mysterious, twin almond-shaped slivers, the amygdalae. We all have them and scientists are beginning to get very interested in their potential so are studying with fresh interest the workings of these complex components of our most important organ. And so they should. Mostly because we might be able to treat or at least influence a range of symptoms and conditions, if only we understood them better. Storytellers have an interest in this too. If we understand the workings of the amygdala, the hippocampus and other parts of the brain we might soon improve our chances of influencing people emotionally, through the stories we tell.

But at this stage our understanding of such things is crude at best, so I'll give it no more space for now. Though for sure, we should watch it.

An emotional letter worth copying

The Carlie letter, from Canada, has become famous as a textbook fundraising letter to recruit new donors. As such it's worth studying and adapting to your cause, whatever your message.

The letter addresses the right audience with the right story. It's the right length, the right style, has the right flow, makes the right connections and delivers the right offer. It is careful emotional storytelling at its very finest, an example of new supporter acquisition that works. It was written for the Make-A-Wish Foundation by Vancouver-based agency Harvey McKinnon and Associates and is reproduced with permission.

Interviewed by writer Fergal Byrne for the 'how I wrote that' series on SOFII, Harvey McKinnon said, 'The letter, of course, is the key to the success of any campaign. Ultimately my goal in writing any letter is to inspire the reader, to touch his or her heart, to make her want to become a participant in the good work we are talking about in our letter.

'The Make-A-Wish Foundation grants wishes to children who have

Brave new world

- The information passing through the average human mind has risen threefold in the last 30 years.
- ... and increases by six per cent each year.
- An office worker processes 20,000 emails per year.
- ...which is rising by 14 per cent each year.
- A US teenager gets 3,339 texts per month.
- Facebook handles 100bn hits every day.
- Twitter has a billion tweets per week.
- We are each exposed to 1,600 plus promotional messages every day.
- The Internet is an enormous brain at our fingertips.
- But what is all this doing to our brains?

FROM *THE OBSERVER*, 5 FEBRUARY 2012

life-threatening medical conditions. With some 200,000 wishes fulfilled globally every year, the Foundation has many stories to tell. Harvey was looking for a strong, powerful story about one of these children.

'A good story,' Harvey explains, 'has to have a number of qualities. First, it has to have emotion. Secondly, it needs to be real – we need to have something tangible happen. Stories have to come from a credible source – a mother talking about her child, someone who was homeless and who now has somewhere to live. Both of these scenarios are credible and understandable. Lastly, the notion that illustrates how the charity's intervention makes the difference, thanks to a donor's gift.'

Harvey McKinnon believes that transformational storytellers develop a sense that if the story is able to move them, the writer, emotionally there's a good chance that story will also affect a lot of other people emotionally. 'Carlie's story is great – not because of any skill I may have as a writer, but simply because it is a great story.'

The Carlie letter – see in full on pages 167-170 – succeeds because

- As Harvey says, it's simply a great story. It's really worth digging, to find your equivalent.
- It has a strong opener – they don't get stronger.
- It's an easy, fast-paced read.
- It employs deep emotion, which is very carefully handled.
- Something significant happens.
- There's a fine balance between achievement and need.
- The narrative pulls the reader along.
- The reader's gift makes all the difference.
- Short words, sentences and paragraphs aid readability.
- It's unfussy. The layout is clear and uncluttered.

The tragedy with this letter is that most charities sending something similar nowadays would allow their designer to use a sans serif typeface rather than serif, thus making it more difficult for older eyes to read. And they would cram the text into two pages rather than four to save money, probably in the process lacing it with jargon and organisation-speak to intellectualise their actions and justify their existence.

> *'Tell the truth but make truth fascinating. You can't bore people into buying your product. You can only interest them in buying it.'*
>
> DAVID OGILVY

Make-A-Wish Foundation® of Canada
2239 Oak Street, Vancouver, BC V6H 3W6
1-888-822-WISH www.makeawish.ca

Dear Friend,

There is absolutely nothing worse than watching your three-year-old child die.

And there is nothing better than stealing her back from heaven.

My daughter Carlie came back from certain death thanks to people like you.

I hope you'll give me one minute of your time because I'm not a fundraiser, I'm a parent. And when I tell you my story I think you'll realize that you can make miracles happen . . .

My daughter Carlie was a perfectly healthy child. Then one day she got a bad fever. We took her to the hospital only to discover every parent's nightmare. Carlie had cancer.

We started the treatment, and we prayed.

Then, when Carlie was near the end of 10 months of chemotherapy, her grandmother gave us a wonderful surprise. She

please read on

gave Carlie's name to the Make-A-Wish Foundation and asked that her dream wish be granted.

But three weeks before Carlie got her dream wish (she wished to go to Sea World), she came down with pneumonia and influenza. Six days later Carlie was in a coma.

The doctors told us she had a 20% chance to live. Then it got worse.

By Carlie's 17th day in a coma she had lost 98% of her lung capacity. She had 13 tubes in her tiny body. She was paralyzed.

The doctors told us she would not live through the weekend. I don't know if you can imagine how horrible it was to hear this news. Our baby was dying.

When the nurses came in on Monday morning they were shocked to see me still there. They had been told to say goodbye to Carlie on Friday at the end of their shift.

But a miracle happened.

Carlie regained consciousness. She had lost half her body weight — but she was alive.

Just 12 days later, Carlie was carried onto a plane to fly to Sea World. She was going to get her wish to swim with dolphins.

When Carlie returned 2 weeks later, she had the strength to run into her grandmother's arms. Carlie's recovery was amazing.

You may or may not believe this, but I'm convinced that

next page please

Carlie came back from certain death because of her dream wish.

When you're as sick as Carlie was, the only thing that could get you out of bed is a dream — something you desperately wish for.

Today, 3 years later, Carlie is a healthy and energetic child.

You know, I volunteered to write this letter because I am one of the luckiest people on earth.

My dying child was given life.

And I believe it's because she wanted her wish so badly that she came back from heaven to get it.

I'm hoping today that you'll join me and help other children who are very ill. Please send a gift to Make-A-Wish Foundation today, so that a child's dream wish may come true.

I know we were lucky. I know that many kids won't get a chance to live long lives. But they can get their most cherished wish fulfilled.

And as a parent who almost lost a child, I can tell you that you will be making a wonderful — and very important — gift.

Knowing that your precious child got their dream wish is something you hold on to forever. Your child will have their fulfilled wish wherever they go. And I assure you that it helps with your grieving.

And you know, when you help kids through Make-A-Wish, you

please turn over

also help dozens of people who love that child. Their wish is to make a very ill child's dream wish come true. Their other wish is to experience a miracle like the one that happened to Carlie.

Please, while you have my letter in your hand, fill out your reply form and mail it back with your gift. By doing so, you fulfill a very ill child's dream.

You may even bring a child back from heaven.

Yours sincerely,

Ross Lewis

Russell Lewis
Carlie's Dad and
Make-A-Wish Volunteer

P.S. When you decide to help a child with a life-threatening illness, please consider joining the *Wish Angels* club — it's the best way you can make a child's dream come true.

Thank you!

CHAPTER'S END:
ACTIONS AND KEY MESSAGES

Before writing, start feeling.

Advertising often paves the way for reform. Follow the rules for creating advertisements, though, when writing from the heart, be prepared to break them.

Public interest campaigns produce happy clients and co-workers as well as getting good works done.

Keep your campaign simple and tell the truth well.

Avoid the temptation to be clever. The clever thing is to be real and gritty, to get angry so you write with fury and feeling.

Learn to be a moody leader and change your mood at will.

Be bold and think big. If you don't ask, you won't get.

Understand the power of emotion, what makes a good person good and how to use all 72 of the emotion words at your disposal.

How to imprint emotional memories for later recall.

The six questions you should ask before you start your story, and the world-changer's seven most powerful words.

For free material and helpful features visit www.sofii.org.

TURNING POINT

This tale has a useful lesson about not judging by appearances, though its main point is about getting the price and proposition precisely right.

A close encounter with a hairy youth

My meeting with this scruffy individual was a salutary experience for a male of a certain age and elevated opinion of his social place. It taught me two valuable lessons: not to judge by appearances and the importance of getting the price just right.

I was visiting an agency I worked with in Reading, England. I had just left the railway station when I was stopped in my tracks by a shaggy-haired young man with a bolt through his bottom lip. Very politely, given his menacing appearance, he asked me for 70 pence so he could buy a second-class train ticket to Banbury, a nearby town.

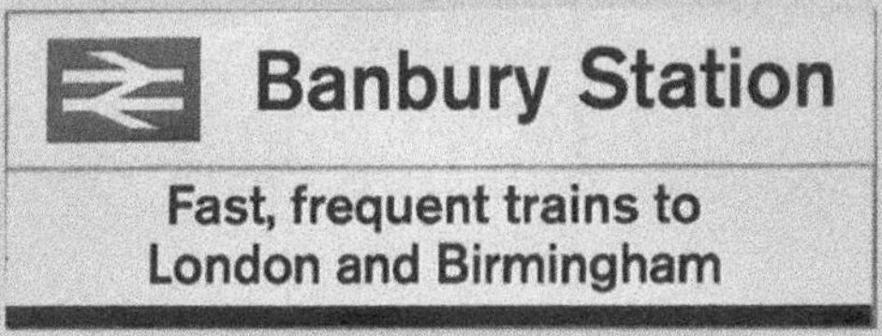

I was puzzled at the specific nature of the sum requested (I gave him a pound, as it happens), so I asked him about it.

'Why 70p?', I said. 'Is that all a train ticket to Banbury costs?'

'No,' he replied, clearly shaken by my ignorance, 'it's £2.40. But I asked you for 70p because you looked like you could afford that.'

I was very upset. Not even a pound! I reeled at this slight, mentally regretting my casual decision to leave off a tie that day. Sensing my dismay my new young friend said reassuringly, 'Usually I just ask people for 50p and think I'm lucky to get it.' I was so relieved I nearly gave him another pound there and then... but I didn't want to spoil him.

He went happily on his way, though I doubt it was to Banbury. And I was left pondering the advantages of knowing how much to ask for from each prospect and the importance of presenting the request as a direct proposition.

Of course, if the shaggy-haired young man had really known what he was about, he would have taken my name and address so he could have solicited me later for a regular monthly gift.

9. Where the story turns

'Then there is the other secret. There isn't any symbolism. The sea is the sea. The old man is an old man. The boy is a boy and the fish is a fish. The sharks are all sharks, no better and no worse. All the symbolism that people say is shit. What goes beyond is what you see beyond when you know.'

ERNEST HEMINGWAY, QUOTED IN *SELECTED LETTERS* BY CARLOS BAKER

Building Sleeping Beauty's palace

Walt Disney was, among other things, creator of Disneyland, one of the world's first large-scale fantasy theme parks. In 1954, in preparation for the building of Disneyland, contractors had cleared a huge acreage of southern California outside the city of Anaheim. Right at the start of the project Walt called a meeting to which he invited all the suppliers, builders, architects, plumbers, electricians and representatives of a dozen other assorted trades; everyone who collectively would make the Disneyland vision come to life. Eager and excited they assembled before him to hear what their eccentric, visionary boss had to say.

Walt then baldly announced to his astonished audience that the very first thing they were going to do was to build Sleeping Beauty's palace, right there, in the centre of the lot.

'Oh no,' cried the architects, plumbers, builders and sundry contractors, as if in one voice. 'No, no, we can't do that. First we have to put in the infrastructure, dig the foundations, lay the electric cabling, put down the sewers, install the...'

Walt Disney was having none of this. He interrupted his agitated advisers and bade them be silent.

'No,' he said firmly. 'No. That's not what we are going to do.

'The very first thing we are going to do is to build Sleeping Beauty's palace right here in the centre of the lot, because that, my friends, is the dream. And right from the start, everyone must see the dream. Big, bold, colourful. Right there, now, and for all time.

'So wherever they might be on this site at whatever time of the night or day, all of the hundreds of people who will work long and hard to make this dream come real, all they each will have to do is to raise their eyes to see the dream, our dream, the reason why we are all here. The splendidly magical, inspirational sight of Sleeping Beauty's palace will keep them focused on and committed to the dream that is Disneyland, always, right here, at the heart of our theme park.'

And so it was. In years to come the people who worked at Disneyland came to realise that Walt's vision had given them a fabulous metaphor for something that all causes, campaigns, movements and even companies must strive to build for their members and customers – to create the dream. It has to be a consistent, readily identifiable dream that, even when seen from other angles, in different lights, at different times and with different accompaniments and backgrounds, still is the same, recognisable dream.

Every cause should seek to build Sleeping Beauty's palace every day, for all its audiences. If you can present your dream as a story, it will stick.

Dreams inspire causes of every size. When, just nine years after Walt's inspirational oration, the Reverend Martin Luther King gave that now world-famous speech in the Mall in Washington DC, he didn't say, 'I have a strategy,' nor did he say, 'I have a rolling five-year plan.'

Nothing like that. Instead in a speech that reverberated so powerfully around the world, gripping the hearts and minds of a generation and inspiring irreversible social change, Martin Luther King said simply, 'I have a dream.'

That dream captured the imaginations of the whole world.

'I have a dream.'

As a transformational storyteller Reverend King could have gone on to say, 'You too share this dream. Together, here's what we are going to do, you and I, to make that change.'

In effect that's just what he did. And he changed the world.

Yet all he did was tell a story that built Sleeping Beauty's palace for his followers everywhere.

Measuring commitment

Until recently marketers and communicators could measure the relative commitment of their target audiences only by quite crude factors such as recency, frequency and monetary value (RFM). RFM tells you a lot, of course, and has served direct marketers, sales managers, fundraisers and others well down the years. If a customer has bought lots of your product, has paid a lot for it and bought it just a short while ago, he or she is reliably much more likely to buy again.

But how much more useful would it be if, for example, a business, social enterprise or charitable cause could measure and monitor the relative commitment to its mission and cause among its legions of supporters or customers? Efforts are being made to enable organisations to do just that and early results are surprisingly positive (see www.sofii.org/article/the-uk-donor-commitment-study) Now imagine if techniques could be evolved (as they surely will) to measure and assign values to attitudes, feelings, satisfaction, loyalty, dedication and even willingness to sacrifice for a cause. Or the propensity to leave a bequest or legacy to a favourite charity. When you look at the commitment study linked overleaf, such fantasising doesn't seem so far-fetched at all. This is a far from static field.

Good communication

+ enthusiasm = *inspiration*!

... which, when added to **results**

Becomes an opportunity to say **thank you** properly,

and congratulations, well done...

which provides a chance for **storytelling**, ie

Superb feedback, which = engagement

+ sincerity = commitment

which builds trust and confidence

= a significant, meaningful relationship

which leads to **loyalty**
+ **pleasure** for donors
=
more gifts & telling friends & family
& campaigning & changed behaviour

= committed giving (on + on + on + on, to a legacy)

= **great** lifetime value (what we are *really* about).

Communications equals lifetime value

Transformational storytellers are seldom in the quick hit business. When winning hearts and minds it's often best to build a relationship over time. Almost invariably new customers are costly to acquire so keeping them and increasing their loyalty and involvement pays.

All businesses depend on repeat business. For a charity developing each supporter one individual at a time the ultimate reward of a lifetime of relationship-building is the leaving of a legacy, a bequest, the ultimate big gift. It's neither quick nor easy, nor is it guaranteed every time, but it does work and surprisingly often. Using the build facility in PowerPoint I illustrate the route from communication to lifetime value as shown in the graphic opposite.

As almost invariably other storytellers aspire to retain and develop their audiences and build a mutually beneficial long-term relationship with them, this approach serves equally well for any communications strategy. Effective communication in the company of a few well-chosen companions does indeed add up to lifetime value. That's why transformational storytelling is so important.

Chunking up and down

Chunking up is moving from the detail to the bigger picture, the vision, why we are here. Chunking down is the reverse, moving from the big picture into the detail of how it might be delivered. It's a simple technique often associated with neuro-linguistic programming (NLP).

Chunking is a powerful and hugely useful tool, particularly for individuals and organisations who want to tell transformational stories. It's so strong and helpful that my partner Alan Clayton refers to it as the magic superhero power. It really does blast away organisational clutter and extraneous detail to get to the emotional heart of what a cause or organisation is all about.

Typically people in big organisations share the same big picture of what they're there for but can rarely agree on the nitty-gritty of how to get to it. To move from the detail up to the big picture, just keep asking the question why? Or what is the purpose of..., or the reason for...?. To chunk down, ask, how? Or give me an example, explain... Put simply, keep on asking why until you get to what. On the way, you'll probably find the moment when something changed.

Asking why takes you in a completely different direction from asking how. A good example of chunking up is how, in 2005, London won the bid to host the 2012 Olympics, when Paris was already hot favourite and had most of the votes already in the bag.

Or so most people imagined, until London delivered its two-hour presentation.

In their respective presentations each competing city had the chance to include a short film. Traditionally these videos feature an elegant, attractive, smartly-dressed presenter with sparkly teeth and neat hair zooming round the city by helicopter showcasing its amenities to the earnest description of building plans, legacy, traffic flow and the athletes' accommodation.

London did none of that. They chose not to feature their city at all, mentioning it just once at the end. Instead they focused on the dream, through the stories of four young athletes from different corners of the world who were inspired to compete alongside the cream of the world's best, to give their all for the Olympic ideal. The result is a beautiful, highly emotional example of transformational storytelling.

In planning this presentation the London committee, just like all its competitors, must have had members reminding them that they were expected to feature their parks and skyline, to explain how they would keep the city moving, show their superb facilites and all that stuff. But someone then cut through that clutter to insist, 'it's all about the children'. As committee members pressed their case, this lone advocate somehow stuck to his or her guns saying, 'No, no. It's about the children!'

That's why London won the day. They had a dream and stuck to it; the big picture, what was really important. And they told the story powerfully, visually and with emotion to move those wavering voters to change their minds.

For years a leading environmental charity believed that its role was to protect birds and that its supporters were largely the kind of folk who wear bobble hats and sit for hours in a field, waiting for something to fly within range of their binoculars. Then this organisation chunked up and realised that to save the birds you have to save the sky, the biggest thing there is. If you save the sky you also must save the land and the sea. Before long it seemed obvious that, really, saving the birds for future generations to marvel at and enjoy is *really* all about children. It's about the future, the imperative that generations as yet unborn might grow up in a world full of sparrows, eagles and the dawn chorus. Soon the organisation realised that they weren't just a charity for bird-watchers, they were a charity for children. Explain what your prospect's children and their children's children will get out of their support for your cause and people will get involved, big time. That's the power of chunking up.

When Norway's Strømme Foundation launched *Jobbskaper* (see page 40) they too were chunking up. They realised their work as micro-credit for small businesses was really about job creation. So they repackaged it, then focused on a target for one town, imaginatively involving everyone living there in a drive to create thousands of jobs. Simply by chunking up they moved from the mundane mechanics of a worthy scheme to re-presenting those same outcomes as an easily identifiable, shareable dream, which had a much stronger chance of appealing to sponsors and donors who want to change the world – the job creators.

Simply put, chunking helps an organisation to find its emotional heart.

More than just thank you and welcome

In chapter 3 I described the fabulous opportunity all organisations have if they can get their thank you/welcome/well done strategy right. Here, courtesy of Lisa Sargent, America's leading expert on the art of saying thank you, are tips anyone can follow, to say thank you nicely.

Thank-you messages are best sent in a personal letter. But an email or almost any other form of communication can be adapted to the task. As speed is so vital electronic media have some appeal, though the most important criteria remain that it be read, welcomed and appreciated.

- Make it important.
- Keep it short.
- Make it personal. Hand top and tail it. Mention specific actions and amounts. Make your signature legible.
- Be prompt, of course. Inside 24 hours should be possible. Make it so.
- Be specific as to what you're thanking them for.

- Use the 'you' word lots. It's not about what we did, but what you enabled us to do.
- Sparkle with sincerity.
- Include your contact number and a link to the website.
- Use your data. You know these people, right? You have their histories. Let them know you know them.
- Mention your website, show pictures of your people, who's who for them to call, other key contacts and helpful info.
- Tell a short story.
- Repeat the thanks and congratulations.
- Tell your customer when she can next expect to hear from you and what about.
- Add something interesting into the PS.
- Check it by reading it aloud to a friend (you just need to do this once).

Make a specific offer, define it clearly and give it a price

Tie your story to a job that needs doing, to a specific amount, preferably one that's affordable and payable monthly by a convenient automated collection system.

My favourite offer is the classic 'Make a blind man see. £15.00'. The story then explains how, through their eye camps in India, Help the Aged (now Age UK) can remove cataracts and restore eyesight for one named individual, for a small, manageable sum.

Just imagine. You could give the precious gift of sight to a different person each month, just for a few pounds payable by monthly direct debit, like your Internet subscription. Imagine what a creative storyteller could make of that in terms of engaging feedback.

The offer is clear and specific. You know where your support will go, what it will do and can picture what it will mean. Where else could you get such value for money?

Package your propositions similarly and you're sure to prosper, though you have to work hard at it. Even better, design your offer as a distinctive product, give it a name, clear benefits and price it appropriately. The storyteller's challenge is, how can I package and present what I want people to do, so that they'll see they want to do it too, enough to give what it takes in money, interest and commitment?

Child sponsorship is a brilliant example from the charity world of a product that has brought in huge numbers of enthusiastic customers who give regularly and substantially, thus making these organisations super-strong in money and members.

Yet you don't have to be an innovative enterprise to succeed, you can instead prosper easily by copying others and by doing what they do just as well or cheaper or even better. But you do have to have a good proposition or product.

Huge sums are invested by commercial companies in new product development, though whether companies will spend enough developing new stories remains to be seen. The case for positive return on investment could be easily made. Charities spend almost nothing on it.

Undoubtedly there's vast potential to develop world-changing products capable of engaging people in large numbers. People are not always selfish when it comes to incentives. For years the top incentive encouraging keen bird-watchers to join the Royal Society for the Protection of Birds was the offer of a free bird table for their garden. But following the 'chunking up' exercise described earlier, when RSPB launched a campaign encouraging people to sign a 'letter to the future' urging the UK government to act responsibly on protecting the environment, more than 360,000 people jumped at the chance to be involved. What RSPB did so effectively was to invite people to be a voice for nature, thus switching their offer from 'enjoy bird-watching' to 'protect the natural world for your children and grandchildren'.

The next generation of durable great enterprises will be built not around great products or technological advances but around potential for social change. These organisations will be more than just places to work, they'll be workplaces that make a difference.

How your stories spread

Through print and electronic media, obviously. By mastering all the social media, particularly those that are free. It must also be possible to cultivate a network of volunteer storytellers, train them in the art of telling a story then release them across the nation to tell your stories for you. Stories of course can go viral and often do. Simple, visual, universal and fun seem to be the keys.

I don't know of many organisations that have done this well yet, but for sure many are trying.

The unusually media savvy US non-profit charity: water is a fashionable and very successful cause that drills directly for clean water in communities that don't have it. Famously they reported on their biggest failure – repeated drilling of a well in a remote village in the Central African Republic that time after time collapsed, until eventually they had to give up and leave. Telling about this turkey generated so much goodwill, sympathy and understanding it probably did more to cement supporter relationships than any success story they could possibly have told.

Their tale of 'oops, we got it wrong!' swept round the non-profit world as a brilliant example of how admitting failure can bind people to you, can convince them that you know what you're doing, that you're good at what you do. And they've exploited it to great advantage. Though what I really like about charity: water is the simple tale they tell on their website, just with statistics.

First, you'll see their slogan, 'we prove every dollar'. Those four words alone tell a powerful story about accountability, transparency, results and customer focus – just the statement is all the reassurance most donors need. Then they spell out their impact in figures: 800 million people – one in nine of us – drink water likely to make them sick. So their supporters have funded 8944 projects giving 3,400,000 people clean water in 20 countries.

See, you like them already. Their story has got you hooked, just with a few sharp statistics and a smart turn of phrase. Charity: water though, does have its critics. By creating the impression that all of a donor's gift goes directly to the cause, they may mislead their donors into imagining that spending on effective fundraising and sound administration is a bad thing, which of course it isn't. But I'm sure in time they'll come to realise that they've got that wrong too and will probably tell a story to turn it to their advantage.

Don't neglect the simple power of telling a story about when you got something spectacularly wrong. Many years ago I worked with a charity called Botton Village, a rural community in North Yorkshire for adults with learning disabilities and other special needs. They made a mistake and sent the same appeal letter to their top donors three times. Their fundraiser, Laurence Stroud, took his courage in his hands and wrote to each of them a fourth time, to apologise. He explained he'd been playing God in his church's nativity play and had been momentarily distracted from his work by higher things. This fourth letter brought in the charity's best result ever, from that group.

Around the same time Greenpeace ran an appeal to cover the cost of fighting a court case against the UK government. They expected to lose the case and to have to pay the other side's costs too, so appealed to their supporters to raise the necessary funds. With right if not the law on their side Greenpeace's appeal exceeded its targets, but the judge also sympathised with the environmentalists so, after all, they didn't have to cover the government's costs. Greenpeace did the right thing and offered their thousands of donors a full refund. Only six people asked for their money back (and two of those had never given in the first place). Many others, impressed by Greenpeace's honesty, sent further gifts. It became one of their top performing appeals.

How are you going to use the Internet to change the world?

In the last few years some amazing stories have been written and are still being written by organisations that could not have existed less than a decade ago. Many of them now count their followers in millions, the funds they raise and the campaigns they promote are matching their reach and between them they've notched up an impressive array of achievements too.

Despite some concerns about their effectiveness and probity the online giving and campaigning portals are clearly here to stay and are shaking more traditionally established players out of their complacency, causing them to rethink their strategies.

Which has to be a good thing.

Go online, read, watch and listen to the stories there from a range of organisations such as Avaaz, Kiva, 38 Degrees, CREDO, Care 2 and many others. For a glimpse of the storytelling potential of these sites have a look at www.avaaz.org/en/stories_of_us_hub/ Through their story hub Avaaz allows individuals from Greenland to Mongolia to tell their own stories of what they do and, if appropriate, what Avaaz means to them. Other users can then 'heart' the story (a kind of 'like', but stronger). Some of these stories are still evolving. Monir from Palestine writes movingly of the trials of living in the Gaza Strip. Next door, Misha from Israel writes about the international language of Esperanto and its power for spreading understanding between people.

The potential is obvious, the chance to hear different voices refreshing. Or disturbing.

New communications and contact sites are springing up on the Internet all the time and they're interactive and evolving too, plus usually free to use. The media landscape for transformational storytellers has never been more interesting.

Individuals are telling amazing stories too. Imagine discovering just at the start of your twenties that something as basic as breathing was becoming more and more difficult for you each day, that your lungs were struggling to catch enough breath, that you were slowly dying for lack of being able to breathe properly. Imagine waiting for a transplant that might never come, then on the brink of catastrophe, getting that long-awaited call.

You might think you'd be lucky to survive. Or you might think, 'Here's a chance to tell my story to millions and encourage everyone to be an organ donor, so people don't have to wait too long, or to suffer like I did. What's here, really, is a chance for me to tell my story and change the world.'

Hélène Campbell is a plucky 22-year-old from Ottawa, Canada. In 2012 her life was saved by a double lung transplant. Since then, through her storytelling, Hélène has raised massive awareness for organ donations largely through documenting on social media the trials, triumphs and traumas of her own wait for new lungs. The Hélène effect was first felt when she started the online campaign #BeAnOrganDonor on Twitter to get the attention of Canadian pop star Justin Bieber. After he retweeted Hélène's campaign, more than 2,000 people in Ontario alone registered to be organ donors. Through Facebook, Twitter and just about every other online channel Hélène's become adept at getting her story out and through, particularly to young people.

Just months after reaching Justin Bieber, Hélène appeared on the *Ellen DeGeneres Show* from her sick bed via Skype, talking about the painful uncertainty of her wait and her mission to encourage people to be organ donors and give patients like her a second chance. According to the *Ottawa Sun,* registrations for organ donations in Ottawa skyrocketed by more than 8,000 in just a few months, all thanks to the 'Hélène Campbell effect'. But that's just one city. Through adroit manipulation of social media in all its aspects her story of pluck, grit and good humour has reached across North America and all round the world.

Hélène is a star storyteller. I was privileged recently to hear her tell an hour-long version of *A Lung Story* to an enraptured audience in Toronto. She had us in tears of laughter and joy and was awarded with a standing ovation. But much more important to Hélène would be those among the thousand or so people in that audience who immediately went on to agree to be an organ donor.

Hélène has so much energy for telling her story it takes your breath away. Apart from carefully planned and orchestrated media and speaking appearances she's helped set up and promote www.Give2Live.ca, a fundraising website that helps patients and families waiting for an organ transplant in four leading transplant centres in Canada. She's recently completed a cross-Canada storytelling tour too.

Social media, it seems, can change the world, in the hands of a great storyteller. You can see and hear Hélène on www.alungstory.ca

How Hélène got her website is an instructive tale in itself. Website administrator Taber Bucknell takes up the story.

'In May, 2011 an anonymous donor gave $10,000 to the pastor of Community Bible Church in Ottawa, where my family attends. There was a condition on the $10,000 gift – the community was required to "pay-it-forward" in the local area. That Sunday pastor Steve Stewart gave at least one $100 bill to each family in the congregation in attendance, along with the assignment to "do something good". All one hundred $100 bills were distributed. As a result, over the next few months there were fundraising garage sales, bake sales and other events, each facilitated by the $100 seed money. The total raised by the various events more than tripled the initial $10,000 and was spread over many community and charitable causes.

'I wanted to try an online assistance project with my $100.

'On the Monday after I received the money from Pastor Steve, two of my co-workers at Canadian Coast Guard donated an additional $180 even before my online "pay-it-forward" project was picked!

'A need for an online initiative became clear in July. Hélène Campbell, the bright, talented, creative 20-year-old daughter of family friends, was having increasing difficulty breathing...'

Taber's seed capital was enough to set up the website. Hélène, with her storytelling skills, then took it from there.

> *'Creating content that allows us to share our experiences, thoughts and ideas in real time is becoming an intrinsic part of life in the twenty-first century.'*
>
> GARY VAYNERCHUCK, AUTHOR

How are you going to use mobile communications devices to change the world?

This is the story of dwell time.

Like most big ideas, dwell time is not new. Back in 1968, long before campaigners and direct marketers started to get excited about the concept, the great David Ogilvy famously raised $26,000 in one night (a lot, back then) with a campaign promoting the United Negro College Fund that involved placing a letter on every seat of every train leaving New York's Grand Central station. Ogilvy not only understood that his travelling audience – mostly well-to-do commuters heading to their homes in the country – would have time to read that letter and might even be grateful for it. He also anticipated that if as they read they were to look out of their train window as it left New York they'd see directly into the run-down inner-city environments he was writing about. They'd see right inside the backyards and mean streets that the students he was exhorting them to support would be dreaming of escaping.

Of course his idea would work. It was bound to.

Imagine you are on a train, going to your work. You make this journey daily, one hour out in the morning, another hour coming home each evening. You don't like it, but you get used to it. You pray each day you'll get a seat and when you do you try to use your time productively. With the vagaries of modern train travel, that's no sure thing.

It's simply what many do, day in, day out.

You have your book, your tablet and your smartphone. In front of you, on the wall, is a colourful poster with a simple proposition and storyline. This month it's about mosquito nets. Malaria kills a child every 45 seconds, it tells you. The solution is mosquito nets, £3.00 is all they cost and each one saves a life. Text five digits now and you can buy one, instantly, no fuss. You'll save a life in Africa.

You have your smartphone, you can do it now. And for the next hour that poster will be in front of you, reminding you, gently cajoling you and castigating you too, if you don't.

This is dwell time. Advertisers recognise its power and its provenance. Commercial service providers and product retailers use it too. It's only valuable to all these enterprises because of that mobile phone you're holding and where you are sitting for so long. Mobile phone companies themselves use these spaces a lot, because it's a great time to get you to reconfigure your phone service and maybe even change your provider.

> *'The combination of dwell time and a strong, well-presented proposition regularly recruits people cost-effectively. When paired with effective telemarketing campaigns, we're seeing large volumes of donors being recruited at a favourable cost.'*
>
> FIONA PATTISON, OPEN FUNDRAISING, LONDON

Next week the short story on the poster will be about the plight of bees. The bees need you too. What a difference your £4.00 per month will make to the health of people everywhere when, thanks to you, the bees get pollinating again.

Using dwell time well depends on telling the right stories in the right place to the right people in the right way. In other words, what communication is all about.

Getting your stories published

Once you've got your story sorted, of course, the next step is to get it out there, into the hands of your audience. We all want our stories to reach readers and find fortune, to make their way into print, online and even into the movies. Nothing is so satisfying as walking into a busy bookshop and seeing your book sitting invitingly upon the shelf. Except, perhaps, seeing it in someone's shopping basket. So, we have to get published.

Although self-publishing is an increasingly attractive option these days a good agent can add value and even be the difference between being published or not, or at least earning from the process, or not.

Finding an agent can be daunting. Google literary agents and you'll see there are upwards of 600 in the London area alone. Many are very small businesses, single operators even and, if they're any good, they'll be very busy. They may not want to hear from you at all.

Most will tell you that for them a new manuscript is an albatross around the neck, an unrewarding chore they dread but which is heaped in stacks upon them, day in, day out, nonetheless. The prospect can be daunting. Somewhere in among those unwelcome piles is your master work. Its chances of getting through can be slim.

That said, when I wanted an agent I googled as above, selected four I liked the sound of, wrote to them all, got three responses and found one who liked me. He got me both published and paid. And was a delight to work with too.

But first I had to get him to love, not merely like, my proposed book. To do that I had to tell him a good story about it, its purpose, structure and content, who would read it and why.

> *'If I knew something that would make a crucial difference I would keep it to myself.'*
>
> JOHN UPDIKE

CHAPTER'S END:
ACTIONS AND KEY MESSAGES

Know what to ask for, when and how.

You've got to have a dream. So first, build the dream.

Learn how to measure commitment and build lifetime value.

Practise chunking up and down to get to the essence of a product, proposition or problem.

Follow Lisa Sargent's top tips for saying thank you.

Learn how to package your offer as a product with a clear price, name, benefits and description.

Always apologise when you get something wrong. But recognise you can turn this to your advantage too.

Practice storytelling across the full range of media till you find where your stories work best and with whom. Study the fast evolving field of social media so you can exploit its many possibilities for transformational storytelling.

Find your audience's equivalent of dwell time.

Love your stories. Always. Make sure others have every chance to love them too.

TURNING POINT

Though I failed to do anything for him, I learned a priceless lesson from the young man dying from AIDS in Zimbabwe. Telling and retelling his story is the only thing I can do now, to make amends.

The worst tourist in the world

The duties of a charity trustee can be onerous. They must prepare for, then endure lengthy, complicated meetings, wade through impenetrable, closely typed reports in bundles inches thick, followed by complex presentations and often tedious analyses. Just occasionally, as if to compensate for all this routine dullness, the trustee will be sent out to the field to see the work first hand. Serving as chairman of the international development charity ActionAid was for me one of life's most rewarding experiences, in large part because from time to time I got to see their brilliant projects for myself.

On one such trip I was privileged to visit several African countries to see ActionAid's work in the field of HIV/AIDS. I'd go on such excursions in ambassadorial mode, representing the entire organisation so invariably I'd be treated very well. This trip included meeting people from partner organisations, women's cooperatives and groups living with HIV/AIDS. Difficult though it must have been for them they welcomed me warmly. I made lots of speeches and shook a lot of hands.

You can tell a lot about someone's well-being from their handshake and I realised I was meeting some of the poorest and sickest people on the planet. I felt I was doing little of practical help. Then, when I was in Zimbabwe, one of the people ActionAid has trained to visit and support people living with AIDS took me to the home of a young man in the final stages of this utterly devastating disease.

Just 22 years old he had been bedridden for four years and was clearly dying. I have a son just a bit younger than him. But this young man's home was nothing more than a shed. The floor was earth. The bare walls of his dismal room were decorated only by a single, dog-eared photograph that showed the patient as a fine young man in distant, much better days. A dirty old towel had been tacked across the window as a makeshift curtain to shade his eyes from painful light. Other than a dilapidated cupboard the only furniture was a creaking bed on which lay the young man, racked with pain in foul, sodden bedding, close to death. In the room with him were his father, the ActionAid worker, and me.

For once I was utterly lost for words. I couldn't think of anything to say in that room that would have had any meaning or relevance whatsoever.

Then my guide asked me if I wanted to take a photograph. And that was too much for me.

The thing was, I knew why the boy's father was there: he was there to comfort and be with his dying son. I knew why the ActionAid worker was there: she was there to offer what was left of this family the meagre support she'd been trained to give. And I knew why the young man was there. He had nowhere else to go. He was there to die from this appalling disease called AIDS.

But at that moment I couldn't for the life of me imagine why I was there. I was ashamed, intruding on that intimate, personal moment. I felt like the worst tourist in the world. So to my eternal shame, without even a word of comfort or support for the others in that room,
I turned and left.

I realised later that of course I was there for a very good reason. I was there because those people wanted me to be there. They wanted to show me what dying of AIDS in Africa is really like. They wanted me to see it in its gut-wrenching awfulness, because I could never have imagined it for myself. They wanted me to see so I would go back home and tell my colleagues, fellow trustees and donors that we must do something to stop this. I was there representing ActionAid, so it was my job to tell other people about situations exactly like this. And to tell them well.

They wanted me to see so I would go back home and tell my colleagues, fellow trustees and donors that we must do something to stop this.

Our donors, colleagues and supporters can't be with us at times like these. It was then I realised that we're nothing if we are not communicators. It's our job to take people there in words and pictures, to help them see the reality and why and how they should help. It is our job to inspire people, to show them there is hope for a treatment, perhaps even for a cure. And if no cure is yet possible then to give comfort, understanding and practical support that will make it possible for these beleaguered people to bear the unbearable.

Would-be world-changers have the best stories in the world to tell and the best reasons for telling them. We have to learn to convey the real, painful, shattering but ultimately optimistic and rewarding experience of helping others in need.

10. Things we get wrong and how we can put them right

'For a creative writer possession of the truth is less important than emotional sincerity.'
GEORGE ORWELL

The power of reciprocity and making the right offer

Everyone has a story. But sometimes, you have to dig.

My career as a professional storyteller began 37 years ago and for most of that time I imagined that my stories about making a difference must inevitably start from then too. But not so, as early anecdotes such as *Fundraising equals fudge* (page 104) and *The Lord's sister* (page 144) show. I frequently employ these two true tales from my pre-professional days to make separate points. They're stories I love to tell because their lessons – the power of reciprocity and making the right offer – apply to anyone seeking to influence others.

You have to give to get. And it helps if you can present your proposition as an appealing product with a clear price. Both are simple, nice advice, best told through stories.

The most important word in storytelling

Sometimes we learn what's important in surprising ways.

We were at a three-day seminar in Scotland, at the Inch Hotel,

Clayton Burnett's retreat on the shores of Loch Ness where we train change-making fundraisers and campaigners singly and in small teams. On this occasion we were about to tell some stories. In the room with us were 16 senior leaders of non-profit organisations, mostly working for major national and international causes, household names all, each of them engaged or planning to engage in a major, transformational appeal. Each of the participants had just five minutes to outline the essence of their appeal.

Prior to coming on this event we'd asked all participants to send us details of their proposed fundraising campaign. In came reams of the stuff: annual reports, scoping documents, proposals, feasibility studies, brochures, reports.

Heavy stuff, mostly. No shortage of quantity, though quality was not so evident. So, not untypical of the outpourings that characterise organisations whose mission is to change the world by inspiring individuals to give of their limited disposable financial resources to make that change. All this bumpf was detailed, technical, professional, of course, with lots of long words, acronyms and jargon. If I'm honest I lost the will to live before I was a tenth of the way through it.

The session was half complete, the first eight individuals having delivered their five-minute presentations. And the three organisers were getting increasingly worried. Then without warning my impetuous, ever-vocal partner Alan Clayton leapt to his feet, thumped the table and in the style of a Scottish regimental sergeant major brought proceedings sharply to a halt.

I scanned the shocked faces of the audience. None had the least idea of what he was doing, or why.

'I've got to stop you,' Alan said slowly, as if weighed down with an unspeakable sadness. 'Do you know…' The faces showed, undoubtedly, they didn't. '…that not one of you has mentioned the donor. You've all talked in detail about you and your organisation and what you need and want and plan to do. But you've none of you, not once, mentioned the donor.'

And so it was. The room was stunned and somewhat shamed. Yet it was true. I'd never before seen so sharply demonstrated what I now realise is an almost universal truth. When they communicate with their supporters, organisations almost invariably talk about the wrong things. They talk about themselves when, if they wish success, they should instead focus firmly on what's always the most interesting thing of all, for all their readers. A single word explains what that most interesting thing is.

You.

'You' is the most important word of all for almost all audiences.

Put another way, after a small shift in perspective, 'me'. From my point of view, my favourite subject is me. I can talk about me not just for hours, but for days. Weeks probably. 'That's enough about you. Let's talk about me for a while. Oh, OK, just kidding. Let's talk about you. How do you think I'm doing?'

It is a universal fundamental of human nature. People read what interests them and the thing that interests them most is themselves. 'Can I make a difference?' 'What's in it for me?'

If you use 'corporate-speak' in your communications – which most businesses do, they're all about 'we' and 'us' – when you write to your customers, you'll reach very few. If you change that to 'customer-speak' – using lots of 'you' and 'yours' – you'll see a massive difference. Too often, so-called communicators obsess on the wrong things. Get the 'you' word often and well into all your stories. And reduce your use of 'I' and 'we'.

It's more than that of course. It's also about thinking your way into their lives, recognising and acknowledging their interests, desires and emotions and treating people as individuals whose concerns and passions matter to you.

This starts with recognising the most powerful word of all.

You.

Drowning in useless words

Seriously, the near universal tendency described above, of all organisations – companies, charities, government departments and endless others, all producing tsunamis of self–centred, impenetrable organisation-speak – is all but overwhelming. As one business area after another has professionalised the people who write their stuff seem to have assumed their job is to appear ever more educated and academic, more proper, formal and studiously serious. So they strive to excise individuality, edge, unease, emotion, colour and challenge. The result is that staple of British business life: the dull, impenetrable, nigh-unreadable report. Or the instantly forgettable letter or email, or the boring corporate film that tells you nothing you haven't heard before.

Yet readers and viewers, we all know, are increasingly fickle, unfaithful and promiscuous, with the attention spans of bored and capricious gnats. Their appetite for a well-told tale is insatiable, their tolerance of dull impenetrable drivel non-existent.

Something should be done about this. A role for the transformational storyteller? I think so.

You can't fake sincerity

Every day we see failed attempts at faking sincerity coming through our letterboxes, down our telephones and into our living rooms via television and online media. If the Life-Stage Fairy, or any other superhero, was to grant me some wishes, one thing I'd like to see is a big brightly coloured sign on every storyteller's wall proclaiming the dictionary definition of sincerity as a constant reminder of this vital, so often missing, component of every piece of good storytelling.

> *Sincerity: honest, frank, genuine. Free from pretence or deceit. Clean, pure, believable.*
>
> THE CONCISE OXFORD ENGLISH DICTIONARY

In the mid 1980s I was tasked to write a letter for Oxfam to report back to donors on what had been achieved with the gifts they had given to the then massive and protracted Ethiopian famine.

It was my first job for Oxfam, then the gold standard-bearer in charity direct mail in the UK. So I wanted my letter to be the best thank you/report back possible, the best communication sent by a charity to its supporters, ever. As part of my brief I took away with me a stack of examples from Oxfam's archive, in the belief that they would give me inspiration.

Before I was half way through the pile I was seriously depressed.

They were all good direct mail, no doubt. Technically, they were superb, state-of-the art examples of the best in British donor marketing, impeccably following best practice, splendidly conceived, well-written, laid out with flair and style. Yet they lacked something. Despite their technical excellence, they lacked sincerity. There were short sentences and paragraphs, lots of indentation and underlining, headlines, PSs and call-outs, the best laid out reply forms ever. But somewhere along the line the sincerity had been sucked out of them.

Then I came across this letter, from Oxfam's Marcus Thompson, freshly returned from the frontline of Oxfam's work in Uganda.

Dear Supporter

Doesn't it upset you to walk among people who have lost everything? Doesn't it distress you to see small children dying in their mothers' arms?

I am often asked these questions when I return from a disaster zone. Quite frankly, it does and it doesn't...

It doesn't because I'm busy when I'm visiting the scene of a disaster. I don't feel the helplessness you feel in front of your TV. Just the opposite, I have the privilege of being able to do something to ease the suffering.

But of course it hurts when someone you've got to know dies.

In the civil war in Uganda I was visiting camps for people fleeing the fighting. We picked up a very sick mother and her starving children to take them to hospital in Kampala. In the crowded jeep a little boy of five or six sat on my lap. We smiled at each other as the jeep bounced along the rough dirt roads. He died before we reached the hospital.

That evening I just dissolved into tears. I have a child about the same age.

Sincerity can't be faked. At least, not by most people. For us, there's no substitute. If I were you I'd stick that dictionary definition on your wall, so you never forget it.

Plan your rituals and cover your walls with inspiration

One year at the charity ActionAid we held a strategy planning meeting in Ethiopia. Their then director for Africa, Colin Williams, told a story that ended with a passionate plea. His words struck home with me and many others too. Pointing to the back of the room he said, 'Standing just outside those doors are some of the poorest people on this planet, waiting for us to take action. They're not faceless individuals in a far-off land, remote and distant, miles away from the decisions we make here. They're here, now, hugely interested in everything we do and say today. And they're right outside our door. We should never forget that.'

The charity's board of trustees took Colin's words seriously. Soon we developed an 'absent guest at table' policy for all our board meetings. We created a symbolic empty chair and set a full place setting at our table, complete with water glass and notepad, to represent the poor people that we work with, wherever they may be. In time this led to us creating another empty place setting, symbolic of the donors who make the charity's work possible. Logically then we added a further chair representing our 2000+ staff around the world.

Then, when space around the board table became tight we put a picture of our three empty chairs on the meeting room wall. Its purpose was exactly the same, to remind everyone of the three groups of important stakeholders who could not be with us that day yet were hugely interested in the discussions we would have and the decisions we would make. ActionAid also got into the habit of starting each board meeting with a mission-related story. People looked forward to those meetings. No one ever doubted why we were there and who we were there for.

If you work in an office this kind of thing is even more worth doing. Most offices are dull, drab places. Yet they all have walls, and floors and ceilings too. Why not make something of them and transform yours into a special place to work?

I've visited more than a few offices in my time and know that even in the so-called inspirational not-for-profit sector, the corporate look is mostly what you find. A while back I was invited to the headquarters of a well-known international NGO, an iconic, inspirational organisation with many of the most visual and uplifting stories in the world to tell of the triumph of voluntary action over the worst of human abuse and oppression. On arrival we were shown into what looked like the security holding area for an international bank. The solitary decoration on this INGO's white walls was a small, framed poem that any visitor wanting to read would have had to get really close to. As inspirational poetry goes it was overlong and unimpressive yet there were a couple of lines that, if highlighted, could have been suitably moving, even striking. As we were collected from that reception area by the director I remarked that, perhaps, it might be an idea if just two lines from this poem could be pulled out – the powerful lines – and displayed prominently across the walls in big letters, proudly for all to see.

It seems this hadn't been thought of. Fair enough, I suppose.

We then entered the room where we were to meet an international team of senior managers. It was a corporate boardroom, windowless, anonymous, sterile. It could have been the meeting room of any business anywhere. There wasn't even a logo on the wall. No pictures either. No story of any kind. I confess I felt deflated. An opportunity for inspiration had been lost. Why were we there?

They have a great logo too, these people, one that tells their story symbolically and powerfully. I suggested they proudly display a large illuminated example of it prominently in that dismal, anodyne space. They seemed surprised. They hadn't thought of that either. After all, they seemed to be thinking, who might come into that room to be impressed by such a demonstration? Corporate donors, international staff, key supporters, major suppliers...? The supposition seemed to be, well, they already know what we do, don't they?

A lost opportunity I'm sure. Office walls can play an important part in team-building and motivation, even if only decorated lightly with a line or two of salient, inspirational advice. One of the most practically useful to my mind is the two-word injunction, *never assume!*

Mastering the art of communication

I'm always surprised how few career professionals realise it and how many people completely fail to show an understanding or interest in it, but as with most sales professionals, fundraisers and campaigners, communication is every transformational storyteller's most important skill.

Communication is like kissing. You can do it on your own, but it works much better when someone else is involved. Information is giving out and communication is getting through, it's worth repeating. You must never forget the difference. Communication is talking to the right people in the right way at the right time about the right things, engaging them in the right way, giving and getting the right feedback so that we build the right relationships that will last a lifetime. Getting this right is rarely easy. It's a job that's never done.

If you can help your listeners to achieve their dreams, ease their anxieties, confirm their beliefs and enable them to allay, or at least confront, their fears, they will follow you, you'll catch and keep attentions.

Sounds simple, but of course it's not. You'll also need to understand readability, design and layout, media techniques, listening, body language and a range of associated skills. These are rarely taught in formal learning environments so most people have to hope they'll learn on the job or, if not, teach themselves.

If you would prosper as a storyteller, don't be surprised at how much you'll need to learn and how often you'll have to revisit a wide range of basics.

Appoint a tone-checker, today

Years ago I worked for an animal welfare charity that produced all sorts of printed communication with no system of central control. Any of its managers could instigate a new publication on any subject that seemed to them a good idea at the time. One of the least useful I found was a leaflet describing what you should do if, while walking along the beach, you were to stumble upon a stranded cetacean. It stuck me that the chances of anyone having this leaflet with them at the time would be considerably more remote than the chance of such an encounter.

The trouble was, the charity also had a policy of translating its publications into minority languages, Welsh, Hindi, Gujarati and so on.

So yes, you've guessed. I can't remember what Gujarati for *How to Kill a Stranded Cetacean* is but the leaflet got produced all the same.

Take up, I imagine, was slender, if there was any at all.

The problem is that most organisations produce communications that are either bad or dull. Yet nobody checks. Nobody says, 'wait a minute, how can we justify this?' Only a handful of people, if any, in most organisations are trained or naturally inspired communicators. Most work unrecognised and unappreciated, struggling unsuccessfully to stem the tide of dull, bad communications that their companies produce. So, whether it's good or bad, stuff gets sent out usually without anyone even recognising the difference. Yet given the chance and a bit of encouragement and authority these professionals could spot and stop bad stuff from going out, could even kill it before it gets to the printed page, website, TV or radio ad. They could save shed-loads for their organisation by preventing stuff destined only for the waste-bin from ever getting produced, far less sent.

Damian O'Brion, a brilliant direct marketing storyteller from Dublin, gave me this simple advice and it's among the best there is for any organisation that aspires to regularly inspire its customers. Every organisation, says Damian, should appoint a tone-checker. If any communication doesn't inspire anger or elation, laughter or tears, kill it before it costs. If it's drab, or bad, don't send it. Wasteful wallpaper floods the world. Pity the planet, save resources, appoint a tone-checker now.

Go on, do it now. He or she will start saving money and improving your output immediately and no one will benefit more than your customers, your audience. Except, perhaps, you.

Earlier I mentioned a radical thought that arose when meeting senior people in international development NGOs, that the best way to fight poverty would be to bring simplicity to internal reporting and reduce the paper mountain by scrapping what's dull and only allowing out what's interesting and engaging. I'm sure this is right. If our organisations could focus on not just putting out but on getting through, on really communicating, not merely reporting, we'd surely make more impact in our work. If we really have the best stories in the world to tell and the best of reasons for telling them we have no excuse for the impenetrable mountains of paper we produce. Changing that will make a difference.

Such is the potential that awaits the transformational storyteller. It's a revolution that can't come quickly enough.

Our most irresistible urge

The illustration below shows four stages of copy approval. Anyone who has ever submitted copy to a client for approval will smile and nod knowingly at the near inevitability of this.

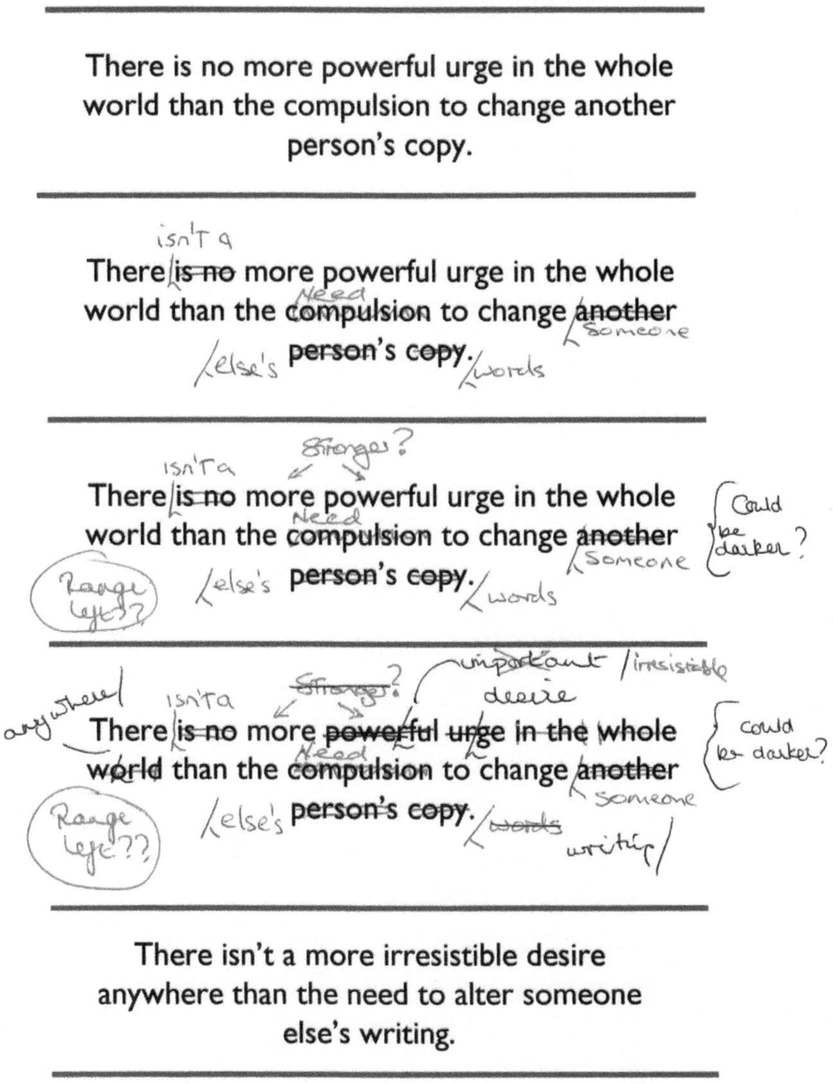

There is no more powerful urge in the whole world than the compulsion to change another person's copy.

There is no more powerful urge in the whole world than the compulsion to change another person's copy.

There is no more powerful urge in the whole world than the compulsion to change another person's copy.

There is no more powerful urge in the whole world than the compulsion to change another person's copy.

There isn't a more irresistible desire anywhere than the need to alter someone else's writing.

Plan for approvals

If your job involves approving another person's writing it's best to establish procedures likely to lead to success rather than failure.

Choose your approvers carefully.

- Demand the 90-degree shift – that they see what they are asked to approve through the reader's eyes, not their own.

Approvers must

- Understand and support the communications professionals.
- Avoid the curse of knowledge.
- Check and sanction accuracy, not style.
- Resist subjectivity and opinion.
- Leave the writing to the professionals.

The most difficult, most important part of the process

In transformational storytelling the most important role may not be the writer's, it may be the client's. Transformational writers often work to a brief, for a cause, for a client, for a living. They may be paid monthly, by the day or the hour, by the shed-load or not at all – which makes a difference for the writer but matters little for their writing or for the audience. All writers will at times have someone sanctioning their work, usually several, seldom adding value, most often chipping it away. As people generally are so ill-prepared and equipped to be an effective client (see www.sofii.org/the-fundraisers-toolbox/how-to-be-an-effective-client) it's rare to be able to celebrate good ones, though their role in the creative process is fundamentally profound.

Notable exceptions to the 'clients generally are the problem, not part of the solution' paradigm were the two women that Indra Sinha worked with in the 1990s at Amnesty. He says of Diane Allard and Karen Sherlock, 'I liked to work through ideas with them because I could be sure they'd only ever want the strongest ones. It was a privilege to work with Diane and Karen…they were massive influences on me and changed my life.'

This is far removed from the normal antipathy that meets the presence of the average client, today. But what an influence those women exerted on the finished products. In *The Cybergypsies* Indra describes meeting Diane and the spectacular brief she gave him and Neil Godfrey, his art director.

Diane, 'a pretty Frenchwoman in a fur coat who chain-smoked through the meeting', went on to say,

> *'Let me tell you what I don't want.*
>
> *'I'm not interested in ego, cleverness and advertising shit. I want to get this through to people – every minute people like you are leading your daily lives, someone is being tortured and killed and it's your fucking responsibility to do something to stop it.'*
>
> DIANE ALLARD, AMNESTY INTERNATIONAL

Thus sanctioned, Indra and Neil went off to produce record-breaking work that would become renowned the world over. If you would be an effective client, you need to work at it, but the results are well worth it. Too often clients pull their punches, dull the power of their stories and snip the heads off the difficult, jarring bits in the copy we submit, making it bland, comfortable and forgettable. Too often clients cover their backsides with rules and restrictions that shut down the storyteller's options and suck the life out of real communication. Often the difference between the same creative team producing brilliant or mediocre work is simply the presence or otherwise of a great client.

> *'A writer's brain is like a magician's hat. If you're going to get anything out of it, you have to put something in it first.'*
>
> LOUIS L'AMOUR, AUTHOR

The art of briefing

Getting the process right will lead to great writing, so briefing a writer really is a skill worth mastering. Given that many clients are not good at managing the writer-client relationship it pays the writer to take responsibility for making sure he or she gets as much from the brief as possible.

- Avoid drowning in briefing papers or website links. Less is more. The secret is not too much and not too little, just enough of the really good stuff. A good client respects the writer's time and will edit and structure briefing materials so the writer can get quickly to the heart of the story.

- The writer has to find a way to immerse him or herself in the dream. She or he has to be very familiar with Sleeping Beauty's palace (see page 173), to know all its rooms and views.

- Write from the real. It's well worth the investment if the writer can visit the project or site herself. It's almost impossible to write passionately about something if all your information comes second hand, or is filtered through a screen. Once you savour the smells, sounds and sensations of reality, stories leap out at you.

- Make listeners and readers work. Let them use their imaginations to fill things in.

- Drama has been described as anticipation mingled with uncertainty. Define the drama, then work to tighten it. Leave elements of discomfort. Remember that comfortable people tend to do nothing.

- Fill with wonder.

'Stories grow in layers around bits of painful grit,' says Indra Sinha. When briefing a writer in India for the Bhopal Medical Appeal Indra provided a quick checklist of the six stages of layering a story.

Layer 1: basic facts
The bare outline of who and what the story is about.

Layer 2: more facts and a timeline
Expand basic facts with more detail. Find a beginning, middle and end.

Layer 3: narrative detail
Add the who, what, when, where and what happened next.

Layer 4: deepen and strengthen
Add more substance to the important themes in the story.

Layer 5: the human element
Add emotions, feelings, upsets, hopes, fears, wishes, disappointments, with the emphasis on direct quotation.

Layer 6: the unexpected
Listen for those small, insightful bits of information or speech that make a story come alive.

What Indra is searching for as he builds the layers when writing for a dramatic cause such as Amnesty or Bhopal is, 'the point when the reader boils off the page'. This is when anger turns to action, when the reader realises, 'Something must be done about this. I can and I will, now.'

Nearly 20 years ago Indra Sinha set out the ten principles that underpin his approach to writing an advertisement for a good cause. With his permission they're introduced and repeated here.

> *The written word is the deepest dagger you can drive into a man's soul. All charity advertising has ultimately only one task: to force people to make a decision about whether or not they will take responsibility for the way things are. The difficulty is that people know this and armour themselves against it. Piercing their carapace will take every ounce of your courage, ingenuity and strength.*
>
> *Charities are founded in pain. You have to feel this pain, and struggle with your constant failure to express it, because you will fail. Words will fail you. Pictures*

will fail you. There will seem to be no way to convey the anguish, the desperate need, the importance, of your cause.

You will have to argue with your readers, trying every argument you can think of, allowing them their objections, anticipating and answering them as if you were having a conversation. Your readers will forgive you anything if they feel your frustration, and your passion.

Here are my principles:

1) Don't write an ad, hold a conversation.

2) The conversation should enable both parties, including you, to discover their own deepest will in the matter and act freely on it.

3) Don't tell people what you want them to believe, think, say or do.

4) Write from the premise that human beings are basically good.

5) Accept that the reader has the right to reject your message. You don't give them this right, they already have it and will exercise it anyway, whether you accept it or not.

6) Encourage people to reject your message – if that's what they're going to do.

7) Choose targets which are impossible to achieve.

8) Accept uncertainty of outcome (the universe is inherently chaotic whether or not you admit it) and use the phenomenal power of chaos.

9) Only work for people you like and whose work you can admire.

10) Don't trust words, they will always fail you.

FROM INDRA SINHA *THE SECRETS OF MOVING PEOPLE TO RESPOND*

Getting the thanking wrong

Recently I received a letter from a major charity, a vigorous fundraiser and a top-notch, thoroughly good cause. Its opening lines stopped me.

> 'Dear Mr Burnett,' the writer said. 'I'd like to say a big thank you for giving your full support to the XXXXX charity's campaigns to (generally, make the world a better place). Your tireless dedication means we were able to (make that world an even warmer, friendlier, safer place for some little ones). I wish you could see for yourself the difference this is making.'

But I knew that I hadn't given them anything for several years.

The letter though made no mention of that. Instead, having buttered me up with transparent nonsense and sprayed around entirely gratuitous thanks and congratulations, the writer went on, clumsily, to ask me for even more money.

She had lost me already. These days if you are personalising direct mail letters there's no excuse for not writing to people individually and accurately. Even if I had been a current donor, I don't do tireless dedication, particularly for them. So going over the top with thanking me destroyed what little credibility the writer had left. Getting this right isn't just good sense and politeness, it's a duty to our publics. And it's good business too.

There are many more things you could get wrong. If it's all about you, if you don't do your homework or talk about things your customers care little about. Most of these are common sense. If you follow the Scottish bard Robbie Burns' advice about seeing yourself as others see you, you'll probably do all right.

Keep it to a simple thank you

If you are writing or calling to say thank you, leave it at that. You don't always have to be selling something else, upgrading or asking for anything. Ask yourself, what kind of friend is always asking for money or trying to sell to you? Try to see your communication through your customer's eyes, to put yourself in your donor's shoes.

But if you don't ask you don't get and your customer would think it odd indeed if you don't make clear what you need and how she or he can help or take part.

Good enough is not good enough

I remember being told at the start of my career that responses to any appeal or promotion will come in from only a tiny part of those who receive it – maybe two or three per cent for a 'cold' audience and 10 to 15 per cent at best from even our current customers. This always struck me as unacceptable. Since then response levels have fallen further, so these figures will now be much worse.

The tragedy with writing to change the world is not so much that only a tiny minority will respond, it's that such a huge majority never even consider responding. They never had any intention not just of taking action but of even listening.

We have to aspire to change that. We can, if we tell our stories well and become known for doing it. We are not writing for all and we have to learn to live with that. But we don't have to accept that we can't reach more of our potential readers, more effectively, more deeply and with more assured precision. Of course we can.

A few other *most importants*

Among the most important realisations for the transformational storyteller is appreciation that your story isn't about you, your needs, your organisation, or your cause, it's about the reader, his or her life, what he or she can achieve, is interested in or at least is prepared to hear.

A comfort blanket might be useful too, plus something to help you get over the sudden onset of anxiety and creative impotence known as writer's block. Legions of writers from Hemingway and Tolstoy to

Laurence Olivier have written about this not uncommon black hole. A spectrum of ways of dealing with it has evolved, from denial of self-criticism through brainstorming and list writing to cold showers or hanging upside down for a while. The best approach I've found is learn to love the drivel in your first draft, then cut, rewrite, rewrite, cut and rewrite until you get something that has shape worth trying on a close and trusted friend.

All people are creative to some degree but the most creative individuals seem to be those best at mastering their mood, or able to alter their mood at will. Positivity, most agree, is best, while those prone to depression seem to suffer frequently from creative block. I find tobacco, alcohol and other mind-altering substances which, because they're shortcuts to changing mood, have always found favour in the creative community, rarely help. Except perhaps when it comes to having the experiences you might later want to write about.

Creativity can turn as much on environment as anything. A major London advertising agency once undertook an exercise to improve its people's creativity. 'Where,' the creative director asked all his colleagues, 'do you get your best ideas?' He was expecting responses to include various parts of the studio and its environs but nobody in the entire agency owned up to ever having a good idea anywhere near the office or its clients. Instead they said their best ideas came when they were jogging, or in the bath, on the loo, or horse-riding, or in a hundred other conducive though unconnected environments. But definitely not in the office.

In the next chapter several writers offer their opinions, helpful or otherwise, to other writers.

'To give real service you must add something which cannot be bought or measured with money, and that is sincerity and integrity.'

DOUGLAS ADAMS, *THE HITCHHIKER'S GUIDE TO THE GALAXY*

CHAPTER'S END: ACTIONS AND KEY MESSAGES

However difficult a story is to tell, it's the storyteller's job to go to where the story is and to learn to tell it fearlessly and very well.

How to make the best offer and to use reciprocity to advantage.

Why 'you' is the most important word in storytelling. And why you should use it lots.

Make where you write comfortable, exciting and fresh, never dull. Decorate your walls and even your ceilings. Show why you are there and who you are for. Learn to use all your images well.

Appoint a tone-checker, without delay.

Recognise that your client is a crucial part of your storytelling team. Make sure you're as well-briefed as you wish to be well-rewarded.

Learn what to avoid by following the mistakes of others.

Keep it simple and remember that good enough isn't good enough.

Recognise that creativity turns on environment and the best ideas can come from almost anywhere. And often not while you're at work. Find where you get your best ideas and spend as much time there as you can.

TURNING POINT

This story shows how success follows attitude. And that very often things are not what they seem, they're how you see them.

How Bata shoes came to be known as the shoes of Africa

I first visited Africa in 1978, touring the wild north of Kenya. In tiny villages and markets along the way I kept seeing signs for Bata, the shoe company. When it came to indications of commercial product dominance in these fly-blown, out of the way spots, Bata was in evidence far more than any other maker of anything. I vaguely wondered why at the time. Later I was told this tale in explanation.

At the turn of the nineteenth century, just as colonial Africa was opening up as a market, all the manufacturers of shoes in Victorian England sent their representatives to Africa to see if there might be an opportunity there for their wares. All duly came back in time with the same answer. 'Nobody in Africa wears shoes. So there is no market for our products there.'

All, that is, save for the Bata rep. He came back saying, 'Nobody in Africa wears shoes. So, there's a huge market for our products in Africa!'

And that's why to this day you'll find signs promoting Bata all over Africa, even in the remotest of spots. It's why Bata's shoes are known as the shoes of Africa.

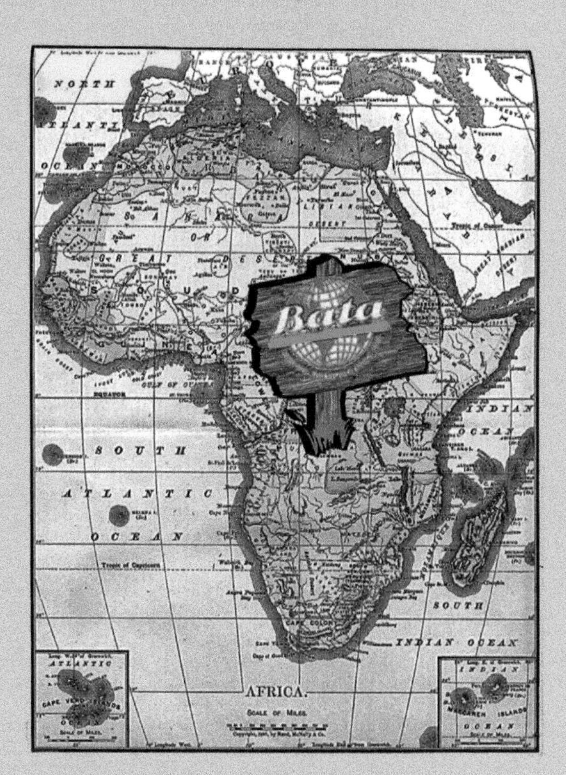

11. Cornerstones of successful storytelling

'If there is a magic in story writing, and I am convinced there is, no one has ever been able to reduce it to a recipe that can be passed from one person to another.'
JOHN STEINBECK

Given Steinbeck's stern warning above it may seem over-optimistic to set out here a summary of tips, techniques, ideas and advice from others who write stories. Yet search the Internet and you'll find that opinion about how to write abounds, from some very famous figures too. Well, you might think, they should know what they're on about.

Not always, I fear. Their advice is unlikely to suit everyone, at least not all of the time, though for sure their counsel can be worth heeding. Still caution and discrimination will serve you well. All writers write differently, so there's no right or wrong way to write.

Though I do it a lot I don't, generally, like reading what others say about the process of writing, nor do I pay it huge attention. Perhaps I should and would write better if I did. But writing is so personal, so much about expressing oneself that something inside me rails against being constrained by the guidance of others, or trying to constrain others even with my best intentions. Then sometimes I read something from someone that is so written for me, I just have to grab it and write it down. Then it becomes me. 'That's me,' I say to myself. 'I feel that.' And it comforts me as from time to time I revisit and review it.

Here are a few of these.

Susan Sontag, on a writer's failure of nerve,

> *'I must write myself out of it. If I am not able to write because I'm afraid of being a bad writer, then I must be a bad writer. At least I'll be writing. Then something else will happen. It always does.*
>
> *'I must write every day. Anything. Everything.'*

Later, more optimistically, she wrote,

> *'Making lists of words, to thicken my active vocabulary. To have puny, not just little, hoax, not just trick, mortifying, not just embarrassing, bogus, not just fake. I could make a story out of puny, hoax, mortifying, bogus. They are a story.'*

Of course it pays to revisit the basics every now and then. I remember being told, a while ago, that you don't get to be a martial arts black belt by practising 14,000 different moves, you get to be a black belt by practising just 14 moves one thousand times each. It's nice advice. The secret to attaining the highest level of proficiency is that you don't progress to mastering the next move until you've truly perfected the last. It's an agreeable story that contains an important truth: to excel at any trade, craft, or activity you must first master the basics.

Young writers not surprisingly will be eager to rush off in multiple directions. Inevitably, for some, this means they risk focusing on what interests and excites them instead of on what they need to understand and learn to be great at what they do. People tend to gravitate towards what's most glamorous at the cost of what matters most. They might profit more if they were to learn a lesson from Japanese sushi chefs.

Sushi chefs, when training, are required to spend their first two years just making rice. Nothing else. Rice is so fundamental to sushi that aspiring tyros must satisfy their seniors that they can make perfect rice infallibly every time, even without thinking about it.

The novice then becomes the master of this basic of her or his trade, and novice no more. Only having perfected the making of rice can he move on.

I like that lesson too. Storytelling to change the world is no less important than the making and serving of sushi or the art of judo or ju-jitsu. Yet in the craft of storytelling we have no such discipline that demands this level of dedication to mastering the basics before permission is granted to move on.

Hence my commitment to spend time now and again with the insights of others. Indra Sinha's observation about the passion between the words on page 146 is an inspirational example as it encourages storytellers out from behind their desks or screens and onto the coalface to experience the work and the issues first hand. You can't create a really good story if you haven't smelled or touched or felt the cause.

Really short *bon mots* work best with me and I'm sure with most people. Here are some specials.

> *'No tears in the writer, no tears in the reader. No surprise in the writer, no surprise in the reader.'*
>
> ROBERT FROST

> *'The difficulty of literature is not to write, but to write what you mean; not to affect your reader, but to affect him, or her, precisely as you wish.'*
>
> ROBERT LOUIS STEVENSON

Frost's advice demands that we be deeply involved and Stevenson's observation shows us why. I can't think of anything better to aspire towards, for any writer.

> *'It is an excellent discipline for a writer to feel that he must say all that he has to say in the fewest possible words, or his reader will skip them; and in the plainest possible words, or his reader will certainly misunderstand them.'*
>
> JOHN RUSKIN

If he'd followed his own advice Ruskin could have said

> *'Say less, but better. If you wish to be understood and remembered, say it short and keep it simple.'*

Though Ruskin's version is prettier.

The observation from Emerson, below, is admirably succinct. He also has a great name, for a writer (I'm sure it helps. Really.)

> *'All of my best thoughts were stolen by the ancients.'*
> RALPH WALDO EMERSON

> *'I've learned that people will forget what you said, people will forget what you did, but people will never forget how you made them feel.'*
> MAYA ANGELOU

> *'You can't wait for inspiration. You have to go after it with a club.'*
> JACK LONDON

> *'As to the adjective, when in doubt, strike it out.'*
> MARK TWAIN

E B White put his aversion to the adjective more bluntly:

> *'Adjectives are the leeches that infest the pond of prose, sucking the blood out of words.'*

Yet many very popular writers successfully eschew Twain's and White's advice, above, scattering often purely decorative adjectives with abandon. Who you choose to believe should be guided by your reader's preferences, not yours. Though, given the contrary nature of much of the advice you'll find, you may feel the need to approach all advice with caution. Several writers have taken the trouble to produce detailed guidance on how they write, implying that other writers would do well to do as they do. Jay Conrad Levinson, author of the *Guerrilla Marketing* series, reckons that getting started in any story is the hardest part. It's like jumping out of a plane, he says, the first step is difficult but the rest is gravity. Stephen King's book *On writing: a memoir of the craft* is one of those that I enjoyed. I also like Elmore Leonard and because it's short I'll include the following from him (somewhat edited for convenience).

Elmore Leonard's ten rules of writing

Leonard, who died in 2013, was an author and screenwriter renowned for his gritty plots and authentic dialogue. His characters so completely came alive for him he once said that long after he'd finished writing about them he continued to think about his characters and wonder what they're up to. Isn't that wonderful? Particularly when you consider point 8, below.

1. *Never open a book with weather.* Not sure I'd ever wish to, but, OK. Weather is pretty dull, and you want a sharp opening.

2. *Avoid prologues.* Because prologues are back story (i.e. what happened earlier than the action you're describing) so according to Leonard can be dropped in anywhere. I quite like prologues, so not sure this would be in my top ten.

3. *Never use a verb other than 'said' to carry dialogue.* It's less intrusive, he says, citing another writer who used 'she asseverated', which caused him to stop reading and scuttle off to find his dictionary. Most people would just stop reading.

4. *Never use an adverb to modify the word 'said'*, he said, definitively. Nice advice (he wrote, sycophantically).

5. *Keep your exclamation marks under control.* Enough said!!

6. *Never use the words 'suddenly' or 'all hell broke loose'.* Dredging the barrel here I feel.

7 *Use regional dialogue, patois, sparingly.* This is sound. If people struggle to understand accents or dialogue they'll struggle with your story. This applies to films as much as to the written word.

8 *Avoid detailed descriptions of characters.* Let the reader form his or her own picture. Leonard cites Hemingway's essay *Hills Like White Elephants* in which, famously, the two characters are not described at all. The only description the writer gives is to say, 'She had taken off her hat and put it on the table.' Yet we can see those people, clearly.

9 *Don't go into great detail describing places and things.* This seems an extension of point 8.

10 *Try to leave out the parts that readers tend to skip.* I love this one.

Though if I were to add a rule of my own it would be, *never limit yourself to ten rules on anything.* Generously Leonard throws in an eleventh rule that probably is the best of the lot. *'If it sounds like writing, I rewrite it.'*

> *'I almost never think about my audience. I'm in charge. I'm a dictator.'*
>
> PHILIP PULLMAN, AUTHOR, SPEAKING ON BBC RADIO'S *SATURDAY LIVE*

There are no rules, but...

Of course there can be no rules when it comes to writing from the heart. But that doesn't mean you shouldn't know intimately what others consider to be their rules, guidance and best practice. Nor does it mean that you shouldn't study closely what's been learned over the years in terms of what works and what doesn't, when, where, why and with whom. The 'greats' of advertising and communication – Ogilvy, Caples, Hopkins, Bernbach, Barton and the rest – all believed in and followed their version of 'the rules'. They prospered in the process because more often than not they got things right. If, when you start your story, you don't know what works and what doesn't with the people you're talking to then you're stumbling in the dark and your chances of success will be greatly diminished.

For sure technique and artifice will only take you so far and a writer can no more write by numbers than an artist can paint that way. But it's a mistake to overlook the usefulness of others' rules and mantras, or disdain to learn from them.

> *'If you can give your child only one gift, let it be enthusiasm.'*
>
> BRUCE BARTON, LEGENDARY US COPYWRITER AND FOUNDER OF THE ADVERTISING AGENCY BBDO

Trust to their imaginations

Writers everywhere quickly learn that their job is not to tell the whole story, to etch in every detail of characters, places, impressions and actions. Much better instead to leave it to the reader's imagination to fill and colour in the gaps.

Readers – all of them – do this automatically. Writers have to choose what they should leave in and what they can comfortably leave out, what they can instead leave to the reader to imagine. Readers are mostly unaware that as the story goes along they're filling in bits from their own imaginations, but that's what happens almost invariably, though it works better with some writers than with others. Omit too much and you'll leave your readers or listeners confused at best and having lost interest at worst. Include too much and you'll bore them and lose their interest. It's the writer's knack, to leave out that which, as Elmore Leonard said, your readers will want to skip.

More advice from writers

What I've included here is in my view among the best of a big, mixed bunch but I may be biased and they're far from complete. To see and savour similar stuff go to the Copyblogger and Brainpickings websites and numerous others worth poking around on the web.

As John Steinbeck so wisely said, writing isn't a recipe. So it really is sound advice to read your drafts aloud to yourself or to a really close friend, so you can see how it sounds. Then sleep on it and try it again after a while. If it still sounds good, it probably is, at least, good enough.

Only, for any writer worth his or her salt, good enough simply isn't good enough.

The 'read-it-aloud' advice works with any kind of writing though it's particularly helpful when writing stories. There is much other advice that forms accepted best practice, or is at least commonly understood by most who write. Though far from complete, I'll mention some here.

A quick skirt through the bleedin' obvious

When telling transformational stories you have to be relevant, interesting and engaging. Clarity, succinctness, drama and excitement work best. Eschew jargon, acronyms, padding and waffle. Instead be friendly, familiar, conversational. Use Anglo Saxon words: show not indicate, now not immediately, build not construct. Write in plain English. Write as you speak. And avoid clichés like the plague. But above all be appropriate to your reader and your story.

In his *Tiny Essentials of Writing for Fundraising* (The White Lion Press, 2003) the splendid George Smith offers some helpful observations.

'This,' says George, 'is the age of Bullshit. We live in a verbally jaded world. We've lost our individual voice. Too often it's as if we're all reading from a teleprompter. Everyone sounds the same and feels the need to say more than is necessary. Then when the teleprompter stops we simply spray words around at random to fill up the spaces.'

That other George, Orwell, had in his essays a lot to say about this tendency and Smith quotes him often. It's not new, this propensity, just that nowadays with so much media it's easier for us to keep spraying words around. People appear to be less critical. And nature abhors a vacuum, so as the breadth and depth of media has mushroomed we seem to think, let's fill those spaces with empty words.

Make it readable

No one has to listen to our stories, so we need to entice them in. Yet many storytellers lose readers in droves just because they make things difficult for their readers, as they don't thoroughly appreciate and understand the importance of designing for readability.

Never, ever reverse other than the shortest amount of type white out of black, or run type over a colour background, or on top of a picture. Is the type style right? Remember, serif type is much easier for older eyes than sans serif, at least for body copy. Is it large enough, well spaced, not too wide a column, not too narrow, black on white, a layout designed for readability? A detailed analysis of design and layout for easy readability is beyond our space limits here, but further study will be well repaid. See www.sofii.org for advice on the complex but vital subject of readability.

Other media require a different set of readability criteria but the issue is important whatever the channel. Website design needs to work across a range of screen formats but issues of typestyle and background legibility are still important. Audibility particularly is essential for films whatever their audience or message. It's easy to spot that not all television and film producers realise this. All messages work better when they are clear, uncluttered, straightforward and accessible. Audience comfort matters far more than gimmicks, fancy effects and surprises. Obviously our stories need to be tellable across a range of media so we storytellers have to be very knowledgeable and sure-footed at making them readable and accessible for all.

Keep it short

Invariably we all write too much. The first thing to do with your draft copy is to cut it in half is good advice for most copywriters. Cut words, add meaning.

Get to the point

Quickly.

Jargon, gobbledygook and long words

Most of this should go without saying. Jargon affects almost every industry and should be avoided unless you're prepared to risk coming across as a complete prat. Death by acronym is a common fate for readers of almost anything written by social work agencies, international development charities and many businesses too.

While we're at it, and at the risk of offending, it's best not to over-elevate the intellectual content of your writing either. Writers should not disdain a simple, straightforward storytelling style just because they don't want to be seen as either of those things. For the already sufficiently complex task of emotional, transformational storytelling, it's wise to keep the writing style very direct, uncomplicated, clear to the point of being blunt. The words of Dan Brown and Jeffrey Archer have probably reached more readers than those of Salman Rushdie, Martin Amis and Jack Kerouac. When it comes to emotional influence none of them I'm sure could hold a candle to Elvis Presley or Dolly Parton. Some writers are inclined to pose as deep, mysterious and intellectual, so in their writing seek to wrap their thoughts and feelings in obscure concepts and high-falutin' aspirations in the hope that this will make them appear cleverer and more mysterious. Which it well might. But they may also risk clouding meaning and losing readers. In transformational storytelling clear thinking, accessibility and directness are invariably prized above academic impenetrability. Complex and complicated will mean your words won't get through. You can't save souls in an empty church.

Smile, or whatever

When I sold advertising space over the telephone I was told to 'smile and dial'. Though your smiles can't be seen they can be felt. My hit rate shot up. I felt good, and sounded good at the other end. Started to enjoy my work more too and had much better conversations. Happy makes you smile and smiling makes you feel happy. So smile while you write. Or scowl, if you're writing something to scowl about. If you want your readers to be angry, get angry yourself.

Beat this, if you can

In my view the best advice ever for any writer comes from Scotland's bard.

> *'Oh would some pow'r the giftie gie us*
> *To see ourselves as others see us.*
> *It would frae mony a blunder free us,*
> *An' foolish notion…'*
>
> ROBERT BURNS

Burns' guidance helps you deal with the hardest thing of all that any writer has to do – to realise whether or not what you have written is any good.

> *'If a story is not about the hearer he or she will not listen… A great lasting story is about everyone or it will not last. The strange and foreign is not interesting, only the deeply personal and familiar.'*
>
> JOHN STEINBECK, *EAST OF EDEN*

Talk to your readers in their language, not yours

The people who work for Oxfam are usually young, idealistic, left of centre and of modest means. The people who support Oxfam are averagely of late middle-age, conservative with a small 'c', religious, probably, and relatively comfortably off. So anyone writing for Oxfam has to be able to understand his or her audience and tell stories accordingly. This often requires an important shift in perspective.

One of the writer's most dangerous traps is to imagine that we're writing, or talking, or telling a story for ourselves, or people like us. So you have to make what's referred to as the 90-degree shift and see things not through your eyes but through those of your readers. As a storyteller you have to imagine and experience all the emotions of your readers through their feelings, not yours.

That takes empathy. And rapport. Empathy is the capacity to recognise and identify with the feelings and emotions experienced by someone else. Rapport is the quality of harmony and mutual acceptance that exists between people when they are comfortably at ease with one another and where communication is occurring easily.

The surest way to empathy and rapport with an audience is to speak in their language, not yours.

'Persuade by illuminating, inspire by surprising'

I like that sentiment, though I've no idea where it's from.

> *'As I ate the oysters with their strong taste of the sea and their faint metallic taste that the cold white wine washed away, leaving only the sea taste and the succulent texture, and as I drank their cold liquid from each shell and washed it down with the crisp taste of the wine, I lost the empty feeling and began to be happy and to make plans.'*
>
> ERNEST HEMINGWAY, *A MOVEABLE FEAST*

Make a specific request and spell out what you need

Present your tale personally, as if you are talking directly to your listener not in a mass, but one to one. Construct it with integrity and flourish, make it real and believable, tangible and imaginable. Above all, make it personal. One on one, eyeball to eyeball or, heaven forfend, belly button to belly button, is always best and is where storytelling skills invariably come into their own. But mass communication too, even to millions, works best when it sounds like one person talking to another about something they both care deeply about, the talker offering the listener something practical he or she can do about it, now, to make a real difference.

Don't assume that your reader will be on the same page as you. Comedy giant John Cleese tells a lovely anecdote of how, after a gap of decades, he met up with an old school friend who was now an accountant. By a cruel twist of fate the night before the quirky British television comedy series *Monty Python's Flying Circus* had for the first time aired a sketch savaging the safe, dull world of accountancy. Cleese was worried that his prim and proper old school chum would be offended.

But not at all. 'I'm a certified accountant,' breezed his former pal. 'That chappie was a chartered accountant.'

Unless you put their name and address actually on the screen, satire is always about other chaps.

Build trust and confidence

There is a difference. Confidence is based usually on some direct or indirect experience, or at least on the recommendation of others. Trust often is based on intangibles, such as faith, belief and intuition; less reliable, perhaps, but not always. And people will be much less likely to give to you, or buy from you, or follow you, if they don't trust you or have confidence in you. They'll be less likely to listen to you if they don't have confidence that you can tell a good story. But if your listeners are to believe and follow you, they must trust you.

Leave them feeling wonderful

In *The Icarus Deception* Seth Godin says we should love ourselves. And who am I to argue with him? According to Godin, the best brand stories help the customer/activist/donor do that.

He says, 'We love the memory we have of how that brand made us feel once. We love that it reminds us of our mom, or growing up, or our first kiss. We support a charity or a soccer team or a perfume because it gives us a chance to love something about ourselves.

'More than ever, we express ourselves with what we buy and how we use what we buy. Extensions of our personality, totems of our selves, reminders of who we are or would like to be. Great marketers don't make stuff. They make meaning.'

The best fundraising copywriters know the truth of this. They know that giving gives meaning. That's why their stories are all about the donor, mentioning the cause or organisation not as ends in themselves but as means to enable the donor to achieve the end he or she desires.

Go forth all transformational storytellers and, as Godin suggests, 'make meaning'.

It's the experiences and the meanings retained in our brain that can be triggered. The emotions then flood in as a consequence of that, rather than being the button itself.

Make your stories sparkle

Karin Weatherup, creative director at the Burnett Works agency, is one of the UK's most experienced and effective transformational storytellers. In *How to produce inspiring annual reports* (Directory of Social Change, 2000) she offers her readers brilliant advice on how to make their words sparkle, including keeping your text conversational, letting the passion come through, giving the people in your organisation a voice, don't try to be clever or funny, say less but better, connect with the reader and spell out the need. She also makes the really useful point that when writing on behalf of an organisation of any kind you should think of your organisation as a truck. She explains, 'The job of your copy is to convince the reader that you are the best, most well-driven vehicle for taking their support from A to B and distributing it as the reader intended. So tell your story to position your reader as the hero and your cause or organisation simply as the vehicle that takes his, or her, help to wherever the need is.'

Karin goes on to explain why the writer needs to work quickly.

'Research says that the average reader gives annual reports just a few minutes. I think you may have even less time. Readers of direct mail, press ads, emails, posters, or leaflets certainly don't give you longer. So writers always have to work fast. Here's how you can make the most of that time.

- Make the cover proposition/title and all the headlines reach out to the readers and pull them into your story. They must say, 'Stop. Listen. This is about you too.'

- Say clearly and briefly at the start what your organisation does, who for, and what it needs to continue to do this. Don't lose your readers by assuming too much knowledge.

- Plan the copy and design to work on two levels: for the reader who skims and for the person who wants/has time for more detail.

- Give signposts to help your readers find their way around.

- Make sure the design helps readers get into the copy. It should serve up vital information in bite-size pieces for easy digestion.

- Begin pages with an introduction that summarises the point of what follows and the reader's role in it. It may well be all they read, so make it work hard.

- Use headlines, subheads, captions and call-outs from the text to help the reader dip in and out, find what they're interested in and grasp the main points of the spread (the two pages they're looking at) at a glance. Pull out the most gripping bits of your body text and set them as call-outs. If they are strong enough, they will send readers into the text to find out more.

- Use photographs that tell a story, with a caption that scores an important point rather than just describes what anyone can see in the picture.

- Make your copy sparkle. Keep it lively, fresh and conversational – it helps people to get through it.

- Get other people to tell your story for you. Independent endorsements from the reader's peer group add credibility.

- Use bullet points and panels to break up the copy – reams of unbroken text can be very off-putting.'

> *'Every time I read* Pride and Prejudice *I want to dig her up and beat her over the head with her own shin bone.'*
>
> MARK TWAIN, ON JANE AUSTEN

I have no idea what point Twain was hoping to make with the above observation but it's a most agreeable image, don't you think? Though it's a mystery why he kept reading it.

'The purpose of a headline is to pick out the people you can influence.'

CLAUDE C HOPKINS, *SCIENTIFIC ADVERTISING*

LEGGE HEADS ARMS BODY

If you are telling stories in print with the objective of influencing anyone the number of responses you get will directly relate to the effectiveness of your headline. A good headline can easily double or triple your response, and a great one can do even better – up to 17 times better, according to advertising giant John Caples.

The story that ran under the above headline explained that a certain Sir Thomas Legge had been appointed to lead an investigation into arms dealing in a West African country. A pretty dull story, really. But you've got to admit the headline writer must have enjoyed crafting that one and his or her efforts probably got a lot of people to read the text. I borrowed the headline from the splendid Fred MacAulay on BBC Radio's *News Quiz*.

David Ogilvy believed that the number one secret to successful marketing copy is the headline. If it's to succeed, any ad, poster, press release, email, website announcement, newsletter, or marketing document of any kind really needs to have a strong headline.

Ten keys to a successful headline

1. It has to have impact. The newsroom at the London *Daily Express* used to have a huge banner hung across it, which proclaimed IMPACT – GET IT IN YOUR HEADLINES. It's not a bad idea to have a prompt like this – you might try it in your office. Impact works best when your words make people stop and think, or feel that they must know more.

2. Keep it short. A challenge this, but worth working at. Five words or fewer are best. But don't sacrifice a great headline solely for brevity. Though if you are heading for double figures, maybe think again (a few exceptions to this are described below).

3 Tell a story. Or at least, introduce intrigue. Long before Twitter came along, headline writers were constantly tasked to communicate their stories concisely in a lot fewer than 140 characters. It's a savage but exhilarating discipline.

4 Make an offer in the headline. MAKE A BLIND MAN SEE. What a great thing to do! You can, now. Offers grab attention.

5 Include a price, if you can. MAKE A BLIND MAN SEE. £15.00. If you can put a price on your proposition it answers the reader's most obvious first objection, 'can I afford this?'. Where could anyone get better value for money than that? The rest of your message is now easy.

6 Your headline has to resonate. It must sound right when you say it out loud. Plays on words are good (see main headline, above and a few others around). Alliteration helps, as in 'she sells sea shells by the sea shore', or 'famous for frequent fabulous feedback'. It is of course possible to be too clever, which can put off potential buyers. Generally, cleverness should be avoided if you would touch hearts with your serious message. Go instead for passion, emotion and a direct call to action.

7 Punctuate carefully and sparingly. Ogilvy pointed out that the full point at the end of a sentence indicates to readers that they should stop. So a full point at the end of a headline can cause people to stop reading your message, particularly when they are flicking through a newspaper, scanning for what interests them. If an intriguing headline will encourage them to read on, it shouldn't be stopped dead by a full point. It also makes sense to ensure your text is easily readable, though this is more of an issue with longer (i.e. body) copy. All communicators should read Colin Wheildon's book about readability called *Type and Layout: how typography and design can get your message across – or get in the way.*

8 Observe reading gravity. As you'll know, most people (i.e. readers in English and many other languages) naturally read top left to bottom right, though there are several exceptions that read right to left, including Hebrew, Arabic, Japanese, Chinese, Farsi, Pashtu and Urdu. So anything that goes against this will be resisted. Logically, therefore, all advertisements should follow what's known as the Ayer no 1 format – picture at top, captioned as necessary (the eye is attracted first to the pic, then reads down) with headline below, then body copy (the sales pitch) beneath that, which leads persuasively into the reply coupon at the bottom (outside fore-edge and foot, preferably, for easy access to the coupon). Layouts other than the Ayer no 1 might look pretty, but they will fight against what's comfortable for readers. The Ayer no 1 format is almost invariably shown as black text on a white background, with serif type. All for readability. Depart from it by all means, but know the risks.

9 Allow your headline enough space. Most so-called communicators these days say too much, so they cut pictures and drop headlines to make room for their excess words. Most headlines then lose impact, or even get lost entirely. One-third pic/one-third headline/one-third text used to be the rule. Maybe for direct marketers it would be four quarters, to include the reply coupon.

10 Copy what others do. The best way to come up with your great headline is to copy those used by others, particularly the very successful. In direct response advertising you can recognise the most successful headlines because they appear again and again. If a headline only appears once or twice you are probably seeing a test that didn't work.

The following are a few worth pondering, but I'll add a caveat too. Sometimes headline writers are just too clever by far. Their role is to get attention, of course, but also to encourage readers to read on. Over-slick headlines can put people off. The knack is to get the balance right.

SUPER CALEY GO BALLISTIC, CELTIC ARE ATROCIOUS.

It doesn't exactly trip off the tongue, but this headline from *The Sun* proves that the king of British tabloid newspapers is difficult to beat when it comes to puns. It's the classic formula: rip off a song lyric everyone knows, substitute a few words and stick it on the sports pages. Brilliant. Caley is my local top team, Inverness Caledonian Thistle, and Celtic is one of the two top Glasgow teams.

BRITANNIA WAIVES THE RULES

When the royal yacht *HMS Britannia* visited the West Indies it was given permission to dock in a port normally prohibited to ships of its size, which gave the headline writers a field day. The above reversal of words from the song makes an almost perfect headline.

SINGING NUN IN DRUG SUICIDE PACT

Apparently *The Sun* also ran the above headline, though I haven't been able to find it. Not something you would easily ignore though, is it?

FREDDIE STARR ATE MY HAMSTER

The ultimate intrigue headline only likely to be beaten when a hamster finally eats Freddie Starr. Headlines of the 'man bites dog' variety invariably go down well with the public.

WHEN YOU COME BACK AS A WHALE YOU'LL BE BLOODY GLAD YOU LEFT A LEGACY TO GREENPEACE IN YOUR WILL

In telling a neat intriguing story with this headline Greenpeace Australia successfully broke the rule about never being clever in a fundraising ad. When some years later Greenpeace UK considered adapting the headline for their donors they spent long hours debating the merit or otherwise of including the word 'bloody', till someone wisely said, 'Come off it. You are Greenpeace'. If such colourful language upsets anyone they deserve to be offended.

Finally and probably my favourite, even though an example of inadvertent mis-reporting, is this shock horror headline from the *Dublin Daily News.*

MORE THAN 30,000 PIGS FLOAT DOWN RIVER

Which should have read

'More than 30 sows and pigs float down river.'

It helps if you read it in a Dublin accent.

'Dear friend' and other abominations

First impressions count. So I would love to obliterate the anodyne salutation 'dear friend', which not so long ago kicked off almost every fundraiser's solicitation for funds and much commercial direct mail too. It's a bad start not just because it's so bland but because it says, 'This guy doesn't know me and, if he doesn't know me, why should I trust him?'

So it's a good thing that direct mail writers now realise that personal is always best when asking or storytelling. If your story is one to one – which a directly mailed letter always is, even when sent simultaneously to millions – then the cost of personalisation is almost certainly worth it. Otherwise you're sending junk mail. And no one likes that.

> *'There is no such thing as junk mail. There's only bad targeting.'*
>
> ALAN CLAYTON, MOTIVATIONAL PUBLIC SPEAKER

Pattern interruptions

The composer Franz Joseph Haydn claimed he often introduced a loud noise into his music just to wake people up. Any interruption changes the pace and keeps people concentrating. Sometimes this effect can be achieved by injecting humour where it's not expected, or even by swearing. Bob Geldof famously did this to great effect during LiveAid when he tired of all the formal, dutiful reporting about impact assessment and the like and said to the watching millions, 'Just give us the fucking money.' Everyone sat up and paid attention.

Great openers

All actors know that if you fluff your entry, recovery can be difficult. So a really strong opening is worth working on. Here are a few examples of brilliant opening lines that I like, selected and borrowed from *American Book Review's* top 100.

> *Happy families are all alike; every unhappy family is unhappy in its own way.*
>
> LEO TOLSTOY, *ANNA KARENINA*

> *It was a bright cold day in April, and the clocks were striking thirteen.*
>
> GEORGE ORWELL, *1984*

> *It was the best of times, it was the worst of times, it was the age of wisdom, it was the age of foolishness, it was the epoch of belief, it was the epoch of incredulity, it was the season of light, it was the season of darkness, it was the spring of hope, it was the winter of despair.*
>
> CHARLES DICKENS, *A TALE OF TWO CITIES*

> *If I am out of my mind, it's all right with me, thought Moses Herzog.*
>
> SAUL BELLOW, *HERZOG*

The sun shone, having no alternative, on the nothing new.

SAMUEL BECKETT, *MURPHY*

'Where's Papa going with that axe?' said Fern to her mother as they were setting the table for breakfast.

E B WHITE, *CHARLOTTE'S WEB*

The past is a foreign country; they do things differently there.

L P HARTLEY, *THE GO-BETWEEN*

'Christmas won't be Christmas without any presents,' grumbled Jo, lying on the rug.

LOUISA M ALCOTT, *LITTLE WOMEN*

He was an inch, perhaps two, under six feet, powerfully built, and he advanced straight at you with a slight stoop of the shoulders, head forward, and a fixed from-under stare which made you think of a charging bull.

JOSEPH CONRAD, *LORD JIM*

You better not never tell nobody but God.

ALICE WALKER, *THE COLOR PURPLE*

I have never begun a novel with more misgiving.

W SOMERSET MAUGHAM, *THE RAZOR'S EDGE*

It was the afternoon of my eighty-first birthday and I was in bed with my catamite when Ali announced that the archbishop had come to see me.

ANTHONY BURGESS, *EARTHLY POWERS*

> *It was a dark and stormy night; the rain fell in torrents, except at occasional intervals, when it was checked by a violent gust of wind which swept up the streets (for it is in London that our scene lies), rattling along the house-tops, and fiercely agitating the scanty flame of the lamps that struggled against the darkness.*
>
> EDWARD BULWER-LYTTON, *PAUL CLIFFORD*

> *It was a dark and stormy night…*
>
> SNOOPY, EVERY NOVEL HE EVER STARTED.

I love all these openings but the one I like best is Burgess's. Into that single sentence the author has poured such decadence, danger, menace and mystery with so much suggested and unexplained you can't help but read on. Not just to find out what happens next, but to understand how come anyone can be such an active and intriguing octogenarian.

Don't let your audience off the hook

Having built up to his or her emotional climax a good storyteller has to learn when to be silent, when to pause to allow the audience to process the story and the right moment to close the deal. You don't get if you don't ask. All good stories should lead to action, but often that'll only happen when the storyteller clinches it, leaving the listener with an inescapable conclusion and no excuses.

Join the fight to keep the word 'yes'

Because of what Stevenson said about affecting people precisely and exactly, storytellers should rail against the ever-increasing trend towards sloppiness and imprecision with language.

Take the simple 'yes' for example. What a tragedy it would be if, as seems ever more likely, it were to disappear. For indubitably, yes is one of the most useful words in the transformational storyteller's lexicon.

'Absolutely,' I hear you say. 'Sure thing.' 'Very much so.' Or even, 'I couldn't disagree less.'

Just listen to us. When did we allow these longer, less precise expressions to become preferable over the simple, unambiguous yes!

But day in, day out that's what people do. Listen to the radio interviews on your morning news. A man gets off the space ship's first ever flight and the interviewer asks, 'Are you the first Englishman ever to walk in space?' and the man answers, 'Absolutely. Very much so.'

Yet despite the obvious absurdity, across the nation no one bats an eyelid. Well, except perhaps some of us, would-be guardians of the language, who grimace inwardly then let it pass. Thank goodness for them.

You can't fight it, perhaps. Still we have to rail against the barbarisms inflicted by modern culture upon our largely defenceless language. Even as we seek to adopt the modern idiom in our prose, we should resist on principle the trend to butcher words and be dismissively careless with the way we speak.

Avoid questions such as, 'Is Len Fairclough dead in real life?' And the need to explain to small children, 'No Martin, when I say I want to go and find the loo, it doesn't mean that the loo is lost.'

'If it's not one thing, it's another.' Er...yes, well...why should that surprise anyone?

'We have no crab salad, I'm afraid.' Why are you afraid? What's happened to the crabs and the salad?

The English language is indeed delightfully quirky. For their obvious contradictions consider 'terribly nice' and 'awfully good'. And of course anything described as 'pretty reasonable' isn't reasonable at all. The thing is, I suppose, we all know what's meant.

At the end of the day, in the final analysis, when you get right down to it, ultimately, the thing about words is that people seem quite prepared to be ever more careless in how they use them. Which gives the transformational storyteller an opportunity to gain a useful edge, by using each one with precision.

Thirty-two more secrets of successful storytelling

Over the last three and a half decades I've spent a huge chunk of my time just telling stories. Stories about, on, or around the great things that good causes can do when you give them just a little of your time, interest, support and money. Here in summary are 32 more things I've learned.

1. Stories are everywhere. Gather those that speak to you and keep them close by, in a story bank. These will become the inspiration for your own stories. Add to your story bank only great stuff that you admire and that inspires, or at least lifts you. Visit it often. (You can check out mine at www.onlinestorybank.com.)

2. For would-be world-changers, the secret of successful storytelling is to tell the truth very well. Fiction can work, though it may undermine your credibility.

3. Vary sentence, paragraph, section and chapter length. It makes for variety, which keeps people reading, whereas neatness and uniformity switch them off.

4. Research is the storyteller's friend. Look, before you leap.

5. Learn to listen. EAR – Explore, Acknowledge, Respond. And WAIT – 'Why Am I Talking?'

6. Value and respect your reader's time and attention. Treat these two volatile, easily transferable things wisely and well.

7. Never stand between your reader and the footlights. Make him or her the hero whenever you can.

8. Offer tangible pleasure to your listeners or readers. Let them control the flow and frequency of your communications. Give them choices, but remind them frequently of the pleasure they get whenever they hear from you and, particularly, when they support your cause.

9. Lace their pleasant experiences liberally with regular brilliant feedback showing tangible results of what their repeated involvement has achieved and will go on achieving. Remind them: this only happened because of you.

10 Stress the benefits that following your story will bring, Make your supporters and customers not just advocates but evangelists for your mission or product by encouraging and even inspiring them to tell their friends about all the great benefits they get. Remember it's the cause, mission, or product that moves them, not your organisation.

11 Remember too that every story you'll ever tell has to intertwine seamlessly with that illogically disproportional asset (given its intangibility) that is the thing people refer to, ignorantly or knowingly, as your brand. Think of brand as your organisation's character – who it stands for and what it is.

12 Tell a story that involves a big idea, as often as you can. Don't compromise on it.

13 Read your draft out loud, as if reading it to your mum. Try it in front of a mirror. Be your own sternest critic and don't relent until you can tell any tale with power and passion that will move people to action. Yes, you have to be an actor.

14 Use logic only to reinforce your emotional anecdotes. Stories are emotions put into words and delivered with evident passion and conviction. Drop the long rational justifications, or package them separately from your stories. Better still, make your rational case so sound and unarguable that your readers simply accept it as fact, with no need to discuss it.

15 Cultivate the virtue and talent of being brief. Even if this means you must kill your babies. Try to cut everything you write in half. A useful question for any storyteller is, so what?. What will that word, phrase or paragraph add to what I'm trying to convey?

16 If it's dull, boring, or ugly cut it out. Most unsolicited promotional communications are tedious. So be rigorous, uncompromising. If it's boring, bin it. Don't send it unless it's brilliant.

17 Learn how to rivet, electrify, surprise, thrill, delight and scare.

18 Study the news. Ape the newsreader's urgently concise reportage. Take your readers there. Give them a role. Make the issue come alive for them.

19 If you can't tell it well inside three minutes you're probably waffling. And if you can't hold their undivided attention a full 15 minutes, maybe you're a bore.

20 How far will you go for your cause? If not the whole hog, do something else, why don't you?

21 Don't just paint verbal pictures. Show pictures, even films. But only great pictures, which stop people in their tracks. Never use an image to fill space. Always caption your pictures by adding to them, not merely describing what all can see.

22 A good story requires good ingredients. Dig deep to find them.

23 Create the best writing environment ever. Writing is something to be enjoyed, so do it somewhere you like to be.

24 Learn the secrets of layout and readability. Use serif type for text, preferably a large appearing font (with rounded rather than thin bowls on letters such as b, d and p) and only black on white. Study line and paragraph lengths, backgrounds, column widths.

25 Cut out the bits that aren't part of the story. That'll include most of your setting of context. Say as little as you profitably can about you and your organisation. As Kurt Vonnegut put it, 'If a sentence, no matter how excellent, does not illuminate your subject in some new and useful way, scratch it out.'

26 Don't rush to write. Do your homework first and thoroughly. Plan a tight contents and structure.

27 Action, not background. Cut out the organisational detail so you can get quickly to the heart of the story. Provide a solution. Wrap it in need and achievement.

28 Every writer is a thief, but some are cleverer than others at disguising it. Learn to steal wisely and well.

29 Simplicity is sacred. Resist embellishing. As Vonnegut put it, remember that Shakespeare's most famous line 'to be or not to be' has no word longer than three letters. And the opening sentence in the Bible is well within the writing skills of a lively 14-year old: 'In the beginning God created the heaven and earth.'

30 Develop an ear for stories. Revel in the sound of words.

31 Never go anywhere, even to sleep, without a notebook and a pen close at hand. Or an inquisitive, acquisitive attitude of mind.

32 Read only what you like. Don't struggle through something because someone else has told you that you should.

Though this list is my own thoughts based on my own experiences I delight in tipping my hat to George Smith, Indra Sinha, Harper Lee, George Orwell, David Ogilvy, Stephen King to mention just a few of those who have particularly inspired and informed me. After all, what storyteller worth his or her salt hasn't honed their craft in retelling the tales of others? So thanks also to a raft of other writers too numerous to mention, from Robert Burns and Robert Service to Joan Rivers and George W Bush. I take any inspiration I can get from wherever and whenever I can get it.

Bacon, eggs and burning your boats

Two short stories illustrate the importance of commitment for the successful storyteller.

An older, experienced storyteller was showing a new, fresh and eager young apprentice the ropes.

'To succeed at storytelling my boy,' the older hand explained with gravitas as they strolled around the customer service department, 'you have to be committed. Mere involvement is not enough. If you want to make something of this career you have chosen, you must be committed.'

The young tyro was puzzled. 'But, what's the difference, old timer? Surely involvement and commitment are pretty much the same thing?'

The voice of experience responded with conviction. 'Ah ha! Not the same thing at all, young fellow, not at all. To understand the difference between commitment and mere involvement you have to understand the difference between bacon and eggs.

'Bacon and eggs?' cried the perplexed youth.

'Yes,' retorted the sage. 'Bacon and eggs. In bacon and eggs, the chicken is involved. But the pig is committed.'

In the eighth century when the Moors of North Africa invaded southern Spain the first thing they did once they'd secured landfall was to burn the ships they'd arrived in. 'There's no going back,' they were saying. 'Here, I belong.'

Proof if it were needed that mere involvement is not enough. You storytellers have to be committed.

Finally, read copiously

There's no substitute, you'll love it and it will rub off, onto your storytelling. And next time someone rumbles your indulgence in sloping off to your corner for a quiet read you can legitimately protest, 'But I am, really, changing the world.'

> *'A wise man is he who knows the difference between a wise utterance and a foolish utterance. A sage is he who knows the difference between a wise silence and a foolish silence.'*
>
> ANCIENT CHINESE SAYING

CHAPTER'S END:
ACTIONS AND KEY MESSAGES

Tell the truth always in an acceptable way.

There are no rules to writing from the heart, though it pays to study other writers and learn from them. But make your own judgements as to whom you listen to.

Revisit the basics regularly.

Trust your reader's imagination, let him or her fill in some blanks.

Follow Karin Weatherup's 11 ideas to make your words sparkle.

Aim for easy reading and audience comfort, because it matters far more than gimmicks, fancy effects and surprises.

What you should do about jargon, gobbledygook and acronyms.

Golden rules to practise: smile as you write, talk to readers in their language, not yours, and never assume.

Work at headlines to give them impact and make them sing. Pin the ten keys to a successful headline on your wall and add the 32 keys to successful storytelling. No need to make a shrine though.

Study great opening lines.

Every so often do something startling to wake everybody up.

Read everything good you can.

Learn the value of positive thinking, as demonstrated by Bata shoes.

PART FOUR

Stories that will stick

TURNING POINT

Most organisations expect to lose even their best customers as they grow old. But not good works and worthwhile causes. At least, not necessarily.

When our audience enters the twilight zone

My mother was a lifelong supporter of several charities. I know of at least ten that she gave to on a regular basis, mainly those working with animals or children.

She was from an older, more fastidious and respectful generation, my mum. She believed in neatness, punctuality and doing things properly. So one day when visiting her I was surprised to find a pile of unopened mail in her hallway.

'What's this Mum?' I asked. 'It's unlike you not to open and deal with your post.'

She became uncharacteristically irritated.

'Oh Kenneth,' she exclaimed, visibly upset, 'I get so much of this stuff now. And they're always shouting at me. I don't know what it is they want.'

The pile of mail was almost entirely from charities she'd supported for years. And there was a lot of it.

'I get so much of this stuff now. And they're always shouting at me. I don't know what it is they want.'

Mother looked so frail. I realised she'd stopped responding in the usual way because, at her age, it'd simply become harder to follow what they were asking her to do. Now these charities that she'd sustained for so long were treating her as a lapsed customer, subjecting her to ever more strident and frequent blandishments, insisting that she renew. As they'd become more insistent she'd stopped even opening their letters, something she'd formerly enjoyed.

But my mum wasn't a lapsed donor. She'd entered a kind of in-between time, a stage between being a regular customer and becoming a legacy prospect, when nothing appeals or interests. It's a life-stage that almost no charity recognises or attempts to respond to, perhaps because it's too difficult. Yet they all want to steward their donors through this gap, because they all depend on legacies, or bequests.

So instead of shouting at her to renew they should have been reassuring her that her past help was still making a difference. A well-crafted personal note or a considerate phone call to my mum in her declining years might have made all the difference, might have worked much better both for her and for them. From someone sensitive and sympathetic, of course, trained in building rapport and adding meaning, in sharing emotions, dreams, passion and experiences, in telling stories that my mother might have welcomed rather than seen as an irritating intrusion.

A life-changer, not a junk marketer.

Fundraisers are at least as famous for intrusion and irritation as they are for innovation and inspiration. Which is a shame. For instead of upsetting and worrying my mother at her most vulnerable the right contact at the appropriate time might have enhanced her experience of and fulfilment from being a donor.

This challenge is of course not unique to fundraisers. It's universal, something all would-be communicators face. We all walk a fine line between being inspirational and being irritating. It's not difficult to see which of these you have to aim for.

12. Keeping the change working

'Making a sale without making a convert doesn't amount to much.'

CLAUDE C HOPKINS, *SCIENTIFIC ADVERTISING*

We transformational storytellers face some interesting challenges in making our stories stick. These days it's not enough to secure interest and even action. The high costs of reaching and acquiring new customers and supporters means we have to keep them for the long term. Yet our discerning, demanding audiences now have so many other options and switching to any of a hundred eager competitors is so easy. So, we've got to work very hard and be very good indeed, to keep them.

First, we have to stop people from wanting to cross the road

Not so long ago I was Christmas shopping in London with a young friend from France when we stumbled across a collection of street fundraisers. 'I hate these people,' my friend said, fending them off (they weren't interested in me – too old) and steering me across the road. 'They're so pushy. They make me feel bad because I can't support them all.'

You will have a similar tale or two I'm sure. Evidence that in their clumsy, often artless interpretation of storytelling on the street, fundraisers are failing to inspire large swathes of potential new donors like my friend Pierre. It's a problem not confined to Britain, to street fundraising, or even to fundraising of any kind. You don't recruit converts to change the world by irritating or harassing people.

Yet day in, day out, worthwhile causes with great stories to tell are losing current and potential customers and supporters largely through inept marketing and crass communication. And those who remain, perhaps in spite of rather than because of the organisations that court them, may tolerate for now the causes that once inspired them but are ready to drift away at the first opportunity. And they do, in droves, at vast expense to us and our causes and organisations. This just won't be good enough in the future. It's worth remembering that today's potential convert to your cause,

- Knows the world's a mess but has minimal confidence that anyone's going to do anything about it.

- Thinks life's tough now and sure to get tougher. Would welcome anything meaningful, fulfilling and worth doing as a positive distraction.

- Gets far too much promotional bumph that's of limited or no interest, via leaflets, direct mail, email and so on. Is surrounded by insincerity, triviality and the shallowness of today's 'celebrity' culture.

- Is increasingly suspicious of big brands, authority figures and being told what to do and think.

- Is fed a daily diet of generally depressing bad news.

- Won't tolerate the irrelevant. If it isn't appropriate, interesting or a pleasure he or she won't give it much time or thought.

- Is moved to respond emotionally far more than logically.

- To get really involved in anything, he or she needs to continually see benefits, or the difference he or she is making.

It's against this backdrop that transformational storytellers must win hearts, minds and direct debits. So what do we need, to succeed?

- We have to move from selling to substance, from 'talking at' to real, useful conversations.
- We have to offer reciprocity, to give as well as get.
- Organisations with great stories to tell must invest bravely and sufficiently to ensure their best storytellers stick around long enough, not just to plan but to see the plan through. Adequate investment and sufficient time are the twin ingredients of success.
- Our cases for support should have less of 'us' and 'I', more of 'you'. Less 'we need', more 'you can'. And more 'yes', less 'no'.
- Storytellers should consistently offer world-class customer contact and service.

> *'The planet does not need more successful people. The planet desperately needs more peacemakers, healers, restorers, storytellers and lovers of all kinds.'*
>
> THE DALAI LAMA

Storytellers should also aspire to go beyond the building of mutually respectful and beneficial relationships (even though most never quite get there, at least, not yet) to create a new kind of partnership with their customers. They could have the kind of conversations that real relationships are made of, that take them under the skins of their customers and offer their customers the chance to get really 'inside' their favourite organisation. The idea is to define and drive a relationship capable of moving beyond the mere exchange of money into a partnership of mutual benefit.

Success will come to those able to breed strong commitment in their customers, ensuring that come what may they'll stay loyal. Practical partnerships will do more to cement that loyalty and commitment than anything else.

And those who invest in testing are far more likely to succeed than those who don't.

Try and try again: the power of persisting

This was something entirely new. There was no accepted standard of success to test it against because nothing quite like it had ever been tried before. Still, test it they must.

Few thought they could succeed. To many at the time it seemed foolhardy, little more than wishful thinking. What kept the two guys behind it going was a feeling that, really, it *should* work. In theory, anyway. The benefits were obvious, massive, the risks clearly terrifying. Horrible failure loomed large, though nowhere near as large as the lure of the prize. It *had* to work.

But first, it had to be properly tested.

It was a cold day in Kitty Hawk. The wind was high, the mercury falling. Gingerly, the boys pushed their prototype onto the test track.

The first test

'When the restraining wire was slipped the machine moved so swiftly I could only stay with it a few feet. It climbed about two feet, stalled and settled 105 feet away. The test lasted just three and a half seconds.'

They would be going nowhere this day. Two days later, after repairs, they tried again.

The second test

'The puddles outside were covered with ice and the wind was 27 miles per hour. As the day wore on with no improvement we decided we'd better make an attempt. The machine started very slowly then rose suddenly and darted for the ground. The flight lasted just 12 seconds, over a distance of 120 feet...'

The third test

'The wind had chilled us through so we went to the building to warm up. This flight was much like the last. The duration was just a second longer, but the distance 75 feet greater.'

The fourth test

'This one was steadier, then a sudden gust from the right lifted the machine up 12 to 15 feet and turned it sideways in an alarming manner. It began sidling to the left so I warped the wings down to try to recover balance. The time of this flight was 15 seconds and the distance over 200 feet.'

The fifth test

This so damaged the machine it put paid to further tests that year. But they did stay in the air for 59 seconds and travelled a distance of 852 feet. This though, by their standards, could be conceived a success. It was the first piloted powered flight of a fixed wing machine.

Mildly paraphrased, these quotes come from Orville Wright describing his experiences with his brother and friends at Kitty Hawk in December 1903. The point of this story is, if the brothers had been trying to innovate in the voluntary sector or in cause marketing nowadays, their transformational idea would most probably never have taken off because of our tendency to scrap initiatives at the first sign of failure.

If your stories are to stick, you must persist.

Storytellers safeguard history

In 1994 Steven Spielberg created the Shoah Foundation to record testimonies of survivors and other witnesses of the Holocaust. Between 1994 and 1999 the Foundation organised nearly 52,000 video interviews in 56 countries and in 32 languages to create a permanent history of the greatest stain upon humanity that our world has ever seen. Their interviews included stories from Jewish survivors, Jehovah's Witnesses, Roma and homosexual survivors, political prisoners, liberators and others. Preserving this many-layered record is a profoundly important undertaking.

The significance of recording stories to safeguard history is being recognised increasingly, and not necessarily for such substantial and significant projects. The American memory project provides free access, through the Internet, to written and sound recordings, still and moving images, music and anything else that documents aspects of American life, including the voices of native Americans, slaves and many others. Voices from the dark days of slavery are recorded by museums in Bristol, Liverpool and elsewhere.

A more industry-specific example I'm particularly close to is SOFII, the Showcase of Fundraising Innovation and Inspiration (www.sofii.org). Here shared stories from the recent past to the very earliest recorded instances show not-for-profit communicators what's best practice when campaigning to inspire audiences and change the world.

The Online Story Bank is a new project to gather selected transformational stories from down the ages and make them freely available online to act as prompts and inspiration for today's storytellers. You can enjoy it for free and add your own content at www.onlinestorybank.com. New stories are particularly welcome, if they're good enough.

Targeting those most likely to change

For most of us, our target audiences will most likely contain a predominance of the affluent over-sixties – the people with disposable resources aplenty, both time and money. Other than the super rich, the only group to prosper consistently throughout the most recent, long recession, is the over-sixties. With some exceptions, of course.

There are now more people in the UK over 60 than under 16. Generally they're the wealthiest group of all and prime targets for the transformational storyteller. They're living longer, have 80 per cent of Britain's private wealth and buy about 80 per cent of all discretionary, non-essential goods.

But all's not well among them. The number of couples over 60 getting divorced has more than doubled in 20 years. The cost of health care seems set to soar. Savings are being eroded and investments under-performing. Along with their extra affluence has come increased uncertainty.

It's into this world, their world, that a huge number of interested parties and individuals all want their stories to reach, to connect and to add meaning. Endless potential awaits those who do it well.

> *'Good ideas, lifelong experiences and the wealth of spare time are assets we cannot afford to ignore...it is time to invent a new stage in life – after career and before retirement – in which older people give back to future generations, utilising a "windfall of talent".'*
>
> *THE OBSERVER* COMMENT COLUMN, 22 DECEMBER 2013

In a changing world, how do we keep people changing the world?

Retention is a perpetual challenge these days. It's not just all the competition around, distracting audiences from you and your stories, apathy and inertia too figure high among your audiences' other options. It'll not suffice just to inspire people to want to change the world, or even to encourage them to believe that by helping the right cause they can. It'll not be enough merely to introduce employees to corporate social engagement or entrepreneurial campaigning and leave it at that. If these processes are to stick, transformational storytellers need to keep their audiences active and believing, all the time.

So as well as communicating effectively and following up regularly with interesting content and the best feedback going, storytellers have to work on ways to make doing good – making a difference – become a habit that customers, clients, donors, campaigners and others will all stick with down the years, come what may.

> *'Your beliefs become your thoughts,*
> *Your thoughts become your words,*
> *Your words become your actions,*
> *Your actions become your habits,*
> *Your habits become your values,*
> *Your values become your destiny.'*
>
> MAHATMA GANDHI

The habit of helping

We're all creatures of habit. Which shoe do you put on first in the morning, left or right? Do you tie your right shoelace first, or the other one? Do you clean your teeth before showering, or after? Do you think about these things at all? Or are you so used to doing them now you just do them without thinking, by habit?

When you stir your tea, smile at a passer-by, ride your bike, or walk along the street, have you ever stopped to think about what you're doing? What would happen if you did?

Gandhi seems to have cottoned onto actions becoming habits some time back. He's not alone. One of the best books on the subject in recent years is *The Power of Habit* by Charles Duhigg (Random House, 2013). Habits it seems can form unnoticed and be changed without anyone spotting the change.

In 1903 the *American Journal of Psychology* defined habit as 'a more or less fixed way of thinking, willing, or feeling acquired through previous repetition of a mental experience'. Habitual behaviour often goes unnoticed in those exhibiting it because we don't need to engage in self-analysis when undertaking routine tasks. But because people's behaviour comes naturally from their habits the implications for marketers and communicators everywhere are profound. Which explains why the science of habit formation is now a major field of study in the world's leading universities.

Habits, we know, can keep us healthy or unhealthy (exercise, eating and smoking). A savings habit can be pleasantly enriching. Productivity, or the lack of it, can come from habit. Bad work habits cost companies billions of pounds, so now some employers are treating habit very seriously. Pioneers of best business practices have found that bad habits can be broken and good habits can be formed.

So, might not doing good become a habit too? There seems to be no real reason why not, other than our inability to tell stories better. Could transformational storytellers encourage our audiences to make 'making a difference' a habit? Could customers come to associate you and your product with social change, something useful, with doing good? Of course they could, if we define our benefits clearly, report on them frequently and tell our compelling stories well in ways that people will welcome and even look forward to. In time and with the right encouragement your customers and supporters could slip into a habit of buying from or supporting you that's not just comforting and enjoyable, it's also automatic, so it's unlikely to be stopped.

Perhaps we could even foster, if not create, a craving to make a difference. 'Go on, do something worthwhile. Feel good, enjoy it, you deserve it!'

Sound far-fetched? Maybe it is. But then, stranger things have happened. Take the extraordinary stories of Schlitz beer and Pepsodent toothpaste and that brilliant if somewhat unprincipled giant of advertising, Claude C Hopkins.

Claude Hopkins, who died in 1932, came from a long line of impoverished preachers and wrote highly effective advertising copy to sell beer, carpet sweepers, lard and tinned meats. He created 'reason-why advertising' and, according to David Ogilvy, was the first advertising great to recognise the importance of brand images a generation before the term came into regular use. Hopkins' greatest contribution to advertising was his insistence that all advertising could be measured and should be rigorously tested. His quirky little book *Scientific Advertising* inspired and informed generations of advertising people and is still influential today.

His Scottish mother instilled in young Claude the values of working hard and learning constantly. At a time when advertising was an exalted occupation for upper crust types he used simple words and short phrases to describe everyday situations. He's also widely credited, through his advertising, with popularising the twice-daily habit of brushing teeth.

> *'You'll wonder where the yellow went,*
> *when you brush your teeth with Pepsodent...'*
> A POPULAR JINGLE FROM PEPSODENT'S TV ADS, 1940S TO 1960S.

> *'There is scarcely a home where some human being is not doing what we demand. The good advertising man comes pretty close to being an absolute czar.'*
> CLAUDE HOPKINS' BOAST WHEN ADDRESSING
> FELLOW BUSINESSMEN IN 1909

The man who made the world smile more brightly

Claude Hopkins had already convincingly shown through campaigns such as Schlitz beer and Palmolive soap that advertising is not a random gamble, it's a precise science. And he'd made himself mega-rich in the process. He was also famous for his controversial theory that, though expensive, it was possible to build habits among consumers that would lead to their buying certain products, come what may.

But when a friend came along with a strange product called Pepsodent that he wanted Hopkins to promote, the great ad man initially said no. The health of America's teeth was in steep decline then due to the rising tide of sweet sticky products people were consuming, but nobody was selling much toothpaste because in those days hardly anyone ever brushed their teeth. It was a bit like the Bata Shoes story (see page 211), only Hopkins then was looking at the opportunity in the wrong way.

Pepsodent's only shortcomings were it cost vastly more than other toothpastes and didn't do the job any better. But it sold spectacularly well.

Eventually (long story being cut short here) he changed his mind and advertising history was made.

Hopkins scoured dental books to find the keys to an offer that would build the daily Pepsodent habit. Thinking the public wouldn't understand plaque he coined instead the concept of 'clinging film', then promised Pepsodent would remove and replace it with what everyone wanted – 'more success, happiness, beauty, cheer'. Pepsodent promised sex appeal, desire and the magic ingredients of irium and IMP. Though there was scientific uncertainty around what these secret ingredients were, the message was that daily brushing with Pepsodent would remove film and leave in its place a dazzling white smile.

Whether Hopkins' ads for Pepsodent really did launch the tooth-brushing habit seems to be a moot point. But according to Kerry Segrave in *America Brushes Up: the use and marketing of toothpaste and toothbrushes in the twentieth century* (McFarland & Co, Inc, 2010), Hopkins 'fulsome and highly exaggerated ads' did unquestionably help Pepsodent become the world's best-selling toothpaste, despite being sold at twice the price of other products.

Soon everyone from politicians to film stars was boasting about his or her 'Pepsodent smile'. An edition of *Mad* magazine from around that time showed a cartoon of Leonardo da Vinci sitting in front of his painting of the Mona Lisa and looking at the debris around his easel thinking, 'I wonder where the yellow went?' Nestled among his tubes of paint is a tube of toothpaste – Pepsodent – evidence that the phrase and the product were firmly lodged in the public consciousness.

It was the classic need and reward cycle. Good behaviour reinforced by a reward eventually becomes a habit. Though the truth may have been stretched in the process, the lesson for storytellers from Hopkins and Pepsodent is in the impact and rewards of creative storytelling, which can lead to habits that will keep customers engaged.

The process of creating and encouraging habits is something storytellers should be studying and fostering. Great feedback generating good feelings could become a routine that turns into a habit, for all kinds of customers. And there are likely to be just as many chances for storytelling to help break bad habits as there are opportunities to implant good ones.

Organised religion of any kind provides one of the clearest examples of a structure designed to make doing good a habit. With the decline of churchgoing in many societies perhaps the role of the transformational storyteller is even more important as the potential for creating and instilling 'habits for good' moves into new hands, groups and formats.

Becoming the world's best

Claude Hopkins has other instructive lessons for us. When he won the Schlitz beer account he invested time in studying the company and its procedures to really understand their product, inside and out. He found brewing to be a much more complex and fastidious process than he'd ever imagined, so he asked why the brewery didn't use these great qualities to explain their product.

'Because,' he was firmly told, 'what we do is how every brewer makes beer.'

'Ah that may be so,' replied Hopkins, 'but as yet, no other has told that story to the world.'

And that's just what he did. In ads with headlines proclaiming 'Perfection of 50 years' he told of the fine, time-tested traditions of Schlitz, the cleanliness of their kitchens, the purity of the water they use and of their experts travelling to Bohemia to find the best hops and barley. He even boasted of how Schlitz cares for your health by refrigerating beer for months to avoid the biliousness that common beers cause.

It sounded rather magical, the commitment to detail of a truly great beer, perhaps, as the ads proclaimed, the best beer that the world ever knew. By then the fact that all other beers followed pretty much the same path had fallen into insignificance and Schlitz had a pre-emptive marketing advantage. Schlitz became *the* beer to call for, the best beer ever brewed – because it told its story first and best.

Invariably better storytelling will enhance any product's performance and getting in with your story ahead of the field will secure a durable advantage over similar propositions.

Smile – you've just done good

One of Claude Hopkins achievements was understood only after the great man died. He had built into Pepsodent a cool, tingling sensation. Soon all toothpastes had it, though it added nothing at all to the efficacy of the toothpaste. Hopkins was onto something, even though he never lived to fully realise it. The foaming of detergents and shampoos is similarly unnecessary for the effectiveness of the products. But they reassure people, are a sign that the product is working. So in Hopkins' terms these also form part of that need and reward cycle.

Maybe if we were to define clearly the signs, symptoms and rewards for doing good and present them consistently, storytellers could offer something akin to that too. Perhaps we should get into the habit of promoting the feeling and routine more enthusiastically, of saying, 'go on, feel good, you deserve it, today and every day!'

Though, we should take care to ensure our stories have real substance. Perhaps the most successful marketing idea ever came from whoever it was who added the single word 'repeat' to the instructions on every bottle of shampoo. People wash their hair by habit, they don't need instructions to follow. A second helping is rarely necessary. One wash, with one dose of shampoo, usually does the job perfectly adequately. Yet through persistent, repeated advertising many people adopted that habit too. Imagine how much more shampoo it sold.

The power of belief

Belief keeps people active and involved and few things reinforce beliefs as effectively as being part of a group. Churches, Alcoholics Anonymous, Lions Clubs, Rotarians, save the whale, stop the power plant, free Nelson Mandela and so on all show that being part of a group greatly facilitates both conversion and retention. And few things are so compelling as the power of a group to persuade others to believe.

So people must believe your stories. Change their routines and behaviours and you may change their habit, but it isn't so easy to alter beliefs. As Gandhi said, belief is perhaps the best place to start, not by trying to change beliefs but by working with them.

Self-help groups representing almost every condition have flourished, though there's room still for new groups to focus on today's urgent causes, such as dementia and depression. They too, if they're to succeed, will need to tell their stories well.

Alcoholics Anonymous, founded in 1935, is the most successful habit-changing organisation in the world. But addiction is more than just habit. To kick that kind of habit, you have to believe.

> *'The advertisement is one of the most interesting and difficult of modern literary forms. Its potentialities are not yet half explored.'*
>
> ALDOUS HUXLEY

It's how you tell 'em

I wouldn't want anyone to imagine that transformational storytellers are some kind of new evangelists setting out to convert the heathen hordes not yet 'doing good', to make sure that, from now on, they do. Rather, I think there's a clue to what may be a bright future for transformational storytellers in the Schlitz beer story, above.

Whatever their messages and motives storytellers have to constantly reinvent, reshape and retell their stories for a different audience and a different time, to get their points through amid unprecedented competing clamour and alternative interests. This is the far from easy task for today's transformational storyteller. But when storytelling is seen as a primary communications skill, one that's fun, stimulating and effective, it becomes that rare combination, an opportunity for doing something good while doing what we enjoy. Storytelling has always been a most worthy occupation and now, particularly, it's a grand time to be doing it.

But as comedians always say, it's as much about how you tell them.

A few years back there was a huge hoo-ha in the European media about the perhaps heavy-handed attempts of France and Belgium to ban wearing of the veil in their countries. Sections of the Muslim population supported the new law, others were up in arms. Much distress was caused and tensions created. Several decades earlier Kemal Ataturk, the father of modern Turkey, introduced to the Turkish parliament (Turkey is a secular state with a largely Muslim population) a law designed to achieve the same result, but which approached the issue in an entirely different way. Instead of banning the veil he made it compulsory for all prostitutes to wear a veil. Soon the veil became a symbol of a certain kind of woman, so most women quietly stopped wearing it. The desired end was achieved, but by a radically different, less divisive means.

Why our stories will change the world

Imagine you are talking to Beryl and Clive Broomhead, from chapter 7. Beryl and Clive are your audience, your listeners, your readers.

They don't yet know why they should listen to you, they don't yet know what they want to do, or whether they'll want anything to do with you. You have just a few minutes to catch their attention before they move on.

There's a lot you could tell them. Stories about life and death issues with real drama, all the ingredients of a soap opera or a thriller.

You have a hero, a problem and a solution.

First you'll capture their interest and imagination and draw them in.

Now, tell them your story so they can feel and savour every emotion. Tell it so well that they'll hang on your every word, eager for your solution, ready to do for you whatever you want them to do.

As no one can tell you how to tell a story, you should focus on what you like and what you are good at. Leave what you don't like and what you're not good at to someone else. The secret of being a great storyteller is to be really good at being you.

Our stories need to be uplifting, to leave that warm, inspirational feeling burning into the memory. If they're to stick and succeed our stories have to be real, interesting, surprising and substantial, not puff, or bland superficiality.

In even trying to change the world we may be in a losing game, or at least the odds may be stacked against us. So we have to get better at it. If fictional stories feature mainly bad things, if the news media mostly focus on bad news and dreams too are so often about trouble, then our stories have to balance dreams, fiction and the news. If people are fed a remorseless diet of gloom and conflict our aim should be to get into their already crowded consciousness with more welcome tales that will make them feel better, even make them feel good. To do this, our stories have to employ every storytelling trick at our disposal to show people that we can solve the problem, whatever it is, and that through us they can make a difference.

For this book I've deliberately steered clear of what could be one of the most powerful potential roles for the transformational storyteller: advocating for political social change. So I'll make just a single observation on it now.

As society becomes ever more unfair, unequal and divided, younger people increasingly are abandoning the political process entirely, convinced that a corrupt, rich elite with an unshakeable stranglehold on power has things so stacked against them that there's no point in voting or agitating, because nothing will ever change.

A new story needs to be told. If when it comes, transformational storytellers can play a part in spreading that story, perhaps the revolution in thinking that'll be needed for real social change could be spread effectively. I don't have an answer for what should replace the current system but for sure it should be based on more fairness, less exclusion and extremes of advantage and disadvantage, more sharing from the haves with the have nots.

That seems a story worth telling.

I'd go further than that quote from *The Observer* displayed on page 251, about a new stage in life. That's true, certainly. But we also need to create a new breed of socially aware business people, non-profit change agents, campaigners and dedicated educators set on doing things that make a positive difference. We need to recognise, celebrate and reward that aspiration. We need to create change warriors no less idealistic and dedicated than those who created Oxfam in the 1940s and Amnesty and Greenpeace in the 1960s and 70s or Avaaz and 38 Degrees in the early years of this century. These people will look, talk, write and inspire differently, as if they're out to really make a difference, to change the world.

The storyteller's responsibilities and opportunities

- Make sure transformational storytelling runs like a rich thread right through your organisation. It's not a technique, it's an approach to life.
- Spread a passion for emotional, transformational storytelling.
- Encourage others by sharing techniques, tips, ideas and storylines.
- Aim to learn from the best.
- Practise telling stories regularly in front of someone you love and trust.
- Talk long, write short, then write long.
- Promote the truth, told well. Avoid peddling the corporate whitewash that so many companies put out. Readers don't want an airbrushed, antiseptic version of reality, they want real, honest, gritty meaning with no punches pulled and no holds barred. That said, of course, some people will be leery of overly gritty truth. For example, my mum when watching telly would leave the room whenever anything too coarse came on. People can be like that.

- Make your stories appealing. No one wants ugly, impersonal, boring, or dull, whatever they might be buying.
- Build your stories on strong, clear moral foundations. Make your stories the glue that binds people to your cause and the grease that eases their engagement and willing participation.
- Make sure the good guys win in the end and the baddies get their comeuppance. I'm only partly jesting here. We need to ensure our stories have a positive outcome, that they make a difference. Usually that's no problem, because they do.
- Always give your reader something, as a gift. Insight, opportunity, inspiration, meaning, fulfilment, warm feelings. If nothing else, give the gift of a great story, a story your listener can keep, embellish and pass on as he or she wishes. So think of your storytelling as giving a gift that lasts.
- Be a change warrior.

Not always instantly, not always entirely, but consistently over time, storytelling wears through. Or perhaps, 'wins through' is better. But however passionate and eloquent you are, you won't win over everyone. Just as the musicians of Terezín didn't soften the Nazis' hearts, some people are beyond reaching.

That doesn't mean though, that you should stop trying.

> *'That's what storytellers do. They restore order, with imagination.'*
>
> WALT DISNEY

The Swedish story: proof that stories do last

More years ago than I care to remember I found myself in Stockholm, Sweden, the first time I'd ever left the shores of Britain to talk to fundraising campaigners in another land. When I waltzed into the conference centre with as much confidence as I could muster I was completely taken aback to find that the entire proceedings, apart from my bit, were being held in the Swedish language. And I didn't have a single word of Swedish; I couldn't even say hello. Of course the several hundred delegates there all were able to switch from the language that most comfortably suited them to listen to me speaking to them in English.

I was mortified, but there was nothing I could do about it, so I soldiered on. Back at my hotel I met a man in the bar who told me the following story, I think in the hope of making me feel better. I grabbed it, adapted it, prefaced it with the story of my embarrassing personal experience in Stockholm and, for the last 25 years or more, have used it in seminars all round the globe both as an ice-breaker and as a tool to introduce the change I want to see in this world. It became *the Swedish story*.

An American professor of business was in a conference hotel in an East African capital, about to go on stage for his first presentation to a foreign audience. Looking around he saw lots of eager faces and colourful African shirts and dresses. On an impulse, out of respect for his hosts, he decided he would greet his audience with 'good morning ladies and gentlemen' in Swahili. Trouble was he didn't know what that was, so he quickly looked around the reception area to find someone to help him. As luck would have it at that moment a couple came in and were greeted by the receptionist with the word *jambo*. Brilliant he thought, *jambo*, hello, good morning – I'm halfway there. Then he had a stroke of real inspiration. Looking across the lobby he spied two doors, side by side, each adorned with the instantly recognisable international symbols for men and women: the men's room and the women's room. Written beneath the female symbol was the words *maji chooni* and beneath the men's was *choo wanaumi.*

Brilliant, he thought, I've got it. And with that he bounded onto the stage and greeted his waiting audience with his new-found phrase, *'Jambo, maji chooni na choo wanaumi.*

Of course his astonished audience fell about in fits of laughter, because what he'd actually said was, 'Hello, water closets and urinals.'

Pause for laughter, followed by relief and relaxation.

I have told this story, in public, maybe a hundred times since. Sometimes I change the language around and take liberties with the

Swedish rather than the Swahili language, but the basic idea works in all countries and cultures and I've never bettered the start it gives my presentations. It always gets a great laugh. It allows me to be a bit self-deprecating and to explain how easy it is to come bouncing into another land, another culture and, even with the best of intentions, to get things completely wrong. It disarms hostility. From that moment everyone likes me, they're all on my side.

If you find a good story, keep it and work it. To be honest I never met that guy in the bar. I first heard a version of this joke on the radio some years before, while driving in rural France. I wrote it down, embroidered it a bit and it's been a boon to me ever since.

Don't forget that, even if you become fed up to the back teeth with it, to your audience your story is a new beginning, a new way in, a new story.

> *'Begin at the beginning...and come to the end, then stop.'*
>
> LEWIS CARROLL

If this book has helped you even a little bit with this stretching, difficult, important task of transformational storytelling then I will feel good. If it's equipped you with even a smidge more confidence to tackle the challenge then I'll feel even better. If it's renewed your zest and enthusiasm to, by hook or by crook, become not just a better writer or a better storyteller but a transformational writer, a transformational storyteller who will go on to change the world, then I couldn't be happier.

Because I wrote all this, for you.

I hope you will now say with some pride, I'm Ken (or Betty, or Sue, or Pierre, or whatever) and I'm a transformational storyteller.

How about that?

Good for you.

Go for it.

CHAPTER'S END: ACTIONS AND KEY MESSAGES

Be inspirational, not irritating. Build mutually beneficial partnerships with your audiences.

Invest in testing.

Target carefully and go first for those easiest to reach.

Hone your stories. Tailor them to the messages you wish to get across.

Tell your story first and best. The key challenge is to tell your story better than anyone else has ever done before.

Try to turn doing worthwhile things into a habit. Then try and persuade others to do the same. Recognise and harness the power of belief.

Take the storyteller's 12 primary responsibilities very seriously.

Be realistic about your storytelling but recognise that once you have a problem, a hero and a solution, you can and will change the world.

When you have a great story you can use and reuse it for decades.

Aspire to be a life changer, not a junk marketer.

Introducing the Online Story Bank

The Online Story Bank (www.onlinestorybank.com) aims to create a free, permanent collection of surprising, engaging and informative stories; a showcase of the best 'change' stories from around the world to inspire writers, storytellers or anyone hoping to influence anyone else about, well, anything at all.

The stories selected and presented in the Online Story Bank have been chosen solely for their potential to intrigue, involve and inspire you. We've tried for variety and balance in subject, length, style and content; to include stories that stimulate a range of emotions and reactions. Some specifically call for a direct response, others don't. Some are obviously transformational, some less so. Several are fresh discoveries, many are old favourites. Some are in the first person, some are told through the eyes of others.

This of course is a work in progress, just starting out. You can add to it too and share your favourites with others around the world who will also love your stories. Though it's growing all the time the Online Story Bank will never be a definitive collection. It's intended to be a collection of all types of transformational, life-changing stories – stories that raise spirits, expose issues and shine light upon the

Welcome to the Online Story Bank

A free, permanent collection of surprising, engaging and informative stories; a showcase of the best 'change' stories from around the world to inspire writers, storytellers or anyone hoping to influence anyone else about, well, anything at all.

Shortcuts to some great stories

ADVENTURE: The gorilla.
DELIGHT: Love the taste of words.
ACTION: One in the eye for Hitler.
SQUIRM: A mastectomy, before the discovery of anaesthetics.
TENACITY: A tortoise crosses the road.
WONDER: Rough sex down by the river.
FEEL GOOD: What happens when a homeless guy does the right thing?
SURVIVAL: How to eat a salamander.
EXPLORATION: The witch-finder Gagool.
GRUESOME: 'Oh me, I eat anything...'
BIZARRE: The strange case of Mr Phineas Gage.
SATIRE: A solution to the rising birth-rate among the urban poor.

- Nature
- Science
- Exploration
- Medicine
- History
- Conflict
- Literature
- Education
- Drama
- Human spirit
- People
- Enterprise
- Sport
- Life
- Romance
- Laughter
- Uncategorized

Write something...

SEARCH

limitless potential of life, as well as for all other equally important stories that have yet to be written, that have not yet been told.

The hope is simply that they'll surprise, entertain, interest and inspire you to create and tell similar stories of your own, here and elsewhere, to change someone's world and while at it, perhaps to change yours, too.

The Online Story Bank is twinned with SOFII, the Showcase of Fundraising Innovation and Inspiration, which also has many examples of storytelling to change the world.

As a reader of this book you're very welcome to use the Online Story Bank and to add your stories too. I hope to see you there.

Permissions

The original writings of John Caples, Claude Hopkins and others are now out of copyright. David Ogilvy is so widely quoted as to be in the public domain. The stories of Schlitz beer, Pepsodent and similar references and anecdotes are adapted from various sources and included as fair use.

The illustration on page 270 is included with permission from the Iris agency.

In the quote on the title page from Howard Luck Gossage the original version used the words 'grown man' only, rather than 'grown man or woman'. It wouldn't have seemed incongruous then to have only used the male descriptor, but it seems wrong now, so we've taken the liberty of changing it as the point is no less valid for women.

Attempts were made to get appropriate permissions for other material not included above, but without response. If after a second or third reminder the quoted source still hadn't responded we took that as a lack of interest or concern, so have either dropped the material or, if we considered its inclusion important to the book, we have gone ahead and included it anyway. Thanks to all those who responded and made the permissions process a bit easier, so that this author could make the points he wished to make, when standing on the shoulders of eagles.

To find out more about Ken Burnett please visit his website at www.kenburnett.com. Ken plans to add some more of his favourite stories online, in the form of an online story bank. A work in progress, it can be accessed free at www.onlinestorybank.com.

Ken Burnett is an internationally-recognised author, consultant and inspirational speaker on fundraising, marketing and communications for non-profit organisations.

He was UK director and director of fundraising and communications for ActionAid from 1977 to 1982, when he founded the influential Burnett Associates agency group. He still works with its successor, the Burnett Works agency. Ken is author of several seminal books including *Relationship Fundraising*, *Friends for Life*, *The Zen of Fundraising* and *Tiny Essentials of an Effective Volunteer Board*. From 1998 to 2003 Ken was chairman of trustees of ActionAid International. He's a partner in the transformational consultancy Revolutionise (formerly Clayton Burnett), a director of The White Lion Press and a trustee of the UK Disasters Emergency Committee. He is founder and managing trustee of SOFII, the Showcase of Fundraising Innovation and Inspiration. In 2013 Ken Burnett was appointed as a commissioner of the Commission on the Voluntary Sector and Ageing, the body set up to provide long-term, strategic thinking about the implications for the voluntary sector of an ageing population.

Start your story here.

Towering at least ten feet above the floor the story opposite dominates the wall of a shared reception area in an office building in central London, England. See page 197 for why you should cover your walls with inspirational stories. The blank page above precedes another, overleaf. Of course they're not left blank because we couldn't think of anything more to say, rather we wanted in these final pages to give you space to start your next story. Why not? Wherever you are is as good a place as any and any blank space is a great place to start. What you make of it from now on is up to you.